Better Homes and Gardens®

Eat Healthy Lose Weight

Volume 4

Meredith® Consumer Marketing
Des Moines, Iowa

Eat Healthy Lose Weight

MEREDITH CONSUMER MARKETING

Vice President, Consumer Marketing: Janet Donnelly
Consumer Product Marketing Director: Steve Swanson
Consumer Product Marketing Manager: Amanda Werts
Business Director: Ron Clingman
Senior Production Manager: George Susral

WATERBURY PUBLICATIONS, INC.

Editorial Director: Lisa Kingsley
Associate Editors: Tricia Bergman, Mary Williams
Creative Director: Ken Carlson
Associate Design Directors: Doug Samuelson, Bruce Yang
Production Assistant: Mindy Samuelson
Contributing Copy Editors: Terri Fredrickson, Peg Smith
Contributing Indexer: Elizabeth T. Parson

BETTER HOMES AND GARDENS. MAGAZINE

Editor in Chief: Gayle Goodson Butler
Senior Deputy Editor, Food & Entertaining: Nancy Wall Hopkins

MEREDITH NATIONAL MEDIA GROUP

President: Tom Harty
Vice President, Production: Bruce Heston

MEREDITH CORPORATION

Chairman and Chief Executive Officer: Stephen M. Lacy

In Memoriam: E.T. Meredith III (1933–2003)

Copyright© 2012 by Meredith Corporation, Des Moines, Iowa.
First Edition. All rights reserved.
Printed in the United States of America.
ISSN: 1949-2227 ISBN: 978-0-696-30117-9

Test Kitchen

Our seal assures you that every recipe in *Eat Healthy, Lose Weight Vol. 4* has been tested in the Better Homes and Gardens® Test Kitchen. This means that each recipe is practical and reliable and meets our high standards of taste appeal. We guarantee your satisfaction with this book for as long as you own it.

All of us at Meredith Consumer Marketing are dedicated to providing you with information and ideas to enhance your home. We welcome your comments and suggestions. Write to us at: Meredith Consumer Marketing, 1716 Locust St., Des Moines, IA 50309-3023.

Pictured on front cover:
Thai Chicken Pizza, page 72

Contents

EAT BETTER TODAY

Simply by picking up this book, you've made one step forward on the path to eating better and feeling better. As someone with an eye on health, you want foods that are good for you, taste great, and help shed excess pounds. Armed with *Eat Healthy, Lose Weight Vol. 4*, you can eat foods you love while watching your waistline, and you can do it without giving in to the latest fads or suffering the food blahs of diet deprivation.

You will quickly discover that this cookbook is perfect for everyday family meals that everyone will gobble up. The more than 270 recipes are low in calories, fat, and sodium—but there are no "diet foods" here. Enjoy your fill of pizzas, burgers, soups, casseroles, and desserts that are especially developed to fit a healthy eating plan. Choose from recipes to suit any occasion— from quick family-friendly weeknight meals to appetizers, main dishes, sides, and desserts that taste indulgent yet are well within the guidelines of a healthful diet. (How about Pizza Meatballs? Or Beef and Noodles? Or Chocolate-Cream Cheese Cupcakes?)

And because every recipe has been tested in the *Better Homes and Gardens* Test kitchen, you can rest assured that they'll taste great too.

Kick off your efforts to eat better and lose weight with the opening chapter of healthful eating basics. Learn to make substitutions at each meal—and how to choose the best produce year-round. One healthy choice leads to another. You chose this book, now choose any recipe, get cooking, and eat better!

CHAPTER 1

Smart Choices

HEALTHY EATING BASICS

Tips and Tricks for Trimming Down

CHOOSE VEGETARIAN SAUSAGE

Breakfast

A smart breakfast helps keep your appetite in check all day. Protein is the nutrient that works hardest at helping you feel full and satisfied, but it's often overlooked at the morning meal. Pork loin cutlets, leftover chicken breast, and lean roast beef are just as tasty with eggs or in breakfast sandwiches as processed breakfast meats yet save on fat and sodium.

Skim milk, nonfat Greek yogurt, and low-fat cheese also provide protein (and calcium) in breakfast recipes or served on the side. Boost satisfaction by bulking up breakfast fare with fiber-rich whole grains and low-calorie vegetables and fruits. Try spinach in egg dishes or berries in whole grain muffins.

Omelet fillers

Stuff omelets with almost anything. Keep them slimming yet satisfying by sprinkling them with lean meats, low-calorie vegetables, and low-fat dairy ingredients.

Choose this	Not this
Raw tomato, diced (¼ cup) 8 cal., 0 g fat, 2 mg sodium, 0.5 g fiber	**Sun-dried tomatoes packed in oil, drained** (¼ cup) 59 cal., 4 g fat, 73 mg sodium, 1.5 g fiber
Leftover cooked pork loin chop, cubed (1 ounce) 60 cal., 3 g fat, 18 mg sodium, 8 g protein	**Crumbled bacon** (1 ounce) 153 cal., 12 g fat, 655 mg sodium, 10 g protein
Yellow summer squash and zucchini, thinly sliced (½ cup) 12 cal., 0 g fat, 1 mg sodium, 0.5 g fiber	**Corn** (½ cup) 62 cal., 1 g fat, 11 mg sodium, 1 g fiber
Vegetarian sausage-style crumbles (1 ounce) 46 cal., 1 g fat, 216 mg sodium, 6 g protein	**Pork sausage crumbles, cooked** (1 ounce) 100 cal., 10 g fat, 190 mg sodium, 4 g protein

CHOPPED FRESH FRUIT IS A HEALTHFUL CHOICE FOR A SALAD TOPPER

Sandwiches

It's easy for excess calories and sodium to sneak into sandwiches. Starting with a slim yet hearty whole grain wrap, pita, or thin bun can help control calories. Or try an open-face hot sandwich with half the bread. Opt for low-fat meats, cheeses, and spreads, and choose lower-sodium options when possible. Leftover chicken breast and roast beef slices are good alternatives to salty processed meats. Your sandwich will be more filling and flavorful when you load it with fresh vegetables such as broccoli, cucumber slices, and sweet pepper strips. Thin slices of apple or pear add crunch and flavor to sandwiches.

CHOOSE HUMMUS
INSTEAD OF MAYO

Smart sandwich staples

It pays to compare calories, fat, and sodium when choosing sandwich fixings. Try these simple swaps to slim your sandwich.

Choose this	Not this
Hummus (1 tablespoon) 23 cal., 1 g fat (0 g sat. fat), 53 mg sodium	**Mayonnaise** (1 tablespoon) 57 cal., 5 g fat (0.5 g sat. fat), 105 mg sodium
Whole wheat bagel thin 110 cal., 1 g fat, 190 mg sodium, 5 g fiber	**Plain packaged bagel** 260 cal., 2 g fat, 500 mg sodium, 2 g fiber
Leftover skinless chicken breast slices (2 ounces) 94 cal., 2 g fat, 42 mg sodium, 17 g protein	**Creamy deli chicken breast salad** (½ cup) 210 cal., 15 g fat, 640 mg sodium, 13 g protein
Reduced-fat smoked provolone cheese (1 ounce) 77 cal., 5 g fat (3 g sat. fat), 245 mg sodium	**Provolone cheese** (1 ounce) 98 cal., 7.5 g fat (5 g sat. fat), 245 mg sodium

Salad

With just 5 calories per cup of shredded lettuce, it's easy to understand why green salads are a dieter's friend. What you add to lettuce, however, can make or break the calorie count. Although it's smart to top salad with lots of colorful vegetables, remember also to add a bit of protein. Protein-rich lean meats, low-fat cheeses, beans, nuts, and seeds lend staying power to salads. Although you should avoid high-fat salad dressings, you don't have to choose fat-free. It's important to get from 3 to 5 grams of fat in a salad (whether from dressing or other ingredients) to best absorb certain vitamins in the vegetables. Avoid drenching greens in salad dressing—about 1 tablespoon per 2 cups of lettuce should be enough.

Salad bar toppers

To build a salad lower in calories, fat, and sodium, use this chart as a guide.

Choose this	Not this
Part-skim mozzarella cheese (1 ounce) 72 cal., 5 g fat, 132 mg sodium, 0 g fiber	**Cheddar cheese** (1 ounce) 114 cal., 9 g fat, 176 mg sodium, 0 g fiber
Fresh fruit, chopped (¼ cup) 16 cal., 0 g fat, 0 mg sodium, 1 g fiber	**Dried fruit bits** (¼ cup) 120 cal., 0 g fat, 20 mg sodium, 3 g fiber
Roasted chicken breast without skin (3 ounces) 142 cal., 3 g fat, 64 mg sodium, 0 g fiber	**Fried chicken breast** (3 ounces) 187 cal., 8 g fat, 64 mg sodium, 0 g fiber
Hard-cooked egg (1 large egg) 78 cal., 5 g fat, 62 mg sodium	**Egg salad** (⅓ cup) 131 cal., 10 g fat, 195 mg sodium

Soups and Stews

Low-fat soups and stews typically contain more water and vegetables than other one-dish entrées, resulting in a satisfying portion with fewer calories per bite. Start with low-sodium broth, low-fat milk, or evaporated skim milk, then pump up the protein with lean meats or fiber-rich beans. Nonstarchy vegetables are easy add-ins when you keep frozen spinach, broccoli, cauliflower, diced green peppers, and chopped onions on hand. Fiber-rich grains—such as barley, quinoa, or whole grain pasta can either be cooked in soups and stews or precooked and added close to serving time. A lemon or lime wedge to garnish the dish doubles as a healthy flavor booster to squeeze over the bowl right before eating.

Soup and stew toppers

Garnishes make soups and stews look pretty while complementing flavor and texture. Here's help for keeping them figure-friendly.

Choose this	Not this
Non-fat Greek yogurt (2 tablespoons) 15 cal., 0 g fat (0 g sat. fat), 3 g protein	**Sour cream** (2 tablespoons) 51 cal., 5 g fat (3 g sat. fat), 0.5 g protein
Low-fat baked tortilla chips, crushed (0.5 ounce) 59 cal., 0.5 g fat, 59 mg sodium, 0.5 g fiber	**Fried tortilla strips** (0.5 ounce) 80 cal., 4 g fat, 50 mg sodium, 1 g fiber
Chopped basil (2 teaspoons) **and pine nuts** (1 teaspoon) 19 cal., 2 g fat (0 g sat. fat), 0 mg sodium	**Pesto** (3 teaspoons) 69 cal., 7 g fat (1 g sat. fat), 129 mg sodium
Freeze-dried mixed vegetables (¼ cup) 40 cal., 0 g fat, 14 mg sodium, 0.5 g fiber High in vitamins A and C	**Butter croutons** (¼ cup) 70 cal., 3 g fat, 110 mg sodium, 0 g fiber

Meat, Poultry, and Seafood

Meat is rich in hunger-satisfying protein, so don't skip it just because you're counting calories. You can find lean cuts of beef, pork, and lamb by looking for the words "loin" or "round" in the name. Skinless white-meat chicken and turkey are smart choices too, but carefully read the label of ground poultry—it may include higher-fat dark meat and skin. Decrease the amount of ground meat used in recipes by adding vegetables with a meaty texture, such as eggplant, mushrooms, or beans. At least twice a week, eat fish, especially ones rich in heart-healthy omega-3 fats, such as salmon. Plain seafood is often sold frozen, so it's easy to move it from freezer to refrigerator first thing in the morning to let it thaw for the evening meal.

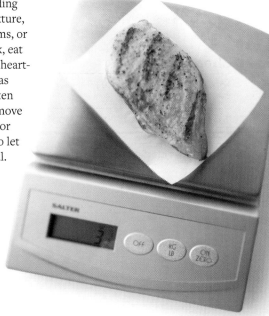

Lean and meaty

Reduce significant fat and calories by making lean meat choices. Low-fat options often provide a bit more protein per serving too. Choose meatless options such as beans and soy products occasionally to reduce calories and fat in some meals.

Choose this	Not this
Beef sirloin steak (4 ounces grilled) 149 cal., 4.5 g fat (1.5 g sat. fat), 25 g protein	**Beef ribeye steak** (4 ounces grilled) 300 cal., 23 g fat (9 g sat. fat), 20 g protein
Skinless chicken breast (4 ounces grilled) 124 cal., 1.5 g fat (0.5 g sat. fat), 26 g protein	**Skinless chicken thigh** (4 ounces grilled) 143 cal., 5 g fat (1 g sat. fat), 24 g protein
Extra-lean ground turkey breast (4 ounces raw) 120 cal., 1 g fat (0 g sat. fat), 28 g protein	**Ground turkey** (4 ounces raw) 240 cal., 17 g fat (4.5 g sat. fat), 20 g protein
Portobello mushroom (4 ounces cooked) 25 cal., 0 g fat (0 g sat. fat), 2 g protein	**Hamburger patty, 85 percent lean** (4 ounces cooked) 243 cal., 17 g fat (6.5 g sat. fat), 21 g protein

Note: Generally, 4 ounces raw, boneless meat, poultry, or fish yields 3 ounces cooked meat. For a cut with the bone in, start with 8 ounces raw to get 3 ounces cooked meat.

Grilling

Grilling is a low-fat way to add flavor to lean meat, chicken, fish, vegetables, even fruit. In general, marinate meats before cooking, even if just for an hour. (Marinate fish only 30 minutes.) Opt for low-fat, low-sodium bottled marinades or make your own. A marinade that contains vinegar, citrus juice, or other acidic ingredients best tenderizes meat. Most vegetables absorb little marinade, so just toss them quickly with a marinade before grilling to help prevent sticking. Although you can grill vegetables and fruit on skewers or in foil, you can cook almost anything outdoors with an inexpensive grilling tray that has small holes to prevent food from falling into the fire.

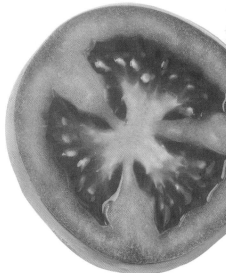

Build a better burger

Many traditional burger toppers are too high in sodium and fat to fit a healthy meal plan. Make a better burger using fresh ingredients, reduced-fat dairy, and whole wheat bread.

Choose this	Not this
Tomato slice (1 thick slice) 5 cal., 0 g fat, 1 mg sodium	**Ketchup** (1 tablespoon) 15 cal., 0 g fat, 167 mg sodium
Roasted red peppers (1 tablespoon) 5 cal., 0 g fat, 30 mg sodium	**Pickle relish** (1 tablespoon) 19 cal., 1 g fat, 164 mg sodium
Reduced-fat cheddar cheese (1 ounce) 49 cal., 3 g fat, 174 mg sodium	**American cheese** (1 ounce) 106 cal., 8 g fat, 356 mg sodium
Whole wheat bun (1.5 ounces) 112 cal., 2 g fat, 195 mg sodium, 2 g fiber	**White hamburger bun** (1.5 ounces) 123 cal., 2 g fat, 204 mg sodium, 1 g fiber

Casseroles

A bubbling hot casserole is the ultimate comfort food, but high-fat sauces, meats, and dairy products can really pile on the calories. Luckily, it's not difficult to find slim ingredients, such as low-fat condensed soups, lean meats, and reduced-fat cheese.

It's also easy to swap regular pastas for higher fiber whole grain versions. And don't forget the vegetables. Mix in nutrient-rich, nonstarchy veggies, such as broccoli, tomatoes, zucchini, carrots, celery, and bell peppers.

Casserole staples

Trim hundreds of calories from your favorite hot dishes by making simple changes like these.

Choose this	Not this
Whole wheat panko bread crumbs (¼ cup) 70 cal., 0.5 g fat, 23 mg sodium, 2 g fiber	**French fried onions** (¼ cup) 90 cal., 7 g fat, 120 mg sodium, 0 g fiber
Long grain brown rice, cooked (½ cup) 108 cal., 3 g protein, 5 mg sodium, 2 g fiber Twice the fiber.	**White rice, cooked** (½ cup) 121 cal., 2 g protein, 0 mg sodium, 0 g fiber
Spaghetti squash, cooked (½ cup) 21 cal., 0 g fat, 1 g fiber, 85 IU vitamin A 80 percent fewer calories!	**Spaghetti, cooked** (½ cup) 111 cal., 0.5 g fat, 1 g fiber, 0 IU vitamin A
Frozen hashbrowns (3 ounces or about 1 cup) 70 cal., 0 g fat (0 g sat. fat), 0 mg sodium	**Frozen tater tots** (3 ounces or 9 pieces) 150 cal., 7 g fat (1.5 g sat. fat), 420 mg sodium

Baked Goods

There are many ways to trim fat and calories from baked goods and desserts. When modifying your favorite recipes, start with one change and when you've fine-tuned that, try other tweaks. For example, use low-fat dairy ingredients instead of the full-fat cousins. When a recipe calls for nuts, cut the amount in half yet heighten flavor by roasting the nuts in an oven. Swap hearty whole grain flour for up to half the all-purpose flour.

Better baking staples

A few small changes can boost fiber and nutrients in baked goods while cutting fat and calories, so you can have your cake and eat it too.

Choose this	Not this
Pureed (baby food) pears (½ cup) 54 cal., 0 g fat, 4.5 g fiber, 31 mg vitamin C	**Vegetable oil** (½ cup) 964 cal., 109 g fat, 0 g fiber, 0 mg vitamin C
Toasted chopped walnuts (¼ cup) 191 cal., 19 g fat (1.5 g sat fat), 2 g fiber	**Chopped walnuts** (½ cup) 383 cal., 38 g fat (3.5 g sat. fat), 4 g fiber
Semi-sweet mini chocolate chips (¼ cup) 280 cal., 16 g fat (10 g sat. fat), 32 g sugars	**Semi-sweet chocolate chips** (½ cup) 560 cal., 32 g fat (20 g sat. fat), 64 g sugars
Whole wheat pastry flour (1 cup) 440 cal., 2 g fat (0 g sat. fat), 16 g fiber 5 times the fiber!	**All-purpose flour** (1 cup) 455 cal., 1 g fat (0 g sat. fat), 3 g fiber

LOW-CAL PRODUCE GUIDE

The best recipes result when you cook with fruits and vegetables that are ripe and in season. Use this chart as a handy reference for spotting, buying, and storing the best produce to ensure delicious healthful dishes all year-round.

Vegetable	Seasonality	Selection	Storage
Asparagus	The peak season for asparagus lasts from February until June.	Look for firm, bright green stalks with fresh, tightly closed tips.	Store asparagus wrapped in a wet paper towel in the refrigerator up to 7 days.
Broccoli	The peak season for broccoli lasts from October through April.	Look for rich color broccoli with tightly closed buds and crisp leaves.	Store unwashed broccoli in a perforated plastic bag in the crisper drawer up to 4 days.
Cabbage	Cabbage is available year-round, but reaches peak in the fall.	Opt for heavy cabbage heads with crisp leaves that are firmly packed.	Store in a plastic bag in the crisper drawer of the refrigerator up to two weeks.
Carrots	Carrots are available year-round but peak October through April.	Look for firm, smooth carrots with fresh, bright color greenery.	Remove greenery and store in a plastic bag in the refrigerator up to 2 weeks.
Cauliflower	Cauliflower is available year-round but is best in the fall months.	Look for firm cauliflower with compact florets and no signs of browning.	Wrap tightly in plastic and store in the refrigerator for 3 to 5 days.
Corn	The peak season for fresh corn lasts from May through September.	Choose ears that are bright green, with tight-fitting husks and golden brown silk.	Corn is best cooked the day it is purchased, but it can be refrigerated with husks on in a plastic bag in the crisper drawer up to 7 days.
Cucumbers	Cucumbers reach their peak season from May to August.	Look for small to medium cucumbers that are firm and have bright color.	Store unwashed cucumbers in the crisper drawer of the refrigerator up to 7 days.
Eggplant	Eggplant is available year-round but reaches its peak in August and September.	Eggplants should be heavy for their size and have firm, glossy skin free from bruising.	Store whole, unwashed eggplant in a plastic bag in the crisper drawer of the refrigerator up to 5 days.
Green Beans	The peak season for green beans lasts from May to October.	Opt for slender beans that are crisp, with bright color, and free from blemishes.	Store green beans in a plastic bag in the refrigerator up 7 days.
Lettuce	Different varieties reach their peaks throughout the year.	Choose crisp, dry salad greens that are free from blemishes.	Store washed lettuce wrapped in paper towels, in a plastic bag in the refrigerator up to 3 days.
Peas	Look for the tastiest peas from mid-spring through early summer.	Choose plump, crisp pea pods with bright green color.	Store snap peas in a plastic bag in the refrigerator up to 3 days.
Peppers	The peak season for sweet peppers lasts from July through September.	Look for peppers with shiny skin that are firm, have rich color, and are heavy for their size.	Store peppers in the refrigerator up to 1 week.
Potatoes	Many varieties are available year-round. Look for new potatoes from spring to summer.	Look for firm potatoes with no green spots, soft spots, wrinkling, or sprouting.	Store in a cool, dry, dark place up to 2 weeks. Use new potatoes within 3 days.

Continues on page 12

Vegetable	Seasonality	Selection	Storage
Summer Squash	Summer squash varieties are at their peak from early to late summer.	Choose small summer squash that have bright color with no blemishes.	Store summer squash in a plastic bag in the crisper drawer of the refrigerator up to 5 days.
Sweet Potatoes	Sweet potatoes are at their peak in the winter months.	Look for small to medium sweet potatoes with smooth, unbruised skins.	Store in a cool, dry, dark place and use within 1 week of purchasing.
Tomatoes	Look for the best tomatoes from June through September.	Look for fragrant tomatoes that are firm, have rich color, and are heavy for their size.	Store ripe tomatoes in a single layer at room temperature out of direct sunlight. Use within a few days.
Winter Squash	Squash is at its tastiest from early fall through the winter months.	Look for squash that is heavy for its size with a hard rind that is blemish-free.	Store winter squash in a cool, dark place for 1 to 6 months.

Fruit	Seasonality	Selection	Storage
Apples	Apples are their best in the fall when they are freshly harvested.	Look for firm, bright color apples free from bruising or blemishes.	Store apples in a cool, dark place or in a plastic bag in the refrigerator.
Blueberries	Look for blueberries from the end of May through early October.	Choose plump, dry berries that are deep blue with a white bloom on their skins.	Store unwashed berries in a single layer on paper towels in the refrigerator up to 3 days.
Cantaloupe	Look for the tastiest cantaloupes from June through August.	Look for fragrant melons that are heavy for their size and free from bruising.	Store whole cantaloupes in the refrigerator up to 3 days.
Cherries	Peak season for sweet and sour cherries is during the summer months.	Choose bright color cherries that are shiny and plump with fresh stems.	Store unwashed cherries in a plastic bag in the refrigerator up to 1 week.
Peaches	In most regions of the United States, peaches are available from May through October.	Choose fragrant peaches that give just slightly to pressure. Be sure to check for bruising.	Store ripe peaches in the crisper drawer of the refrigerator up to 5 days.
Pears	Pears reach their peak from late July to early spring, depending on the region.	Choose fragrant pears that are free from bruising and blemishes.	Store unripe pears at room temperature until ripe; store ripe pears in the refrigerator up to 7 days.
Raspberries	Peak season for red raspberries spans May through September.	Choose bright, clean, and uniform color raspberries without hulls	Store unwashed berries in a single layer on paper towels in the refrigerator up to 3 days.
Strawberries	Strawberries are available year-round and at their peak from spring to fall.	Look for firm, bright, uniform color berries with the hulls attached.	Store unwashed berries in a single layer on paper towels in the refrigerator up to 3 days.

CHAPTER 2

Breakfast

Spinach-Cheese Omelet

START TO FINISH 20 minutes

NUTRITION FACTS PER SERVING

Calories 122
Fat 3 g
Cholesterol 10 mg
Sodium 404 mg
Carbohydrates 7 g
Fiber 3 g
Protein 16 g

Nonstick cooking spray
1   cup refrigerated or frozen egg
     product, thawed, or 4 eggs,
     lightly beaten
     Dash salt
     Dash cayenne pepper
¼   cup shredded sharp cheddar
     cheese (1 ounce)
1   tablespoon snipped fresh
     chives, Italian (flat-leaf)
     parsley, or chervil
1   cup fresh spinach leaves
1   recipe Red Pepper Relish

1. Lightly coat a small nonstick skillet with cooking spray. Heat skillet over medium heat.

2. In a medium bowl whisk together egg product, salt, and cayenne pepper until frothy. Pour egg mixture into the hot skillet; reduce heat to medium. As mixture sets, run a spatula around the edge of the skillet, lifting egg mixture so uncooked portion flows underneath. Continue cooking and lifting edges until eggs are almost set (surface will be moist).

3. Sprinkle omelet with cheese and chives. Top with ¾ cup of the spinach and 2 tablespoons of the Red Pepper Relish. Using the spatula, lift and fold an edge of the omelet partially over filling. Top with the remaining ¼ cup spinach and 1 tablespoon of the Red Pepper Relish. (Reserve the remaining relish for another use.) Cut the omelet in half.
MAKES 2 SERVINGS

Red Pepper Relish: In a small bowl stir together ⅔ cup chopped red sweet pepper, 2 tablespoons finely chopped onion, 1 tablespoon cider vinegar, and ¼ teaspoon black pepper. **MAKES ABOUT ⅔ CUP**

Shrimp-Artichoke Frittata

START TO FINISH **30 minutes**

NUTRITION FACTS
PER SERVING

Calories 126
Fat 3 g
Cholesterol 37 mg
Sodium 343 mg
Carbohydrates 6 g
Fiber 2 g
Protein 19 g

4 ounces fresh or frozen shrimp in shells
½ of a 9-ounce package frozen artichoke hearts
2 cups refrigerated or frozen egg product, thawed, or 8 eggs, lightly beaten
¼ cup fat-free milk
¼ cup thinly sliced green onions (2)
⅛ teaspoon garlic powder
⅛ teaspoon black pepper
   Nonstick cooking spray
3 tablespoons finely shredded Parmesan cheese
   Cherry tomatoes, quartered (optional)
   Italian (flat-leaf) parsley (optional)

1. Thaw shrimp, if frozen. Peel and devein shrimp. Rinse shrimp; pat dry. Halve shrimp lengthwise; set aside. Meanwhile, cook artichoke hearts according to package directions; drain. Cut artichoke hearts into fourths; set aside.

2. In a medium bowl stir together egg product, milk, green onions, garlic powder, and pepper; set aside.

3. Lightly coat a large nonstick skillet with cooking spray. Heat skillet over medium heat. Add shrimp to skillet; cook and stir for 1 to 3 minutes or until shrimp are opaque.

4. Pour egg mixture into skillet; do not stir. Cook over medium-low heat. As mixture sets, run a spatula around edge of skillet, lifting egg so uncooked portion flows underneath. Continue cooking and lifting edges until eggs are almost set (surface will be moist).

5. Remove skillet from heat. Sprinkle artichoke pieces and Parmesan cheese over frittata. Cover and let stand for 3 to 4 minutes or until top is set. Loosen edges; transfer to a serving plate. To serve, cut frittata wedges. If desired, garnish with cherry tomatoes and parsley.
MAKES 4 SERVINGS

Breakfast Burritos

START TO FINISH **20 minutes**

NUTRITION FACTS PER SERVING

Calories 325
Fat 11 g
Cholesterol 37 mg
Sodium 1,038 mg
Carbohydrates 30 g
Fiber 3 g
Protein 26 g

2   cups refrigerated or frozen egg product, thawed, or 8 eggs, lightly beaten
⅓   cup fat-free milk
½   teaspoon garlic salt
8   ounces uncooked bulk turkey sausage
½   cup chopped green sweet pepper
½   cup chopped fresh mushrooms
¼   cup chopped onion
¾   cup bottled chunky salsa
½   cup chopped romaine
2   tablespoons finely chopped fresh jalapeños (see tip, page 63) (optional)
6   8- to 10-inch whole wheat tortillas, warmed
¾   cup shredded reduced-fat cheddar cheese (3 ounces)
    Bottled chunky salsa (optional)
    Grapes (optional)

1. In a medium bowl combine egg product, milk, and garlic salt; set aside.

2. In a large skillet cook and stir sausage, sweet pepper, mushrooms, and onion over medium heat until sausage is browned and vegetables are tender; drain off fat. Add egg mixture to skillet. Cook, without stirring, until eggs begin to set on the bottom and around edges.

3. With a spatula or large spoon, lift and fold partially cooked eggs so the uncooked portion flows underneath. Continue cooking over medium heat for 2 to 3 minutes or until cooked through yet glossy and moist.

4. Immediately remove skillet from heat. Stir in the ¾ cup salsa, romaine, and, if desired, jalapeños. Divide egg mixture among warm tortillas; top with cheese. Fold bottom edge of tortillas up and over the filling. Fold opposite sides in. Roll up from bottom. If desired, serve with additional salsa and grapes. **MAKES 6 SERVINGS**

Poached Eggs with Mustard Vinaigrette

START TO FINISH **20 minutes**

NUTRITION FACTS PER SERVING

Calories 183
Fat 13 g
Cholesterol 213 mg
Sodium 257 mg
Carbohydrates 10 g
Fiber 1 g
Protein 8 g

2   tablespoons vinegar
2   tablespoons olive oil
1   tablespoon coarse grain brown mustard
    Vegetable oil
4   eggs
2   cups mixed salad greens, or 8 cups torn fresh spinach sautéed in 1 tablespoon butter
2   slices dark rye bread, toasted and halved diagonally
    Salt and black pepper

1. In a small saucepan combine vinegar, olive oil, and mustard. Bring to boiling, stirring to combine. Reduce heat; keep warm, stirring occasionally.

2. Grease four cups of an egg poaching pan* with vegetable oil. Place poacher cups over a pan of boiling water (water should not touch the bottoms of the cups). Reduce heat to simmering. Break one egg into a measuring cup. Carefully slide egg into a poacher cup. Repeat with remaining eggs. Cover and cook for 6 to 9 minutes or until egg whites are completely set and yolks begin to thicken but are not hard.

3. To serve, evenly place greens on rye bread halves. Loosen poached eggs by running a knife around edge of each poacher cup; invert poacher cups and slip eggs onto greens. Stir mustard sauce; spoon over eggs. Sprinkle with salt and pepper. **MAKES 4 SERVINGS**

*Note: If you don't have an egg poaching pan, lightly grease a medium skillet. Fill the skillet half full with water. Bring the water to boiling; reduce heat to simmering (bubbles should begin to break the surface of the water). Break one egg into a measuring cup. Holding the lip of the cup as close to the water as possible, carefully slide egg into simmering water. Repeat with remaining eggs, allowing each egg an equal amount of space. Simmer eggs, uncovered, for 3 to 5 minutes or until whites are completely set and yolks begin to thicken but are not hard. Remove eggs with a slotted spoon. Serve as directed in Step 3.

Italian Baked Eggs

PREP 20 minutes
BAKE 15 minutes
STAND 5 minutes
OVEN 350°F

NUTRITION FACTS PER SERVING

Calories 114
Fat 5 g
Cholesterol 58 mg
Sodium 164 mg
Carbohydrates 6 g
Fiber 1 g
Protein 11 g

2   teaspoons olive oil or vegetable oil
1   small zucchini, halved lengthwise and thinly sliced
½   cup chopped red onion (1 medium)
½   cup chopped red or green sweet pepper
2   cloves garlic, minced
6   egg whites
1   egg
1   cup fat-free milk
1   tablespoon shredded fresh basil
¼   cup shredded mozzarella cheese (1 ounce)
     Chopped tomato (optional)

1. Preheat oven to 350°F. In a medium skillet heat oil over medium heat. Add zucchini, onion, sweet pepper, and garlic. Cook about 5 minutes or until onion is tender. Set aside.

2. In a medium bowl whisk together the egg whites, egg, milk, and basil. Stir in zucchini mixture. Pour egg mixture into four individual quiche dishes or shallow casseroles about 4½ inches in diameter.

3. Bake for 15 to 20 minutes or until set. Sprinkle with mozzarella cheese. Let stand for 5 minutes before serving. If desired, sprinkle with chopped tomato.
MAKES 4 SERVINGS

Tip: Keep garlic on hand for adding a boost of flavor to many recipes—without adding fat or calories. Store fresh garlic in a cool, dry, dark place. Leave the bulb whole, as individual cloves dry out quickly. Minced garlic is available in easy-to-use jars and will keep in the refrigerator up to 6 months.

Hash Brown Strata

PREP 15 minutes
BAKE 40 minutes
STAND 5 minutes
OVEN 350°F

NUTRITION FACTS PER SERVING

Calories 231
Fat 11 g
Cholesterol 17 mg
Sodium 472 mg
Carbohydrates 17 g
Fiber 1 g
Protein 17 g

Nonstick cooking spray
2 cups frozen loose-pack diced hash brown potatoes with onion and peppers
1 cup coarsely chopped broccoli florets
3 ounces turkey ham, chopped, or turkey bacon, cooked, drained, and crumbled
⅓ cup evaporated fat-free milk
2 tablespoons all-purpose flour
2 8-ounce cartons refrigerated or frozen egg product, thawed, or 8 eggs, lightly beaten
½ cup shredded reduced-fat cheddar cheese (2 ounces)
1 tablespoon snipped fresh basil or ½ teaspoon dried basil, crushed
¼ teaspoon black pepper

1. Preheat oven to 350°F. Lightly coat a 2-quart square baking dish with cooking spray. Arrange hash brown potatoes and broccoli in baking dish; top with turkey ham. Set aside.

2. In a medium bowl whisk together milk and flour. Whisk in the egg product, ¼ cup of the cheese, the basil, and pepper. Pour egg mixture over vegetables.

3. Bake for 40 to 45 minutes or until a knife inserted near the center comes out clean. Sprinkle with the remaining ¼ cup cheese. Let stand for 5 minutes before serving. **MAKES 6 SERVINGS**

Swiss-Potato Breakfast Casserole

PREP 20 minutes
BAKE 35 minutes
STAND 5 minutes
OVEN 350°F

NUTRITION FACTS PER SERVING

Calories 207
Fat 9 g
Cholesterol 132 mg
Sodium 409 mg
Carbohydrates 18 g
Fiber 2 g
Protein 13 g

1   pound tiny new potatoes, cut into ¼-inch slices
⅓   cup thinly sliced leek
     Nonstick cooking spray
¾   cup diced cooked ham (3½ ounces)
3   ounces Swiss cheese, cut into small pieces
1¼ cups fat-free milk
1   tablespoon all-purpose flour
3   eggs, lightly beaten
½   teaspoon dried thyme, crushed
¼   teaspoon salt
¼   teaspoon black pepper
3   slices center-cut bacon, cooked and crumbled (optional)

1. Preheat oven to 350°F. In a large saucepan cook potatoes in a small amount of lightly salted, boiling water about 10 minutes or just until tender, adding leek during the last 5 minutes of cooking. Drain well.

2. Lightly coat a 2-quart baking dish with cooking spray. Arrange cooked potatoes and leek evenly in the prepared dish. Sprinkle with ham and cheese.

3. In a medium bowl whisk together milk and flour. Whisk in eggs, thyme, salt, and pepper. Pour the egg mixture over layers in dish.

4. Bake, uncovered, for 35 to 40 minutes or until a knife inserted near the center comes out clean. Let stand for 5 minutes before serving. If desired, sprinkle with bacon. **MAKES 6 SERVINGS**

Turkey-Pork Sausage Patties

START TO FINISH 25 minutes

NUTRITION FACTS
PER PATTY

Calories 126
Fat 8 g
Cholesterol 55 mg
Sodium 62 mg
Carbohydrates 1 g
Fiber 0 g
Protein 12 g

12 ounces uncooked lean ground turkey
3 ounces uncooked ground pork
1 teaspoon dried sage, crushed
½ teaspoon garlic powder
½ teaspoon onion powder
½ teaspoon cumin seeds, lightly toasted
½ teaspoon freshly ground black pepper
¼ teaspoon crushed red pepper
¼ teaspoon dried oregano, crushed
¼ teaspoon dried tarragon, crushed
   Nonstick olive oil cooking spray

1. In a large bowl combine turkey, pork, sage, garlic powder, onion powder, cumin seeds, black pepper, red pepper, oregano, and tarragon. Shape turkey mixture into six round patties, 3 to 4 inches in diameter.

2. Lightly coat an unheated extra-large nonstick skillet with cooking spray. Heat the skillet over medium heat. Place patties in skillet. Cook about 8 minutes or until no longer pink (165°F), turning once halfway through cooking. **MAKES 6 PATTIES**

*Tip: The internal color of a ground poultry patty is not a reliable doneness indicator. A turkey patty cooked to 165°F is safe, regardless of color. To measure the doneness of a patty, insert an instant-read thermometer through the side of the patty to a depth of 2 to 3 inches.

Multi-Grain Orange-Kissed Waffles

PREP 10 minutes
BAKE per waffle baker directions

NUTRITION FACTS PER WAFFLE

Calories 221
Fat 10 g
Cholesterol 1 mg
Sodium 226 mg
Carbohydrates 28 g
Fiber 2 g
Protein 5 g

1½ cups all-purpose flour
½ cup whole wheat flour
½ cup oat flour
1 tablespoon baking powder
1 tablespoon packed brown sugar
½ teaspoon baking soda
¼ teaspoon salt
1¾ cups skim milk or light vanilla soy milk
½ cup refrigerated or frozen egg product, thawed, or 2 eggs, lightly beaten
½ cup canola oil
1 tablespoon finely shredded orange peel
½ cup low-sugar orange marmalade
1½ cups fresh blueberries, raspberries, and/or sliced strawberries

1. In a large bowl combine all-purpose flour, whole wheat flour, oat flour, baking powder, brown sugar, baking soda, and salt. Make a well in center of flour mixture; set aside.

2. In a medium bowl combine milk, egg product, oil, and orange peel. Add egg mixture to flour mixture all at once. Stir just until moistened (batter should be slightly lumpy).

3. Pour ⅔ to 1 cup batter onto grids of a preheated, lightly greased waffle baker (use a regular or Belgian waffle baker). Close lid quickly; do not open until done. Bake according to manufacturer's directions. When done, use a fork to lift waffle off grid. Repeat with remaining batter.

4. For sauce, in a small saucepan heat marmalade until melted. Stir in berries; heat through. Spoon sauce over warm waffles.
MAKES 12 TO 16 (4-INCH) WAFFLES

Crunch-Topped French Toast

PREP 20 minutes
CHILL 2 to 24 hours
BAKE 30 minutes
OVEN 375°F

NUTRITION FACTS PER SERVING

Calories 227
Fat 3 g
Cholesterol 7 mg
Sodium 296 mg
Carbohydrates 39 g
Fiber 3 g
Protein 10 g

Nonstick cooking spray
1 cup evaporated fat-free milk
¾ cup refrigerated or frozen egg product, thawed, or 3 eggs, lightly beaten
3 tablespoons sugar
2 teaspoons vanilla
½ teaspoon ground cinnamon
¼ teaspoon ground nutmeg
6 1-inch slices Italian bread (3 to 4 inches in diameter)
1 large shredded wheat biscuit, crushed (⅔ cup)
1 tablespoon butter, melted
2 cups sliced strawberries
3 tablespoons sugar
½ teaspoon ground cinnamon

1. Lightly coat a 2-quart rectangular baking dish with cooking spray; set aside. In a medium bowl whisk together the evaporated milk, egg product, 3 tablespoons sugar, the vanilla, ½ teaspoon cinnamon, and the nutmeg. Arrange bread slices in a single layer in the prepared baking dish. Pour milk mixture evenly over bread. Cover and chill for 2 to 24 hours, turning bread slices once.

2. Preheat oven to 375°F. In a small bowl combine crushed shredded wheat biscuit and melted butter; sprinkle evenly over the bread slices. Bake, uncovered, about 30 minutes or until light brown.

3. Meanwhile, in a small bowl toss together strawberries, 3 tablespoons sugar, and ½ teaspoon cinnamon. Serve with French toast.
MAKES 6 SERVINGS

Slimmed-Down Cinnamon Rolls

PREP **35 minutes**
STAND **10 minutes**
RISE **2 hours 30 minutes**
BAKE **20 minutes**
COOL **5 minutes**
OVEN **375°F**

NUTRITION FACTS PER ROLL

Calories 167
Fat 3 g
Cholesterol 0 mg
Sodium 45 mg
Carbohydrates 32 g
Fiber 1 g
Protein 4 g

2¾ to 3¼ cups all-purpose flour
1 package active dry yeast
1 cup fat-free milk
⅓ cup granulated sugar
3 tablespoons vegetable oil
¼ teaspoon salt
¼ cup refrigerated or frozen egg product, thawed, or 2 slightly beaten egg whites
1 cup whole wheat flour or all-purpose flour
  Nonstick cooking spray
⅓ cup packed brown sugar
1 teaspoon ground cinnamon
  Nonstick cooking spray
1 cup powdered sugar
1 to 2 tablespoons orange juice

1. In a large mixing bowl combine 2 cups of the all-purpose flour and yeast; set aside. In a small saucepan heat and stir milk, granulated sugar, oil, and salt just until warm (120°F to 130°F).

2. Add milk mixture and egg product to flour mixture. Beat with an electric mixer on low for 30 seconds, scraping sides of the bowl. Beat on high for 3 minutes more. Using a wooden spoon, stir in the 1 cup of whole wheat flour, plus as much of the remaining all-purpose flour as you can.

3. Turn dough out onto a floured surface. Knead in enough remaining all-purpose flour to make a moderately soft dough that is smooth and elastic (3 to 5 minutes total). Shape into a ball.

4. Coat a large bowl with cooking spray. Place dough in bowl, turning once to coat. Cover and let rise in a warm place until double in size (about 1 hour). Punch down. Turn onto a lightly floured surface. Divide in half. Cover; let rest for 10 minutes.

5. In a small bowl combine brown sugar and cinnamon; set aside.

Coat two 8×1½-inch round baking pans with cooking spray.

6. On a lightly floured surface, roll each dough half to a 12×8-inch rectangle. Brush with a little water. Sprinkle brown sugar-cinnamon on dough, leaving 1 inch along one long side. Roll up each rectangle, starting from the filled long side. Pinch to seal. Slice each roll in 9 equal pieces. Arrange, cut sides up, in pans.

7. Cover and let rise in a warm place until nearly double in size (about 30 minutes).

8. Preheat oven to 375°F. Bake for 20 to 25 minutes or until golden. Cool about 5 minutes; remove pans.

9. For icing, in a small bowl stir together powdered sugar and 1 tablespoon of the juice. Stir in additional juice, 1 teaspoon at a time, until the icing is drizzling consistency. Drizzle over the rolls.
MAKES 18 ROLLS

Apple Surprise Rolls

PREP 45 minutes
RISE 30 minutes
BAKE 12 minutes
OVEN 375°F

NUTRITION FACTS PER ROLL

Calories 149
Fat 2 g
Cholesterol 13 mg
Sodium 187 mg
Carbohydrates 29 g
Fiber 0 g
Protein 4 g

1   16-ounce package hot roll mix
1   cup finely chopped cooking apple (1 medium)
¼   cup mixed dried fruit bits or raisins
2   tablespoons packed brown sugar
½   teaspoon ground cinnamon
    Nonstick cooking spray
½   cup powdered sugar (optional)
1½ to 2 teaspoons milk (optional)

1. Preheat oven to 375°F. Prepare hot roll mix according to package directions. Knead the dough; allow to rest as directed. Meanwhile, for filling, in a small bowl stir together apple, dried fruit bits, brown sugar, and cinnamon. Lightly coat two baking sheets with cooking spray; set aside.

2. Divide dough in 16 pieces. Flatten each piece to a 3-inch circle. Spoon 1 rounded teaspoon of filling onto each circle. Shape the dough around the filling to enclose, pulling dough until smooth and rounded. Place rolls, rounded sides up, on the prepared baking sheets. Cover and let rise in a warm place until nearly double in size (about 30 minutes).

3. Bake for 12 to 15 minutes or until golden. Transfer rolls to a wire rack and cool slightly. If desired, in a small bowl stir together powdered sugar and enough milk to make an icing of drizzling consistency. Drizzle icing over rolls. **MAKES 16 ROLLS**

Raspberry-Cheese Coffee Cake

PREP 15 minutes
BAKE 35 minutes
COOL 10 minutes
OVEN 375°F

NUTRITION FACTS PER SERVING

Calories 195
Fat 5 g
Cholesterol 14 mg
Sodium 223 mg
Carbohydrates 33 g
Fiber 1 g
Protein 4 g

Nonstick cooking spray
1¼ cups all-purpose flour
1¼ teaspoons baking powder
1 teaspoon finely shredded lemon or orange peel
¼ teaspoon baking soda
¼ teaspoon salt
1 cup granulated sugar
3 tablespoons butter, softened
¼ cup refrigerated or frozen egg product, thawed
1 teaspoon vanilla
½ cup buttermilk or fat-free sour milk*
2 ounces reduced-fat cream cheese (Neufchâtel)
2 tablespoons refrigerated or frozen egg product, thawed
1 cup fresh or frozen raspberries
Powdered sugar
Raspberries (optional)

1. Preheat oven to 375°F. Lightly coat a 9-inch round baking pan with cooking spray; set aside. In a medium bowl stir together flour, baking powder, lemon peel, baking soda, and salt.

2. In a medium mixing bowl beat ¾ cup of the granulated sugar and the butter with an electric mixer on medium to high until combined. Add the ¼ cup egg product and the vanilla. Beat on low to medium for 1 minute. Alternately add flour mixture and buttermilk to beaten egg mixture, beating just until combined after each addition. Pour batter into prepared pan.

3. In a small mixing bowl beat cream cheese and the remaining ¼ cup granulated sugar with electric mixer on medium to high until combined. Add the 2 tablespoons egg product; beat until combined. Sprinkle the 1 cup raspberries on the batter in pan. Spoon cream cheese mixture on raspberries, allowing some berries to show.

4. Bake about 35 minutes or until a toothpick inserted near the center comes out clean. Cool in pan for 10 minutes. Sprinkle with powdered sugar. Serve warm. If desired, garnish with additional raspberries. **MAKES 10 SERVINGS**

*Tip: To make ½ cup fat-free sour milk, place 1½ teaspoons lemon juice or vinegar in a glass measuring cup. Add enough fat-free milk to equal ½ cup liquid; stir. Let the mixture stand for 5 minutes before using.

Maple Bran Muffins

PREP 20 minutes
STAND 5 minutes
BAKE 25 minutes
COOL 5 minutes
OVEN 350°F

NUTRITION FACTS PER MUFFIN

Calories 173
Fat 4 g
Cholesterol 1 mg
Sodium 152 mg
Carbohydrates 33 g
Fiber 5 g
Protein 5 g

Nonstick cooking spray
2   cups whole bran cereal
1⅔ cups buttermilk or fat-free
    sour milk*
1   cup whole wheat flour
1¾ teaspoons baking powder
½   teaspoon ground cinnamon
¼   teaspoon baking soda
½   cup refrigerated or frozen egg
    product, thawed, or 2 eggs,
    lightly beaten
⅓   cup packed brown sugar
¼   cup pure maple syrup or
    maple-flavor syrup
3   tablespoons canola oil
¾   cup mixed dried fruit bits
    and/or raisins
1   recipe Maple Icing (optional)

1. Preheat oven to 350°F. Lightly coat twelve to sixteen 2½-inch muffin cups with cooking spray; set aside.

2. Place bran cereal in a large bowl; stir in buttermilk. Let stand for 5 to 10 minutes or until cereal is softened. In a small bowl stir together flour, baking powder, cinnamon, and baking soda; set aside.

3. Stir egg product, brown sugar, syrup, and oil into bran mixture. Add flour mixture to bran mixture; stir just until combined. Stir in dried fruit bits. Spoon batter evenly into prepared muffin cups, filling each three-fourths full.

4. Bake for 25 to 30 minutes or until tops spring back when lightly touched and a toothpick inserted in centers comes out clean. Cool in muffin cups on a wire rack for 5 minutes. Remove from muffin cups. If desired, drizzle with Maple Icing. Serve warm.

MAKES 12 TO 16 MUFFINS

*Tip: To make 1⅔ cups fat-free sour milk, place 1 tablespoon plus 2 teaspoons lemon juice or vinegar in a 2-cup glass measuring cup. Add enough fat-free milk to equal 1⅔ cups; stir. Let the mixture stand for 5 minutes before using.

Maple Icing: In a small bowl combine ⅓ cup powdered sugar and ¼ teaspoon maple flavoring. Stir in fat-free milk, 1 teaspoon at a time, until the icing is drizzling consistency.

Morning Glory Muffins

PREP 10 minutes
BAKE 18 minutes
COOL 5 minutes
OVEN 375°F

NUTRITION FACTS
PER MUFFIN

Calories 221
Fat 9 g
Cholesterol 35 mg
Sodium 225 mg
Carbohydrates 33 g
Fiber 1 g
Protein 3 g

2   cups all-purpose flour
1¼ cups packed brown sugar
2   teaspoons baking soda
2   teaspoons ground cinnamon
½   teaspoon salt
1⅓ cups chopped, peeled apples
1¼ cups finely shredded carrots
½   cup raisins
3   eggs, lightly beaten
1   8-ounce can crushed
      pineapple (juice pack),
      undrained
⅔   cup vegetable oil
½   teaspoon vanilla

1. Preheat oven to 375°F. Line eighteen 2½-inch muffin cups with paper bake cups; set aside.

2. In a large bowl combine flour, brown sugar, baking soda, cinnamon, and salt. Stir in apples, carrots, and raisins. Make a well in the center of the flour mixture.

3. In a medium bowl combine eggs, the undrained pineapple, oil, and vanilla. Add pineapple mixture to flour mixture. Stir just until moistened (batter should be lumpy). Spoon batter into prepared muffin cups.

4. Bake about 18 minutes or until a wooden toothpick inserted in centers comes out clean. Cool in muffin cups on a wire rack for 5 minutes. Remove from muffin cups. Serve warm. **MAKES 18 MUFFINS**

Baked Grapefruit Halves

PREP 15 minutes
BAKE 12 minutes
OVEN 450°F

NUTRITION FACTS PER SERVING

Calories 154
Fat 3 g
Cholesterol 0 mg
Sodium 4 mg
Carbohydrates 32 g
Fiber 3 g
Protein 2 g

3   red grapefruit
1   medium orange, peeled and sectioned
1   medium banana, sliced
⅓   cup dried cherries
2   tablespoons orange liqueur or orange juice
1   tablespoon canola oil
2   tablespoons packed brown sugar
½   teaspoon ground cinnamon

1. Preheat oven to 450°F. Cut each grapefruit in half horizontally; cut a very thin slice from the bottom of each half so grapefruit halves will stand flat. Using a grapefruit knife or a small serrated knife, cut around the outer edge to loosen fruit from shell. Cut between each segment and the membrane, slicing to grapefruit center. Turn the knife and slide it up the other side of the section alongside the membrane. Place grapefruit halves in a 3-quart rectangular baking dish.

2. In a medium bowl combine orange sections, banana slices, cherries, and orange liqueur. Mound the orange mixture on grapefruit halves. Drizzle with oil. In a small bowl combine brown sugar and cinnamon; sprinkle over orange mixture.

3. Bake about 12 minutes or until grapefruits are warm and topping is heated through. **MAKES 6 SERVINGS**

Warm Citrus Fruit with Brown Sugar

PREP 15 minutes
BROIL 5 minutes

NUTRITION FACTS PER SERVING

Calories 192
Fat 6 g
Cholesterol 16 mg
Sodium 68 mg
Carbohydrates 35 g
Fiber 4 g
Protein 2 g

2 medium red grapefruit, peeled and sectioned, or 1½ cups drained refrigerated grapefruit sections
2 medium oranges, peeled and sectioned
1 cup fresh pineapple chunks or one 8-ounce can pineapple chunks, drained
2 tablespoons rum (optional)
¼ cup packed brown sugar
2 tablespoons butter, softened

1. In a medium bowl combine grapefruit, oranges, and pineapple. Transfer to a 1-quart broiler-safe gratin dish or casserole or 4 individual gratin dishes.

2. If desired, in a small saucepan heat rum until it almost simmers. Carefully ignite with a long kitchen match and pour over fruit. Stir gently to coat until flames extinguish.

3. In a small bowl stir together brown sugar and butter until well mixed; sprinkle over fruit. Broil about 4 inches from the heat for 5 to 6 minutes until sugar is bubbly and fruit is warmed.
MAKES 4 SERVINGS

Breakfast Fruit Medley

START TO FINISH 20 minutes

NUTRITION FACTS PER SERVING

Calories 116
Fat 0 g
Cholesterol 0 mg
Sodium 2 mg
Carbohydrates 30 g
Fiber 2 g
Protein 1 g

½ cup dried tart cherries
¼ cup honey
½ teaspoon finely shredded lime peel
1 to 2 tablespoons lime juice
1 cup seedless green grapes, halved
1 cup seedless red grapes, halved
1 Granny Smith apple, cored and cut in bite-size pieces
1 Red Delicious apple, cored and cut in bite-size pieces
2 fresh kiwifruits, peeled and cut in wedges

1. Place dried cherries in a small bowl; add enough boiling water to cover cherries. Let stand about 15 minutes or until cherries are plump; drain.

2. In a large bowl combine honey, lime peel, and lime juice. Stir in the drained cherries, grapes, apples, and kiwifruits. Serve immediately or cover and refrigerate up to 2 hours before serving.
MAKES 8 TO 10 SERVINGS

Banana-Berry Smoothies

START TO FINISH 10 minutes

NUTRITION FACTS
PER SMOOTHIE

Calories 182
Fat 3 g
Cholesterol 9 mg
Sodium 82 mg
Carbohydrates 35 g
Fiber 3 g
Protein 7 g

2   ripe bananas, chilled
1   cup frozen unsweetened
    whole strawberries
1   6-ounce carton vanilla low-fat
    yogurt
¾   cup milk
    Fresh whole strawberries
    (optional)

1. Cut bananas in chunks. In a
blender combine bananas, frozen
strawberries, yogurt, and milk.

2. Cover and blend until smooth.
Pour into glasses or transfer to a
small pitcher and chill up to
6 hours. If desired, garnish
smoothies with whole strawberries.
MAKES 3 (ABOUT 8-OUNCE) SERVINGS

CHAPTER 3

Breads

Oatmeal-Raisin Swirl Bread

PREP 30 minutes
STAND 45 minutes
RISE 1 hour 30 minutes
BAKE 25 minutes
OVEN 350°F

NUTRITION FACTS
PER SLICE

Calories 109
Fat 2 g
Cholesterol 0 mg
Sodium 60 mg
Carbohydrates 21 g
Fiber 2 g
Protein 3 g

1½ cups boiling water
¾   cup quick-cooking rolled oats
2   tablespoons granulated sugar
1   tablespoon tub-style vegetable oil spread
½   teaspoon salt
¼   cup warm water (105°F to 115°F)
1   package active dry yeast
1   cup whole wheat flour
2¼ to 2¾ cups all-purpose flour
¼   cup packed brown sugar
¼   cup ground flaxseed meal
1½ teaspoons ground cinnamon
2   tablespoons tub-style vegetable oil spread
½   cup raisins, chopped

1. In a large mixing bowl combine the boiling water, oats, granulated sugar, 1 tablespoon of the vegetable oil spread, and salt. Stir until spread is melted. Cover and let stand about 45 minutes or until cooled to room temperature. In a small bowl combine the warm water and yeast; stir until yeast is dissolved. Stir yeast mixture and whole wheat flour into oat mixture. Using a wooden spoon, stir in as much of the all-purpose flour as you can.

2. Turn dough out onto a floured surface. Knead in enough of the remaining all-purpose flour to make a moderately stiff dough that is smooth and elastic (6 to 8 minutes total). Shape dough into a ball. Place dough in a lightly greased large bowl, turning once to grease surface of dough. Cover; let rise in a warm place until double in size (about 1 hour).

3. Punch dough down. Turn out onto a lightly floured surface. Divide in half. Cover; let rest for 10 minutes. Meanwhile, lightly grease two 8×4×2-inch loaf pans; set aside. For filling, stir together brown sugar, flaxseed meal, and cinnamon; set aside.

4. Roll each portion of the dough to a 12×8-inch rectangle. Spread 1 tablespoon of the remaining vegetable oil spread on each dough rectangle. Evenly sprinkle with filling and raisins, leaving 1 inch unfilled along one short side. Roll up each rectangle starting from filled short side. Pinch dough to seal seams. Pinch together open ends to enclose the filling. Place each roll, seam side down, in a prepared pan. Cover and let rise in a warm place until nearly double in size (about 30 minutes).

5. Preheat oven to 350°F. Bake loaves for 25 to 35 minutes or until tops are golden brown and loaves sound hollow when lightly tapped. Remove from pans and cool completely on wire racks.
MAKES 2 LOAVES (12 SLICES EACH)

Braided Cranberry Bread

PREP 30 minutes
RISE 1 hour 30 minutes
BAKE 25 minutes
OVEN 375°F

2¾ to 3 cups all-purpose flour
1   package active dry yeast
½   cup milk
¼   cup water
2   tablespoons granulated sugar
2   tablespoons butter
½   teaspoon salt
1   egg
½   cup finely chopped fresh
     cranberries
¼   cup packed brown sugar
2   tablespoons finely chopped
     pecans
1½ teaspoons finely shredded
     orange peel
¼   teaspoon ground cinnamon
¼   teaspoon ground nutmeg
⅛   teaspoon ground cloves
1½ teaspoons butter, melted
1   recipe Orange Icing (optional)

1. In a large bowl combine 1 cup of the flour and the yeast; set aside. In a medium saucepan heat and stir milk, the water, granulated sugar, the 2 tablespoons butter, and the salt until warm (120°F to 130°F) and butter is almost melted. Add milk mixture to flour mixture; add egg. Beat with mixer on low to medium for 30 seconds, scraping sides of bowl constantly. Beat on high for 3 minutes. Using a wooden spoon, stir in as much of the remaining flour as you can.

2. Turn dough out onto a floured surface. Knead in enough of the remaining flour to make a soft dough that is smooth and elastic (3 to 5 minutes total). Shape into a ball. Place in a lightly greased bowl, turning once to grease surface of dough. Cover and let rise in a warm place until double in size (1 to 1½ hours).

3. Meanwhile, for filling, in a small bowl stir together cranberries, brown sugar, pecans, orange peel, cinnamon, nutmeg, and cloves.

4. Punch down dough. Turn out onto lightly floured surface. Cover and let rest for 10 minutes. Grease a baking sheet. Roll dough into a 14×10-inch rectangle. Brush with the melted butter. Spread filling on dough, leaving 1 inch unfilled along one long side. Roll up dough, starting from filled long side. Seal seam. Cut roll in half lengthwise. Turn cut sides up. Loosely twist halves together, keeping cut sides up. Pinch ends to seal. Place loaf on the prepared baking sheet. Cover; let rise in a warm place until nearly double in size (about 30 minutes).

5. Preheat oven to 375°F. Bake about 25 minutes or until golden. Transfer loaf to a wire rack; cool completely. If desired, drizzle with Orange Icing. **MAKES 18 SERVINGS**

Orange Icing: In a small bowl stir together ½ cup powdered sugar and enough orange juice (1 to 3 teaspoons) to make icing of drizzling consistency.

Herb Dinner Bread

PREP **30 minutes**
RISE **1 hour 15 minutes**
STAND **10 minutes**
BAKE **35 minutes**
OVEN **350°F**

NUTRITION FACTS PER SLICE

Calories 105
Fat 2 g
Cholesterol 1 mg
Sodium 187 mg
Carbohydrates 19 g
Fiber 2 g
Protein 4 g

1   package active dry yeast
½   cup warm water (105°F to 115°F)
2   cups all-purpose flour
1   cup whole wheat flour
⅔   cup mashed cooked potatoes
⅓   cup cream-style cottage cheese
¼   cup potato water or water
1   tablespoon vegetable oil
1   teaspoon salt
½   teaspoon dried dill or dried parsley flakes
¼   teaspoon dried thyme, crushed
¼   teaspoon celery seeds (optional)

1. In a small bowl dissolve yeast in the ½ cup warm water; set aside. In a large bowl combine all-purpose flour, whole wheat flour, mashed potatoes, cottage cheese, the ¼ cup water, the oil, salt, dill, thyme, and, if desired, celery seeds, stirring until well mixed. Add the yeast mixture; stir until combined.

2. Turn dough out onto a lightly floured surface. Knead until dough is moderately soft, smooth, and elastic (3 to 5 minutes). Shape dough into a ball. Place dough in a lightly greased bowl, turning once to grease the surface of the dough. Cover; let rise in a warm place until double in size (45 to 60 minutes).

3. Punch dough down. Turn out onto a lightly floured surface. Cover and let rest for 10 minutes. Lightly grease a 1½-quart casserole or a 9×5×3-inch loaf pan.

4. Shape dough into a round or rectangular loaf. Place round loaf in prepared casserole or place rectangular loaf in prepared loaf pan. Cover and let rise in a warm place until nearly double in size (30 to 40 minutes).

5. Preheat oven to 350°F. Bake for 35 to 40 minutes or until bread sounds hollow when tapped. Immediately remove from casserole or pan. Cool on a wire rack.
MAKES 1 LOAF (16 SLICES)

Hearty Mixed Grain Bread

PREP 30 minutes
STAND 30 minutes
RISE 1 hour 15 minutes
BAKE 30 minutes
OVEN 375°F

NUTRITION FACTS PER SLICE

Calories 142
Fat 2 g
Cholesterol 0 mg
Sodium 151 mg
Carbohydrates 26 g
Fiber 2 g
Protein 4 g

1¼ cups boiling water
½ cup uncooked seven-grain hot cereal
3 to 3½ cups all-purpose flour
1 package active dry yeast
¾ cup fat-free milk
¼ cup honey
2 tablespoons canola oil
1½ teaspoons salt
1½ cups whole wheat flour or white whole wheat flour
½ cup rolled oats
¼ cup flaxseed meal
Fat-free milk
¼ cup rolled oats and/or flaxseeds

1. In a medium bowl combine the boiling water and cereal. Let stand for 20 minutes. In a large mixing bowl combine 2 cups of the all-purpose flour and the yeast; set aside. In a small saucepan heat and stir the ¾ cup milk, the honey, oil, and salt over medium heat just until warm (120°F to 130°F). Add milk mixture and cereal mixture to flour mixture. Beat with electric mixer on low to medium for 30 seconds, scraping sides of bowl. Beat on high for 3 minutes. Using a wooden spoon, stir in whole wheat flour, ½ cup oats, the flaxseed meal, and as much of the remaining all-purpose flour as you can.

2. Turn dough out onto a lightly floured surface. Knead in enough of the remaining all-purpose flour to make a moderately stiff dough that is almost smooth and elastic (6 to 8 minutes total). Shape dough into a ball. Place in a lightly greased bowl, turning once to grease surface of dough. Cover; let rise in a warm place until double in size (45 to 60 minutes).

3. Punch dough down. Turn out onto a lightly floured surface.

Divide in half. Cover; let rest for 10 minutes. Meanwhile, lightly grease a large baking sheet; set aside.

4. Shape dough halves into 8-inch-long oval loaves about 4 inches wide at the center. Place shaped loaves 4 inches apart on prepared baking sheet. Cover and let rise in a warm place until nearly double in size (about 30 minutes).

5. Preheat oven to 375°F. Brush tops of loaves lightly with milk; sprinkle with ¼ cup oats and/or flaxseeds.

6. Bake for 30 to 35 minutes or until bread sounds hollow when lightly tapped, covering loosely with foil, if necessary, the last 10 minutes of baking to prevent overbrowning. Transfer loaves to wire racks and cool completely.
MAKES 2 LOAVES (12 SLICES EACH)

Chive Batter Bread

PREP 30 minutes
STAND 10 minutes
RISE 20 minutes
BAKE 18 minutes
OVEN 350°F

NUTRITION FACTS
PER ROLL

Calories 140
Fat 4 g
Cholesterol 28 mg
Sodium 144 mg
Carbohydrates 21 g
Fiber 1 g
Protein 4 g

1   tablespoon yellow cornmeal
2   cups all-purpose flour
1   package fast-rising active dry yeast
¼   teaspoon black pepper
1   cup milk
2   tablespoons sugar
3   tablespoons butter
½   teaspoon salt
1   egg
½   cup snipped fresh chives or ¼ cup finely chopped green onions (green tops only)
⅓   cup yellow cornmeal

1. Grease the bottom and sides of twelve 2½-inch muffin cups. Sprinkle bottoms of cups evenly with the 1 tablespoon cornmeal; set aside. In a large mixing bowl stir together 1¼ cups of the flour, the yeast, and the pepper; set aside.

2. In a small saucepan combine milk, sugar, butter, and salt; heat and stir over medium heat just until mixture is warm (120°F to 130°F) and butter is almost melted. Add milk mixture and egg to flour mixture. Beat with electric mixer on low to medium for 30 seconds, scraping bowl constantly. Beat on high for 3 minutes. Stir in chives and the ⅓ cup cornmeal. Stir in remaining flour. (The batter will be soft and sticky.) Cover and let rest in a warm place for 10 minutes.

3. Spoon batter into prepared muffin cups. Cover loosely with plastic wrap. Let rise in a warm place for 20 minutes.

4. Preheat oven to 350°F. Bake about 18 minutes or until rolls sound hollow when tapped. Cool in muffin cups on a wire rack for 5 minutes. Remove from muffin cups; serve warm. **MAKES 12 ROLLS**

Tomato-Artichoke Focaccia

PREP 30 minutes
RISE 1 hour 15 minutes
STAND 15 minutes
BAKE 25 minutes
OVEN 450°F

NUTRITION FACTS PER SERVING

Calories 197
Fat 4 g
Cholesterol 0 mg
Sodium 310 mg
Carbohydrates 35 g
Fiber 3 g
Protein 5 g

3½ to 4 cups all-purpose flour
1   package active dry yeast
1   teaspoon salt
1¼ cups warm water (120°F to 130°F)
2   tablespoons olive oil
¼ cup cornmeal
    Nonstick cooking spray
1¼ pounds plum tomatoes and/or green or yellow tomatoes, thinly sliced
1   14-ounce can artichoke hearts, drained and quartered
1   tablespoon olive oil
1   tablespoon snipped fresh rosemary or 1 teaspoon dried rosemary, crushed
1   small red onion, very thinly sliced and separated in rings
4   cloves garlic, cut in thin slivers or slices

1. In a large bowl combine 1½ cups of the flour, yeast, and salt. Add the warm water and the 2 tablespoons olive oil. Beat with electric mixer on low to medium for 30 seconds, scraping sides of bowl constantly. Beat on high for 3 minutes. Using a wooden spoon, stir in cornmeal and as much of the remaining flour as you can.

2. Turn dough out onto a lightly floured surface. Knead in enough of the remaining flour to make a moderately soft dough that is smooth and elastic (3 to 5 minutes). Shape dough in a ball. Place in a lightly greased bowl, turning once. Cover; let rise until double in size (45 to 60 minutes).

3. Punch down dough; let rest for 10 minutes. Grease a 15×10×1-inch baking pan. Place dough in baking pan. Gently pull and stretch dough to a 15×8-inch rectangle, being careful not to overwork dough.

4. Lightly coat dough with cooking spray. Cover loosely with plastic wrap; let dough rise in a warm place until nearly double in size (about 30 minutes).

5. Preheat oven to 450°F. Arrange tomato slices and artichoke quarters on a double thickness of paper towels. Let stand for 15 minutes. Change towels as necessary so liquid is absorbed from tomatoes and artichokes.

6. Press deep indentations in the dough 1½ to 2 inches apart. Brush dough with the 1 tablespoon olive oil. Sprinkle with rosemary. Evenly arrange tomato slices, artichoke quarters, onion rings, and garlic slivers on dough.

7. Bake about 25 minutes or until golden brown. Transfer to a wire rack; cool. Cut in rectangles. Serve warm or at room temperature. **MAKES 12 SERVINGS**

Lemon-Herb and Walnut Focaccia

PREP 30 minutes
STAND 8 hours to overnight
RISE 1 hour
REST 30 minutes
BAKE 12 minutes
COOL 15 minutes
OVEN 475°F

NUTRITION FACTS PER SERVING

Calories 135
Fat 4 g
Cholesterol 0 mg
Sodium 147 mg
Carbohydrates 22 g
Fiber 2 g
Protein 4 g

2 to 2⅓ cups all-purpose flour
⅓ cup warm water (105°F to 115°F)
1 package active dry yeast
¾ cup warm water (105°F to 115°F)
¾ cup whole wheat flour or white whole wheat flour
⅓ cup chopped walnuts, toasted
1 tablespoon finely shredded lemon peel
2 teaspoons snipped fresh oregano or 1 teaspoon dried oregano, crushed
2 teaspoons snipped fresh thyme or ½ teaspoon dried thyme, crushed
¾ teaspoon salt
1 tablespoon olive oil
Additional fresh or dried oregano and/or thyme leaves (optional)

1. In a large bowl combine ⅓ cup of the all-purpose flour, the ⅓ cup warm water, and the yeast. Beat with a wooden spoon until smooth. Cover loosely with plastic wrap. Let stand at room temperature for at least 8 hours or overnight to ferment.

2. Gradually stir the ¾ cup warm water into the yeast mixture. Stir in whole wheat flour, walnuts, lemon peel, 2 teaspoons oregano, 2 teaspoons thyme, and the salt. Stir in as much of the remaining all-purpose flour as you can. Turn dough out onto a lightly floured surface. Knead in enough remaining all-purpose flour to make a moderately stiff dough that is smooth and elastic (6 to 8 minutes total). Shape dough in a ball. Place in a lightly greased bowl, turning once to grease surface of dough. Cover; let rise in a warm place until double in size (about 1 hour).

3. Punch down dough. Turn dough out onto a well-floured baking sheet. Place a large bowl upside down over dough to cover it; let rest for 30 minutes.

4. Preheat oven to 475°F. Shape dough on the baking sheet into a 10-inch circle by gently pulling and pressing with your fingertips, taking care to keep air bubbles in dough intact. Using your fingers, make ½-inch indentations in dough every 2 inches (dust fingers with flour if necessary). Brush with oil. If desired, sprinkle with additional oregano and/or thyme leaves.

5. Bake for 12 to 15 minutes or until golden brown, checking after 8 minutes and using a sharp knife to pop any large air bubbles. Using a large spatula, transfer focaccia to a wire rack. Cool about 15 minutes. Cut into 12 wedges. Serve warm. **MAKES 12 SERVINGS**

Parmesan Dinner Rolls

PREP 25 minutes
RISE 30 minutes
BAKE 12 minutes
OVEN 400°F

NUTRITION FACTS
PER ROLL

Calories 89
Fat 2 g
Cholesterol 9 mg
Sodium 145 mg
Carbohydrates 15 g
Fiber 0 g
Protein 3 g

1   16-ounce package hot roll mix
¼   cup finely shredded Parmesan cheese (1 ounce)
2   tablespoons snipped fresh basil or 1 teaspoon dried basil, crushed
2   tablespoons sugar
      Nonstick cooking spray
1   tablespoon milk
2   tablespoons finely shredded Parmesan cheese

1. In a large mixing bowl prepare hot roll mix according to package directions through the resting step, stirring the ¼ cup Parmesan, the basil, and sugar into the flour mixture. Divide dough in half.

2. Lightly coat twenty-four 1¾-inch muffin cups with cooking spray. Divide each dough half in 12 pieces. Gently pull each piece into a ball, tucking edges under to make smooth tops. Place in the prepared muffin cups. Cover; let rise in a warm place until nearly double (about 30 minutes).

3. Preheat oven to 400°F. Brush tops of rolls with milk; sprinkle with the 2 tablespoons Parmesan cheese. Bake for 12 to 15 minutes or until tops are golden brown. Remove rolls from muffin cups and serve warm. **MAKES 24 ROLLS**

Make-Ahead Directions: Bake the rolls up to 2 days in advance, wrap them in foil packets, and freeze. Just before serving, reheat the frozen wrapped rolls in a 350°F oven about 20 minutes.

Cinnamon Streusel Rolls

PREP 45 minutes
RISE 1 hour 30 minutes
BAKE 25 minutes
COOL 5 minutes
OVEN 375°F

NUTRITION FACTS PER ROLL

Calories 196
Fat 5 g
Cholesterol 2 mg
Sodium 199 mg
Carbohydrates 33 g
Fiber 2 g
Protein 5 g

1   cup fat-free milk
2   tablespoons packed brown sugar
2   tablespoons vegetable oil spread
1   teaspoon salt
¼   cup warm water (110°F to 115°F)
1   package active dry yeast
¼   cup refrigerated or frozen egg product, thawed, or 1 egg, lightly beaten
4   to 4½ cups all-purpose flour
½   cup rolled oats, toasted*
2   teaspoons ground cinnamon
2   tablespoons vegetable oil spread
¼   cup chopped pecans, toasted
1   recipe Sour Cream Icing

1. In a small saucepan heat and stir milk, brown sugar, 2 tablespoons vegetable oil spread, and the salt just until warm (110°F to 115°F); set aside. In a large bowl combine the warm water and the yeast; let stand for 10 minutes. Add egg product and the milk mixture to yeast mixture. Using a wooden spoon, stir in as much of the all-purpose flour as you can.

2. Turn dough out onto a lightly floured surface. Knead in enough remaining flour to make a moderately soft dough that is smooth and elastic (3 to 5 minutes total). Shape dough in a ball. Place in a lightly greased bowl; turn once to grease surface. Cover and let rise in a warm place until double in size (about 1 hour). Punch down dough. Turn out onto a lightly floured surface. Cover; let rest for 10 minutes.

3. Meanwhile, lightly grease a 13×9×2-inch baking pan; set aside. In a medium bowl combine oats and cinnamon. Using your fingers, blend in 2 tablespoons vegetable oil spread until mixture is crumbly. Stir in pecans.

4. Roll dough to a 15×8-inch rectangle. Sprinkle with pecan mixture, leaving 1 inch unfilled along one long side. Starting from filled long side, roll in a spiral. Pinch dough to seal seam. Slice 15 equal pieces. Arrange cut sides up, in prepared baking pan. Cover and let rise in a warm place until nearly double in size (about 30 minutes).

5. Preheat oven to 375°F. Bake for 25 to 30 minutes or until golden. Cool in pan on a wire rack for 5 minutes. Remove rolls from pan. Drizzle with Sour Cream Icing. Serve warm. **MAKES 15 ROLLS**

Sour Cream Icing: In a small bowl combine ⅓ cup light sour cream, ¼ cup powdered sugar, ¼ teaspoon vanilla, and enough fat-free milk (2 to 3 teaspoons) to make drizzling consistency.

*Tip: To toast oats, place rolled oats in a large skillet; heat over medium heat for 4 to 5 minutes or until oats are lightly toasted, stirring frequently.

Pumpkin Seed Breadsticks

PREP **15 minutes**
BAKE **8 minutes per**
OVEN **425ºF**

**NUTRITION FACTS
PER BREADSTICK**

Calories 39
Fat 1 g
Cholesterol 9 mg
Sodium 75 mg
Carbohydrates 6 g
Fiber 0 g
Protein 1 g

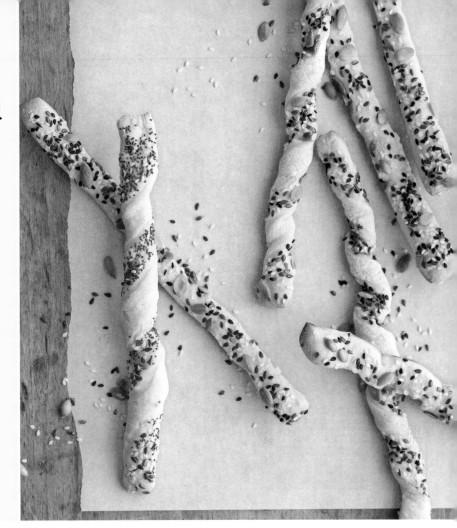

1   13- to 14-ounce package
     refrigerated pizza dough
1   egg, lightly beaten
1   to 3 tablespoons shelled
     pumpkin seeds, poppy seeds,
     flax seeds, plain sesame
     seeds, and/or black sesame
     seeds
½   teaspoon coarse salt or salt

1. Preheat oven to 425ºF. Lightly grease two large baking sheets. Unroll pizza dough on a lightly floured surface. Using your hands, shape dough to a 12×9-inch rectangle. Brush the dough with some of the egg. Sprinkle with seeds and salt. Use a long floured knife or floured pizza cutter to cut dough crosswise in ¼- to ½-inch-wide strips. Twist the strips slightly to create a corkscrew shape, if desired.

2. Place strips on prepared baking sheets. Bake one sheet at a time for 8 to 10 minutes or until golden brown. Cool on wire racks.
MAKES ABOUT 24 BREADSTICKS

Whole Wheat Sweet Potato Bread

PREP 30 minutes
BAKE 30 minutes
COOL 2 hours
OVEN 375°F

NUTRITION FACTS PER SERVING

Calories 132
Fat 5 g
Cholesterol 2 mg
Sodium 132 mg
Carbohydrates 19 g
Fiber 2 g
Protein 3 g

Nonstick cooking spray
¾ cup all-purpose flour
¾ cup white whole wheat flour or whole wheat flour
2 teaspoons baking powder
1 teaspoon pumpkin pie spice
½ teaspoon baking soda
¼ teaspoon salt
½ cup light sour cream
½ cup refrigerated or frozen egg product, thawed, or 2 eggs, lightly beaten
¼ cup sugar
¼ cup fat-free milk
¼ cup canola oil
1½ teaspoons vanilla
1 cup mashed cooked, peeled sweet potatoes
¼ cup chopped pitted dates
¼ cup chopped pecans, toasted

1. Preheat oven to 375°F. Lightly coat three 5¾×3½×2-inch or one 8×4×2-inch loaf pan(s) with cooking spray. Set aside.

2. In a large bowl combine all-purpose flour, whole wheat flour, baking powder, pumpkin pie spice, baking soda, and salt. In a medium bowl combine sour cream, egg product, sugar, milk, oil, and vanilla. Stir in sweet potatoes. Add sour cream mixture all at once to flour mixture. Stir just until moistened. Fold in dates and nuts. Spoon batter into prepared pans, spreading evenly.

3. Bake for 30 to 40 minutes or until a toothpick inserted near centers comes out clean. Cool in pans on a wire rack for 10 minutes. Remove from pans. Cool completely.
MAKES 16 TO 18 SERVINGS

Make-Ahead Directions: Wrap and store baked and cooled bread in refrigerator up to 3 days or freeze up to 3 months.

Zucchini Chip Bread

PREP 30 minutes
BAKE 55 minutes
COOL 2 hours
STAND overnight
OVEN 350°F

NUTRITION FACTS PER SLICE

Calories 197
Fat 10 g
Cholesterol 0 mg
Sodium 120 mg
Carbohydrates 25 g
Fiber 1 g
Protein 4 g

3 cups all-purpose flour*
¾ cup sugar
1 teaspoon baking soda
1 teaspoon ground nutmeg
½ teaspoon salt
½ teaspoon ground cinnamon
¼ teaspoon baking powder
¾ cup refrigerated or frozen egg product, thawed, or 3 eggs lightly beaten
½ cup unsweetened applesauce
½ cup canola oil
1 tablespoon finely shredded orange peel
2 teaspoons vanilla
2 cups shredded zucchini
1 cup chopped walnuts, toasted
1 cup semisweet chocolate pieces

1. Preheat oven to 350°F. Grease bottom and ½ inch up the sides of two 8×4×2-inch loaf pans. Set aside.

2. In a large bowl combine flour, sugar, baking soda, nutmeg, salt, cinnamon, and baking powder. In a small bowl combine egg product, applesauce, oil, orange peel, and vanilla; add to flour mixture. Stir just until moistened. Fold in zucchini, walnuts, and chocolate.

3. Divide mixture evenly between the two prepared pans. Bake about 55 minutes or until a toothpick inserted near centers comes out clean. Cool in pans on wire rack for 10 minutes. Remove bread from pans and cool completely on rack. For easier slicing, wrap and store overnight before serving.
MAKES 2 LOAVES (12 SLICES EACH)

*Tip: You can substitute 1½ cups whole wheat pastry flour for 1½ cups of the all-purpose flour.

Lemon Bread

PREP 30 minutes
BAKE 45 minutes
COOL 2 hours
STAND overnight
OVEN 350°F

NUTRITION FACTS PER SLICE

Calories 140
Fat 5 g
Cholesterol 0 mg
Sodium 80 mg
Carbohydrates 21 g
Fiber 1 g
Protein 3 g

1¾ cups all-purpose flour
¾ cup sugar
2   teaspoons baking powder
¼   teaspoon salt
¼   cup refrigerated or frozen egg product, thawed, or 1 egg, lightly beaten
1   cup fat-free milk
¼   cup vegetable oil or melted butter
2   teaspoons finely shredded lemon peel
1   tablespoon lemon juice
½   cup chopped almonds or walnuts, toasted
2   tablespoons lemon juice (optional)
1   tablespoon sugar (optional)

1. Preheat oven to 350°F. Grease the bottom and ½ inch up sides of an 8×4×2-inch loaf pan; set aside. In a medium bowl stir together flour, ¾ cup sugar, the baking powder, and salt. Make a well in center of flour mixture; set aside.

2. In another medium bowl combine the egg product, milk, oil, lemon peel, and the 1 tablespoon lemon juice. Add egg mixture all at once to flour mixture. Stir just until moistened (batter should be lumpy). Fold in nuts. Spoon batter into prepared pan.

3. Bake for 45 to 55 minutes or until a wooden toothpick inserted near center comes out clean. If desired, stir together the 2 tablespoons lemon juice and the 1 tablespoon sugar. While bread is still in the pan, brush lemon-sugar mixture over the top of the loaf. Cool in pan on a wire rack for 10 minutes. Remove from pan. Cool completely on a wire rack. Wrap and store overnight before serving. **MAKES 1 LOAF (16 SLICES)**

Lemon-Poppy Seed Bread:
Prepare as above, except substitute 1 tablespoon poppy seeds for the almonds or walnuts.

Date-Nut Bread

PREP **15 minutes**
STAND **20 minutes**
BAKE **50 minutes**
COOL **2 hours**
OVEN **350°F**

**NUTRITION FACTS
PER SLICE**

Calories 119
Fat 3 g
Cholesterol 13 mg
Sodium 182 mg
Carbohydrates 22 g
Fiber 3 g
Protein 3 g

1½ cups boiling water
1   8-ounce package pitted whole
    dates, snipped
1   cup all-purpose flour
1   cup whole wheat flour
1   teaspoon baking soda
1   teaspoon baking powder
½   teaspoon salt
1   egg or ¼ cup refrigerated or
    frozen egg product, thawed
1   teaspoon vanilla
½   cup sliced almonds, toasted
    and coarsely chopped
    Coarse sugar (optional)

1. In a medium bowl pour the boiling water over dates. Let stand about 20 minutes or until dates are softened and mixture has cooled slightly.

2. Preheat oven to 350°F. Lightly grease bottom and ½ inch up sides of an 8×4×2-inch loaf pan; set aside. In a large bowl stir together all-purpose flour, whole wheat flour, baking soda, baking powder, and salt. In a small bowl beat together egg and vanilla with a fork; stir into the cooled date mixture. Add date mixture and almonds to flour mixture; stir until well mixed (mixture will be thick). Spoon batter into prepared pan, spreading evenly. Sprinkle with coarse sugar, if desired.

3. Bake for 50 to 55 minutes or until a toothpick inserted near the center comes out clean. Cool in pan on a wire rack for 10 minutes. Remove from pan. Cool completely on a wire rack. Wrap in plastic wrap and store overnight before slicing. **MAKES 1 LOAF (16 SLICES)**

Banana Millet Muffins

PREP 20 minutes
BAKE 15 minutes
COOL 5 minutes
OVEN 400°F°

NUTRITION FACTS
PER MUFFIN

Calories 279
Fat 11 g
Cholesterol 36 mg
Sodium 179 mg
Carbohydrates 41 g
Fiber 2 g
Protein 5 g

Nonstick cooking spray
2 cups all-purpose flour
½ cup millet
2 teaspoons baking powder
½ teaspoon salt
2 eggs, lightly beaten
¾ cup milk
½ cup vegetable oil
½ cup applesauce
½ cup packed dark brown sugar
⅓ cup granulated sugar
2 teaspoons vanilla
1 medium banana, chopped

1. Preheat oven to 400°F. Lightly coat bottoms of twelve 2½-inch muffin cups with cooking spray; set aside. In a large bowl combine flour, millet, baking powder, and salt. Make a well in the center of the flour mixture; set aside.

2. In a medium bowl whisk together eggs, milk, oil, applesauce, brown sugar, granulated sugar, and vanilla. Add to flour mixture all at once. Stir just until moistened (batter should be lumpy). Fold in banana. Spoon batter into prepared muffin cups, filing each two-thirds full.

3. Bake for 15 to 18 minutes or until golden and a wooden toothpick inserted near the center comes out clean. Cool in muffin cups on a wire rack for 5 minutes. Remove from muffin cups; serve warm. **MAKES 12 MUFFINS**

Peachy Corn Bread Muffins

PREP 15 minutes
BAKE 14 minutes
COOL 5 minutes
OVEN 400°F

NUTRITION FACTS PER MUFFIN

Calories 145
Fat 5 g
Cholesterol 47 mg
Sodium 219 mg
Carbohydrates 21 g
Fiber 1 g
Protein 3 g

1 cup yellow cornmeal
¾ cup all-purpose flour
¼ cup sugar
2½ teaspoons baking powder
½ teaspoon salt
½ teaspoon apple pie spice
2 eggs, lightly beaten
¾ cup milk
¼ cup butter, melted
¾ cup chopped fresh or frozen
   unsweetened peaches
   Light vegetable oil spread
   (optional)

1. Preheat oven to 400°F. Grease twelve 2½-inch muffin cups; set aside. In a medium bowl stir together cornmeal, flour, sugar, baking powder, salt, and apple pie spice. Make a well in the center of flour mixture; set aside.

2. In a small bowl whisk together eggs, milk, and melted butter. Stir in peaches. Add peach mixture all at once to flour mixture. Stir just until moistened. Spoon batter into prepared muffin cups, filling cups two-thirds full.

3. Bake for 14 to 15 minutes or until edges are firm and golden brown. Cool in muffin cups on a wire rack for 5 minutes. Remove from muffin cups; serve warm. If desired, serve with vegetable oil spread. **MAKES 12 MUFFINS**

Ham-and-Cheddar Scones

PREP 25 minutes
BAKE 18 minutes
OVEN 375°F

NUTRITION FACTS PER SCONE

Calories 223
Fat 13 g
Cholesterol 56 mg
Sodium 369 mg
Carbohydrates 21 g
Fiber 1 g
Protein 6 g

1¾ cups all-purpose flour
¼ cup whole wheat flour
2 teaspoons baking powder
1 teaspoon sugar
½ teaspoon baking soda
⅛ teaspoon salt
½ cup butter
½ cup reduced-fat shredded sharp cheddar cheese (2 ounces)
¼ cup diced cooked ham
1 tablespoon snipped fresh dill or 1 teaspoon dried dill
1 egg, lightly beaten
¾ cup light sour cream
1 tablespoon Dijon mustard
Fresh dill (optional)

1. Preheat oven to 375°F. Line a baking sheet with parchment paper; set aside. In a large bowl combine all-purpose flour, whole wheat flour, baking powder, sugar, baking soda, and salt. Using a pastry blender or two knives, cut in butter until mixture resembles coarse crumbs. Stir in cheese, ham, and the 1 tablespoon snipped dill. Make a well in center of flour mixture.

2. In a small bowl combine egg, sour cream, and mustard. Add egg mixture all at once to flour mixture. Using a fork, stir just until mixture is moistened (do not overmix).

3. Turn dough out onto a lightly floured surface. Knead dough by folding and gently pressing four to six strokes or just until dough holds together and is nearly smooth. Pat or lightly roll dough to ¾ inch thick. Cut dough with a floured 2½- to 3-inch biscuit cutter. Reroll scraps as necessary, dipping cutter into flour between cuts. Place dough circles 1 inch apart on prepared baking sheet.

4. Bake for 18 to 20 minutes or until golden. Remove scones from baking sheet; serve warm. If desired, sprinkle with additional fresh dill. **MAKES 10 TO 12 SCONES**

Citrus Rosemary Scones

PREP 25 minutes
BAKE 12 minutes
OVEN 425°F

NUTRITION FACTS PER SCONE

Calories 174
Fat 5 g
Cholesterol 29 mg
Sodium 155 mg
Carbohydrates 28 g
Fiber 1 g
Protein 4 g

Nonstick cooking spray
2¾ cups all-purpose flour
⅓ cup sugar
1 tablespoon baking powder
1 tablespoon finely shredded orange peel or lemon peel
2 teaspoons snipped fresh rosemary
¼ teaspoon salt
¼ cup butter
⅔ cup fat-free milk
1 egg, lightly beaten
1 egg white, lightly beaten
2 teaspoons fat-free milk
Reduced-sugar orange marmalade (optional)

1. Preheat oven to 425°F. Lightly coat a baking sheet with cooking spray; set aside. In a large bowl stir together flour, sugar, baking powder, orange peel, rosemary, and salt. Using a pastry blender or two knives, cut in butter until mixture resembles coarse crumbs. Make a well in the center of the flour mixture.

2. In a small bowl stir together the ⅔ cup milk, the egg, and egg white. Add milk mixture all at once to flour mixture. Using a fork, stir just until moistened.

3. Turn dough out onto a lightly floured surface. Quickly knead dough by folding and gently pressing 10 to 12 strokes or just until dough is smooth. Pat gently into a 9-inch circle. Cut into 12 wedges. Transfer scones to prepared baking sheet. Brush tops with the 2 teaspoons milk.

4. Bake for 12 to 15 minutes or until golden brown. Serve warm. If desired, serve with orange marmalade. **MAKES 12 SCONES**

Zucchini-Chocolate Chip Scones

PREP 25 minutes
BAKE 13 minutes
OVEN 400°F

NUTRITION FACTS PER SCONE

Calories 202
Fat 7 g
Cholesterol 11 mg
Sodium 179 mg
Carbohydrates 30 g
Fiber 2 g
Protein 5 g

1½ cups all-purpose flour
1   cup whole wheat flour
3   tablespoons sugar
1½ teaspoons baking powder
½   teaspoon ground cinnamon
¼   teaspoon ground nutmeg
¼   teaspoon baking soda
¼   teaspoon salt
¼   cup butter, cut up
½   cup refrigerated or frozen egg
      product, thawed, or 2 eggs,
      lightly beaten
½   cup buttermilk or fat-free sour
      milk*
1   cup shredded zucchini
½   cup miniature semisweet
      chocolate pieces

1. Preheat oven to 400°F. In a large bowl stir together all-purpose flour, whole wheat flour, sugar, baking powder, cinnamon, nutmeg, baking soda, and salt. Using a pastry blender or two knives, cut in butter until mixture resembles coarse crumbs. Make a well in center of the flour mixture.

2. In a small bowl combine egg product and buttermilk; stir in zucchini and chocolate pieces. Add the buttermilk mixture all at once to the flour mixture. Using a fork, stir just until moistened.

3. Turn dough out onto a lightly floured surface. Knead dough by folding and gently pressing 10 to 12 strokes or until nearly smooth. Pat or lightly roll dough to an 8-inch circle. Cut dough circle into 12 wedges. Place dough wedges 2 inches apart on an ungreased baking sheet.

4. Bake for 13 to 15 minutes or until edges are light brown. Remove scones from baking sheet; serve warm. MAKES 12 SCONES

*Tip: To make ½ cup fat-free sour milk, place 1½ teaspoons lemon juice or vinegar in a glass measuring cup. Add enough fat-free milk to equal ½ cup liquid; stir. Let the mixture stand for 5 minutes before using.

CHAPTER 4

Burgers, Sandwiches & Pizzas

Spicy Beef Sloppy Joes

PREP 20 minutes
COOK 8 hours (low) or
4 hours (high)

NUTRITION FACTS PER SANDWICH

Calories 294
Fat 8 g
Cholesterol 36 mg
Sodium 756 mg
Carbohydrates 37 g
Fiber 3 g
Protein 18 g

2   pounds lean ground beef
2   16-ounce jars salsa
3   cups sliced fresh mushrooms
     (8 ounces)
1½ cups shredded carrots
     (3 medium)
1½ cups finely chopped red
     and/or green sweet peppers
     (2 medium)
⅓   cup tomato paste
2   teaspoons dried basil,
     crushed
1   teaspoon dried oregano,
     crushed
½   teaspoon salt
¼   teaspoon cayenne pepper
4   cloves garlic, minced
12 kaiser rolls, split and toasted

1. In a large skillet cook ground beef over medium heat until brown. Drain off fat. In a 5- or 6-quart slow cooker stir together beef, salsa, mushrooms, carrots, sweet peppers, tomato paste, basil, oregano, salt, cayenne pepper, and garlic.

2. Cover and cook on low-heat setting for 8 to 10 hours or on high-heat setting for 4 to 5 hours.

3. Serve sloppy joes on kaiser rolls.* **MAKES 12 SANDWICHES**

*Tip: If you like, serve half the sandwiches now and set aside the rest of the sloppy joes for another meal. Measure 5 cups of the sloppy joes and place in an airtight container and refrigerate up to 3 days or freeze up to 3 months.

Flank Steak and Caramelized Onion Sandwiches

PREP 35 minutes
COOK 30 minutes
STAND 10 minutes

NUTRITION FACTS PER SANDWICH

Calories 399
Fat 14 g
Cholesterol 56 mg
Sodium 799 mg
Carbohydrates 37 g
Fiber 4 g
Protein 31 g

1½ teaspoons dried oregano, crushed
1½ teaspoons coriander seeds, crushed
1 teaspoon salt
1 teaspoon freshly ground black pepper
2 tablespoons butter
2 large sweet onions, cut in ¼-inch slices (about 4 cups)
2 cloves garlic, minced
1½ pounds beef flank steak
6 small romaine lettuce leaves
6 bakery sourdough rolls or buns or 12 slices sourdough bread, toasted
1 recipe Horseradish Sauce

1. In a small bowl stir together oregano, crushed coriander seeds, salt, and pepper; set aside. In a large nonstick or cast-iron skillet melt butter over medium-low heat. Add onions, garlic, and half the spice mixture. Cook, covered, for 13 to 15 minutes or until onions are tender, stirring occasionally. Uncover; cook and stir over medium-high heat for 5 to 8 minutes more or until onions are golden. Remove from skillet; set aside. Wipe skillet clean.

2. Score both sides of steak in a diamond pattern by making shallow diagonal cuts at 1-inch intervals. Rub meat on both sides with the remaining spice mixture. Heat the same skillet over medium-high heat until very hot. Cook steak in hot skillet, uncovered, for 12 to 16 minutes or until medium-rare (145°F), turning once. Transfer meat to a cutting board; cover with foil and let stand for 10 minutes. Slice steak thinly across the grain.

3. To serve, arrange lettuce leaves and meat evenly on buns. Top with onions and Horseradish Sauce. Add bun tops. **MAKES 6 SANDWICHES**

Horseradish Sauce: In a small bowl stir together ¾ cup mayonnaise, 1 to 2 tablespoons prepared horseradish, 1 tablespoon lime juice, and ½ teaspoon dried oregano, crushed.

Ginger Pork Rolls

START TO FINISH **30 minutes**

NUTRITION FACTS PER 2 MINI SANDWICHES

Calories 433
Fat 9 g
Cholesterol 74 mg
Sodium 797 mg
Carbohydrates 57 g
Fiber 3 g
Protein 34 g

1 cup water
⅔ cup golden raisins
½ cup coarsely chopped red onion (1 medium)
3 tablespoons reduced-sodium soy sauce
2 teaspoons ground ginger
¼ teaspoon black pepper
1 pound pork loin, thinly sliced
8 mini hamburger buns or dinner rolls, split
1 small cucumber, thinly sliced

1. In a large skillet combine the water, raisins, onion, soy sauce, and ginger. Cover and bring to a simmer over medium-high heat; simmer for 5 to 6 minutes or until raisins are plump and onions are tender. Remove raisins and onions with a slotted spoon. Transfer raisin mixture to small bowl; stir in the black pepper. Set aside.

2. Add sliced pork to cooking liquid in pan. Simmer, uncovered, for 7 to 8 minutes or until pork is cooked through (just a trace of pink remains), turning once. Remove with a slotted spoon.

3. Serve pork in buns with cucumber slices and raisin mixture. **MAKES 4 SERVINGS (2 MINI SANDWICHES EACH)**

Pulled Pork and Peaches

PREP 20 minutes
COOK 8 hours (low) or
4 hours (high)

NUTRITION FACTS PER SANDWICH

Calories 339
Fat 14 g
Cholesterol 48 mg
Sodium 517 mg
Carbohydrates 36 g
Fiber 2 g
Protein 17 g

1   3- to 4-pound boneless pork shoulder roast
3   medium onions, cut in wedges
½   teaspoon salt
½   teaspoon black pepper
6   cloves garlic, minced
2   12- to 16-ounce packages frozen peaches
1   cup ginger ale
1   28-ounce can diced tomatoes with basil, garlic, and oregano, drained
20   hamburger buns, split
     Lettuce leaves (optional)
     Sliced peaches (optional)

1. Trim fat from meat. If necessary, cut meat to fit into a 5- or 6-quart slow cooker. Place onions in cooker. Place meat on onions. Sprinkle meat with salt, pepper, and garlic. Add peaches and ginger ale to cooker.

2. Cover and cook on low-heat setting for 8 to 10 hours or on high-heat setting for 4 to 5 hours.

3. Transfer meat to a cutting board. Using two forks, pull meat apart into bite-size pieces. Return meat to cooker. Add drained tomatoes. Stir to combine. Keep warm on warm setting, if available, or low-heat setting.

4. If desired, line buns with lettuce leaves. Using a slotted spoon, spoon pork on buns. If desired, top with additional sliced peaches. **MAKES 20 SANDWICHES**

Mu Shu-Style Pork Roll-Ups

START TO FINISH 20 minutes
OVEN 350°F

NUTRITION FACTS PER WRAP

Calories 296
Fat 8 g
Cholesterol 53 mg
Sodium 325 mg
Carbohydrates 32 g
Fiber 1 g
Protein 22 g

4   10-inch flour tortillas
1   teaspoon toasted sesame oil
12 ounces lean boneless pork, cut in strips
2   cups frozen stir-fry vegetables (any combination)
¼   cup bottled plum or hoisin sauce

1. Wrap tortillas tightly in foil. Heat in a 350°F oven for 10 minutes to soften. (Or wrap tortillas in paper towels and microwave on high for 45 to 60 seconds or until tortillas are warm.) Set aside and keep warm.

2. Meanwhile, in a large skillet heat sesame oil over medium-high heat. Add pork strips; cook and stir for 2 to 3 minutes or until no longer pink. Add stir-fry vegetables; cook and stir for 3 to 4 minutes or until vegetables are crisp-tender.

3. Spread 1 tablespoon of the plum sauce on each tortilla. Spoon pork mixture evenly down centers of tortillas. Fold in the sides of the tortillas then roll up.
MAKES 4 WRAPS

Mediterranean Lamb Pitas

PREP 25 minutes
COOK 8 hours (low) or 4 hours
(high) + 15 minutes

NUTRITION FACTS PER SANDWICH

Calories 255
Fat 6 g
Cholesterol 51 mg
Sodium 434 mg
Carbohydrates 27 g
Fiber 3 g
Protein 21 g

1 2-pound portion boneless lamb leg roast
1 tablespoon olive oil
1 15-ounce can garbanzo beans (chickpeas), rinsed and drained
¾ cup dry red wine
½ of a 6-ounce can (⅓ cup) tomato paste
¼ cup water
1 cup chopped onion (1 large)
4 cloves garlic, minced
½ teaspoon ground allspice
½ teaspoon dried mint, crushed
¼ teaspoon salt
¼ teaspoon black pepper
6 large pita bread rounds, halved crosswise
   Lettuce leaves and/or thinly sliced cucumber
1 6-ounce container plain yogurt
¼ teaspoon ground cumin
½ cup chopped tomato (1 medium)

1. Trim the fat from the lamb. If necessary, cut roast to fit slow cooker. In a large skillet brown lamb on all sides in hot oil.

2. Meanwhile, in a 3½- or 4-quart slow cooker combine drained garbanzo beans, wine, tomato paste, the water, onion, garlic, allspice, mint, salt, and pepper. Place meat on bean mixture. Cover and cook on low-heat setting for 8 to 10 hours or on high-heat setting for 4 to 5 hours.

3. Remove meat from cooker. Shred the meat and return it to the cooker. Cover and cook 15 minutes more. Remove meat and beans with a slotted spoon.

4. To serve, open pita bread halves to form a large pocket. Line pitas with lettuce and/or cucumber. Combine yogurt and ground cumin. Spoon meat then yogurt mixture into pitas. Sprinkle with chopped tomato.
MAKES 12 SANDWICHES

Honey Chicken Sandwiches

START TO FINISH **20 minutes**

NUTRITION FACTS PER SANDWICH

Calories 342
Fat 12 g
Cholesterol 76 mg
Sodium 443 mg
Carbohydrates 31 g
Fiber 1 g
Protein 27 g

3   tablespoons honey
2   teaspoons snipped fresh thyme or ½ teaspoon dried thyme, crushed
1   small red onion, halved and thinly sliced
2½ cups cut-up cooked chicken (about 12 ounces)
4   baked biscuits, split

1. In a medium skillet combine honey and thyme; stir in onion. Cook and stir over medium-low heat just until hot. (Do not boil.) Stir in chicken; heat through. Serve chicken on biscuits.

MAKES 4 SANDWICHES

Parmesan Chicken Salad Sandwiches

START TO FINISH **10 minutes**

NUTRITION FACTS PER SANDWICH

Calories 326
Fat 14 g
Cholesterol 62 mg
Sodium 596 mg
Carbohydrates 26 g
Fiber 2 g
Protein 24 g

½ cup low-fat mayonnaise
1 tablespoon lemon juice
2 teaspoons snipped fresh basil
2½ cups chopped cooked chicken or turkey (about 12 ounces)
¼ cup grated Parmesan cheese
¼ cup thinly sliced green onions (2)
3 tablespoons finely chopped celery
Salt and black pepper
12 slices wheat bread, toasted if desired

1. In a small bowl stir together mayonnaise, lemon juice, and basil. Set aside.

2. In a medium bowl stir together chicken, Parmesan cheese, green onions, and celery. Pour mayonnaise mixture over chicken mixture; toss to coat. Season with salt and pepper. Serve immediately or cover and chill for 1 to 4 hours. Serve on toasted wheat bread.
MAKES 6 SANDWICHES

Chicken and Hummus Wraps

PREP 15 minutes

NUTRITION FACTS PER WRAP

Calories 288
Fat 9 g
Cholesterol 31 mg
Sodium 713 mg
Carbohydrates 36 g
Fiber 3 g
Protein 16 g

1   7-ounce carton any flavor hummus or one 8-ounce tub cream cheese spread with garden vegetables
4   10-inch flour tortillas
⅓   cup plain low-fat yogurt or sour cream
1   6-ounce package refrigerated cooked chicken breast strips
¾   cup coarsely chopped plum tomatoes (2 large)
⅓   of a medium cucumber, cut in 2-inch matchsticks

1. Evenly spread hummus on tortillas; spread yogurt over hummus. Top with chicken, tomatoes, and cucumber. Roll up tortillas. **MAKES 4 WRAPS**

Barbecued Turkey Tenderloins

PREP 20 minutes
GRILL 16 minutes

NUTRITION FACTS PER SANDWICH

Calories 303
Fat 5 g
Cholesterol 70 mg
Sodium 593 mg
Carbohydrates 31 g
Fiber 3 g
Protein 32 g

½ cup bottled hickory-flavor barbecue sauce

1 small fresh jalapeño, seeded and finely chopped*

1 tablespoon tahini (sesame seed paste)

2 turkey breast tenderloins (about 1 pound total)

4 French-style rolls, split and toasted

2 cups fresh spinach leaves

¼ cup bottled green salsa (optional)

1. For sauce, in a small bowl combine barbecue sauce, jalapeño, and tahini. Transfer half the sauce to another bowl to use as basting sauce. Reserve the remaining sauce until ready to serve.

2. Brush both sides of each turkey tenderloin with basting sauce. For charcoal grill, lightly grease the rack of an uncovered grill. Place turkey on rack directly over medium coals. Grill for 16 to 20 minutes or until tender and no longer pink (170°F), turning once halfway through grilling. (For a gas grill, preheat grill and grease rack. Reduce heat to medium. Place turkey on grill rack over heat. Cover and grill as above.) Thinly slice turkey.

3. To serve, fill rolls with spinach leaves, grilled turkey, and, if desired, green salsa. Top with reserved sauce. **MAKES 4 SANDWICHES**

***Tip:** Because chile peppers contain volatile oils that can burn skin and eyes, avoid direct contact with them as much as possible. When working with chile peppers, wear plastic or rubber gloves. If your bare hands touch the peppers, wash hands and nails well with soap and warm water.

Mexi Turkey Burgers

PREP 25 minutes
GRILL 14 minutes

NUTRITION FACTS PER BURGER

Calories 431
Fat 21 g
Cholesterol 115 mg
Sodium 908 mg
Carbohydrates 29 g
Fiber 3 g
Protein 33 g

1   cup radishes, chopped
6   green onions, chopped
1   cup snipped fresh cilantro
¼   teaspoon salt
1   pound uncooked ground turkey
1   4-ounce can whole green chile peppers, drained (see tip, page 63)
4   1-ounces slices Monterey Jack cheese
4   hamburger buns, split and toasted
1   cup shredded lettuce
4   tomato slices
½   cup bottled salsa

1. In a large bowl combine radishes, green onions, cilantro, and salt. Add ground turkey; mix well. Shape mixture into four ¾-inch-thick patties.

2. For a charcoal grill, grease the rack of an uncovered grill. Place patties on the rack directly over medium coals. Grill for 14 to 18 minutes or until internal temperature of each burger registers 165°F,* turning once halfway through grilling. Top burgers with chile peppers and cheese during the last 1 minute of grilling. (For a gas grill, preheat grill. Grease grill rack. Reduce heat to medium. Place patties on grill rack over heat. Cover; grill as above.)

3. Serve burgers in buns with lettuce, tomato, and salsa.
MAKES 4 BURGERS

*Tip: The internal color of a burger is not a reliable doneness indicator. A turkey patty cooked to 165°F is safe, regardless of color. To measure the doneness of a patty, insert an instant-read thermometer through the side of the patty to a depth of 2 to 3 inches.

Turkey Tomatillo Burgers

PREP 20 minutes
GRILL 14 minutes

NUTRITION FACTS PER BURGER

Calories 360
Fat 9 g
Cholesterol 91 mg
Sodium 492 mg
Carbohydrates 28 g
Fiber 3 g
Protein 40 g

2   egg whites, lightly beaten
¼   cup fine dry bread crumbs
2   tablespoons snipped fresh cilantro
2   teaspoons chopped canned chipotle chile pepper in adobo sauce (see tip, page 63)
2   cloves garlic, minced
½   teaspoon chili powder
¼   teaspoon freshly ground black pepper
1   pound uncooked ground turkey breast
8   slices tomatillo and/or tomato
4   ¾-ounce slices Muenster cheese
4   whole wheat hamburger buns, split and toasted

1. In a medium bowl combine egg whites, bread crumbs, cilantro, chipotle pepper in adobo sauce, garlic, chili powder, and black pepper. Add ground turkey breast; mix well. Shape turkey mixture into four ¾-inch-thick patties. (If mixture is sticky, moisten hands with water.)

2. For a charcoal grill, grill burgers on the lightly greased rack of an uncovered grill directly over medium coals for 14 to 18 minutes or until no longer pink (165°F),* turning once halfway through grilling. Add tomatillo and/or tomato slices to the grill and top each burger with a slice of cheese for the last 2 minutes of grilling. (For a gas grill, preheat grill. Reduce heat to medium. Place burgers, and later tomatillos and/or tomato slices, on grill rack over heat. Cover and grill as above.)

3. Serve grilled turkey burgers topped with tomatillo and/or tomato slices in buns.
MAKES 4 BURGERS

*Tip: The internal color of a burger is not a reliable doneness indicator. A turkey patty cooked to 165°F is safe, regardless of color. To measure the doneness of a patty, insert an instant-read thermometer through the side of the patty to a depth of 2 to 3 inches.

Turkey Reuben

PREP 15 minutes
COOK 4 minutes per batch

NUTRITION FACTS PER SANDWICH

Calories 379
Fat 11 g
Cholesterol 67 mg
Sodium 884 mg
Carbohydrates 38 g
Fiber 5 g
Protein 31 g

2   cups packaged shredded cabbage with carrots (coleslaw mix)
2   tablespoons bottled reduced-calorie clear Italian salad dressing or white wine vinaigrette salad dressing
2   tablespoons bottled reduced-calorie Thousand Island salad dressing
8   ½-inch slices rye bread
8   ounces sliced cooked turkey breast
4   slices provolone cheese (4 ounces)
1   medium tomato, sliced
    Dill pickle spears (optional)

1. In a medium bowl combine cabbage with carrots and Italian salad dressing; set aside.

2. Spread Thousand Island salad dressing on one side of each bread slice. Place four bread slices, dressing sides up, on a work surface; top with turkey, cheese, tomato, and cabbage mixture. Top with remaining bread slices, dressing sides down.

3. Preheat a large skillet over medium heat. Reduce heat to medium-low. Cook sandwiches, two at a time, for 4 to 6 minutes or until the bread is toasted and the cheese is melted, turning once halfway through cooking. If desired, serve with dill pickle spears. **MAKES 4 SANDWICHES**

Turkey and Cranberry Sandwiches with Curry Dressing

START TO FINISH 15 minutes

NUTRITION FACTS PER SANDWICH

Calories 255
Fat 7 g
Cholesterol 28 mg
Sodium 908 mg
Carbohydrates 34 g
Fiber 4 g
Protein 17 g

3   tablespoons light mayonnaise dressing or salad dressing
½   teaspoon curry powder
⅓   cup canned whole cranberry sauce
8   thin slices firm-texture whole wheat bread
8   ounces thinly sliced smoked turkey breast
1   cup watercress, tough stems removed, or spinach leaves

1. For dressing, in a small bowl stir together mayonnaise dressing and curry powder. Set aside.

2. Snip any large pieces in the cranberry sauce. Spread one side of four bread slices with cranberry sauce. Divide and arrange turkey and watercress on cranberry sauce. Spread dressing on one side of remaining bread. Place one bread slice, dressing side down, on each sandwich. **MAKES 4 SANDWICHES**

Grilled Jamaican Jerk Fish Wraps

PREP 30 minutes
GRILL 4 to 6 minutes per ½-inch thickness

NUTRITION FACTS PER WRAP

Calories 254
Fat 4 g
Cholesterol 48 mg
Sodium 509 mg
Carbohydrates 23 g
Fiber 11 g
Protein 29 g

1 pound fresh or frozen skinless flounder, cod, or sole fillets
1½ teaspoons Jamaican jerk seasoning
4 7- to 8-inch whole grain flour tortillas
2 cups packaged fresh baby spinach
¾ cup chopped, seeded tomato
¾ cup chopped fresh mango or pineapple
2 tablespoons snipped fresh cilantro
1 tablespoon finely chopped, seeded fresh jalapeño (see tip, page 63)
1 tablespoon lime juice

1. Thaw fish, if frozen. Rinse fish; pat dry with paper towels. Sprinkle both sides of fillets with Jamaican jerk seasoning; rub in with your fingers. Measure thickness of fish.

2. For a charcoal grill, grill tortillas on the greased rack of an uncovered grill directly over medium coals about 1 minute or until bottoms of tortillas have grill marks. Remove from grill and set aside.

3. Add fish to the grill. Grill for 4 to 6 minutes per ½-inch thickness or until fish begins to flake when tested with a fork, carefully turning once halfway through grilling. (For a gas grill, preheat grill. Reduce heat to medium. Place tortillas, then fish, on greased grill rack over heat. Cover and grill as above.) Coarsely flake the fish.

4. Meanwhile, in a medium bowl combine spinach, tomato, mango, cilantro, jalapeño, and lime juice; toss gently to coat.

5. To serve, place tortillas, grill mark sides down, on a flat work surface. Divide spinach mixture and fish among tortillas. Fold tortillas over to enclose filling.
MAKES 4 WRAPS

Black Bean Chipotle Burgers

PREP 35 minutes
COOK 10 minutes
CHILL 1 hour

NUTRITION FACTS
PER BURGER

Calories 399
Fat 11 g
Cholesterol 0 mg
Sodium 245 mg
Carbohydrates 43 g
Fiber 8 g
Protein 9 g

1   15-ounce can no-salt-added black beans, rinsed and drained
1   cup baked corn chips, finely crushed (about ½ cup crushed)
½   cup cooked brown rice
½   cup frozen whole kernel corn, thawed
¼   cup finely chopped red onion
¼   cup chunky salsa
½   to 1 teaspoon finely chopped canned chipotle pepper in adobo sauce (see tip, page 63)
1   clove garlic, minced
½   teaspoon ground cumin
1   tablespoon olive oil
    Shredded green cabbage
4   tostada shells, heated according to package directions
    Radish slices
    Fresh cilantro leaves
    Light sour cream (optional)
    Chunky salsa (optional)
    Lime wedges (optional)

1. In a medium bowl mash half the beans with a fork or potato masher. Stir in the remaining beans, corn chips, cooked rice, corn, onion, ¼ cup salsa, chipotle pepper, garlic, and cumin.

2. Shape bean mixture into four ¾-inch-thick patties. Place patties on a plate; cover and chill at least 1 hour before cooking.

3. Brush both sides of patties with oil. In a 12-inch skillet or large griddle cook patties over medium heat about 10 minutes or until heated through, turning once.

4. Place some shredded cabbage on each tostada shell; top with burgers, radishes, and cilantro. If desired, serve with sour cream, additional salsa, and lime wedges.
MAKES 4 BURGERS

Broiling Directions: Preheat broiler. Place patties on the unheated rack of a broiler pan. Broil about 4 inches from the heat about 10 minutes or until heated through, turning once halfway through broiling.

Garden Fresh Pizza

PREP 30 minutes
STAND 12 to 24 hours
RISE 1 hour
BAKE 20 minutes
OVEN 400°F

NUTRITION FACTS
PER SERVING

Calories 336
Fat 8 g
Cholesterol 19 mg
Sodium 659 mg
Carbohydrates 54 g
Fiber 4 g
Protein 12 g

2   cups all-purpose flour
½   cup white whole wheat flour
    or whole wheat flour
½   cup cornmeal
1   teaspoon salt
¼   teaspoon active dry yeast
1¼ cups warm water (120°F to
    130°F)
    Olive oil
½   cup no-salt-added tomato
    sauce
½   teaspoon dried Italian
    seasoning
3   to 4 cups fresh vegetables,
    such as halved yellow cherry
    tomatoes, sliced plum
    tomatoes, red onion slices,
    and/or broccoli florets
1   cup mushrooms, halved or
    sliced
2   ounces chorizo sausage or
    ground beef, cooked and
    drained
½   cup crumbled feta cheese or
    1 cup shredded mozzarella
    cheese
    Shredded radicchio (optional)

1. In a large bowl combine both flours, cornmeal, salt, and yeast; gradually add the warm water, stirring until mixture is moistened (will be a soft, sticky dough). Cover; let stand at room temperature for 12 to 24 hours.

2. Line a 15×10×1-inch baking pan with parchment paper. Brush parchment with olive oil. Turn dough out onto prepared pan. Using well-oiled hands or a rubber spatula, gently push dough to edges and corners of pan (dough will be sticky). Build up edges slightly. Cover; let rise for 1 to 1½ hours or until puffy and dough pulls away slightly from edges of baking pan.

3. Preheat oven to 400°F. Bake crust for 10 minutes. In a small bowl combine tomato sauce and dried Italian seasoning; spread on hot crust. Top with vegetables, mushrooms, cooked chorizo, and cheese.

4. Bake for 10 to 15 minutes or until bubbly. Remove from oven. If desired, top with radicchio. Serve immediately. **MAKES 6 SERVINGS**

Buffalo Chicken Pizzas

START TO FINISH **20 minutes**
OVEN **450°F**

NUTRITION FACTS PER SERVING

Calories 353
Fat 14 g
Cholesterol 45 mg
Sodium 1,084 mg
Carbohydrates 36 g
Fiber 2 g
Protein 21 g

4   pita bread rounds
¼   cup bottled blue cheese salad
     dressing
1   9-ounce package refrigerated
     Southwest-flavor cooked
     chicken breast strips
¾   cup thinly sliced celery
     (1½ stalks)
     Blue cheese crumbles
     (optional)
     Bottled hot pepper sauce or
     buffalo wing sauce (optional)

1. Preheat oven to 450°F. Place pita rounds on a large baking sheet. Brush with blue cheese dressing. Scatter chicken strips and celery on dressing.

2. Bake about 10 minutes or until heated through and pita rounds are crisp. Transfer pizzas to plates. If desired, sprinkle with blue cheese and pass hot sauce.
MAKES 4 SERVINGS

Thai Chicken Pizza

PREP **20 minutes**
BAKE **11 minutes**
OVEN **475°F**

NUTRITION FACTS PER SERVING

Calories 303
Fat 11 g
Cholesterol 29 mg
Sodium 190 mg
Carbohydrates 31 g
Fiber 2 g
Protein 19 g

⅓ cup natural creamy peanut butter
¼ cup warm water
2 teaspoons sugar
2 teaspoons rice vinegar
¼ to ½ teaspoon crushed red pepper
2 teaspoons canola oil
12 ounces skinless boneless chicken breast halves, cut in bite-size pieces
½ cup very thinly sliced green onions (4)
2 cloves garlic, minced
   Nonstick cooking spray
1 recipe Thin Crust Pizza Dough
1 cup red sweet pepper, seeded and cut in thin strips
½ cup shredded part-skim mozzarella cheese (2 ounces)
½ cup snipped fresh cilantro
   Sliced green onions

1. Preheat oven to 475°F. In a small bowl combine peanut butter, the water, sugar, rice vinegar, and crushed red pepper. Set aside.

2. In a medium skillet heat oil over medium heat. Add chicken; cook and stir until no pink remains. Add green onions and garlic; cook for 1 minute more. Turn heat to low; add 2 tablespoons of the peanut butter mixture (set the rest aside). Mix until chicken is coated; remove from heat.

3. Coat a 12- to 14-inch pizza pan, large cookie sheet, or pizza screen with cooking spray. Roll out Thin Crust Pizza Dough according to directions at right. Slide onto prepared pan. Spread dough with remaining peanut sauce, adding water if needed for spreading consistency. Top with chicken, red pepper strips, and cheese.

4. Bake for 11 to 14 minutes or until cheese is melted and crust starts to brown. Remove from oven and sprinkle with cilantro and sliced green onions. Cut into 8 slices. Serve immediately. **MAKES 8 SERVINGS**

Thin Crust Pizza Dough: In a large bowl stir together 1 package active dry yeast (2½ teaspoons), 1 teaspoon sugar, ¼ teaspoon salt, ¾ cup warm water (100°F to 105°F), 1 tablespoon olive oil, and 2 cups bread flour. If needed, use wet hands to quickly work in any remaining flour (do not knead the dough). Cover the bowl with a towel and let stand at room temperature for 40 to 50 minutes or until almost doubled in size. Transfer to the refrigerator and chill, covered with a towel, for 2 to 24 hours. Turn dough out onto a well-floured surface. Shape into a ball. Cover and let stand for 20 minutes. Roll out dough to a 12- to 14-inch circle or a 12×8-inch rectangle. Top as directed. Makes 1 crust.

Cheesy Sweet Pepper Pizza

PREP **15 minutes**
BAKE **15 minutes**
OVEN **425°F**

NUTRITION FACTS PER SERVING

Calories *364*
Fat *12 g*
Cholesterol *18 mg*
Sodium *718 mg*
Carbohydrates *50 g*
Fiber *2 g*
Protein *16 g*

Nonstick cooking spray
1 13.8-ounce package refrigerated pizza dough
1 tablespoon olive oil
1 cup shredded mozzarella cheese (4 ounces)
2 medium plum tomatoes, thinly sliced
½ cup sliced roasted yellow and/or red sweet peppers
2 tablespoons shredded fresh spinach (optional)
¼ teaspoon coarse ground black pepper
2 tablespoons snipped fresh basil

1. Preheat oven to 425°F. Coat a 12-inch pizza pan with cooking spray. Press pizza dough in the prepared pan, building up edges. Brush crust with oil. Bake for 10 minutes.

2. Remove crust from oven. Sprinkle with cheese. Arrange tomatoes, roasted peppers, and, if desired, spinach on crust. Sprinkle with black pepper.

3. Bake for 5 to 10 minutes or until cheese is bubbly. Sprinkle with basil. **MAKES 4 SERVINGS**

Original Pizza Margherita

PREP **15 minutes**
BAKE **15 minutes**
OVEN **400°F**

NUTRITION FACTS PER SERVING

Calories 291
Fat 15 g
Cholesterol 27 mg
Sodium 418 mg
Carbohydrates 27 g
Fiber 2 g
Protein 12 g

Nonstick cooking spray
1   11-ounce package refrigerated thin-crust pizza dough
1   tablespoon olive oil
2   cups grape tomatoes, halved
8   ounces small fresh mozzarella cheese balls, sliced
2   cloves garlic, minced
½   cup fresh basil leaves
    Coarse ground black pepper (optional)

1. Preheat oven to 400°F. Coat a 15×10×1-inch baking pan with cooking spray. Unroll pizza dough in the prepared pan. Press onto the bottom and slightly up the sides of the pan. Brush with oil. Bake for 7 minutes. Top with tomatoes, cheese, and garlic.

2. Bake for 8 to 10 minutes or until crust is golden brown. Tear or snip large basil leaves. Sprinkle pizza with basil and, if desired, pepper. **MAKES 6 SERVINGS**

CHAPTER 5

Main-Dish Salads

Warm Fajita Salad

START TO FINISH 35 minutes
OVEN 400°F

NUTRITION FACTS PER SERVING

Calories 223
Fat 8 g
Cholesterol 52 mg
Sodium 246 mg
Carbohydrates 19 g
Fiber 4 g
Protein 21 g

12 ounces boneless beef top sirloin steak, trimmed of fat
¼ cup lime juice
¼ cup reduced-sodium chicken broth
1 tablespoon snipped fresh cilantro
2 to 3 teaspoons honey
1½ teaspoons cornstarch
2 cloves garlic, minced
½ teaspoon ground cumin
¼ teaspoon salt
¼ teaspoon black pepper
Nonstick cooking spray
2 small green, red, and/or yellow sweet peppers, seeded and cut in thin strips
2 small onions, cut in thin wedges
1 tablespoon vegetable oil
1 10-ounce package torn mixed salad greens
12 red or yellow cherry tomatoes, halved or quartered
1 recipe Baked Tortilla Strips

1. If desired, partially freeze meat for easier slicing. Trim fat from meat. Cut meat in thin bite-size strips. For sauce, in a small bowl combine lime juice, broth, cilantro, honey, cornstarch, and garlic; set aside. Sprinkle meat strips with cumin, salt, and black pepper; toss to coat.

2. Coat a large skillet with cooking spray. Preheat over medium-high heat. Add sweet peppers and onions; cook and stir for 3 to 4 minutes or until crisp-tender. Remove from skillet. Pour oil into hot skillet. Add meat; cook and stir for 2 to 3 minutes or until desired doneness. Push meat from center of skillet.

3. Stir sauce; add to center of skillet. Cook and stir until thickened and bubbly. Return sweet peppers and onions to skillet. Stir all ingredients together to coat with sauce. Cook and stir until heated through.

4. Divide salad greens and tomatoes among four dinner plates. Spoon meat mixture on greens. Sprinkle with Baked Tortilla Strips.
MAKES 4 SERVINGS

Baked Tortilla Strips: Preheat oven to 400°F. Cut one 6-inch corn tortilla in ⅛- to ¼-inch strips; cut long strips in half crosswise. Place strips on ungreased baking sheet. Coat with nonstick cooking spray; sprinkle lightly with paprika and chili powder. Bake about 8 minutes or until golden and crisp, stirring once.

Gingered Beef and Broccoli Salad Bowl

START TO FINISH 20 minutes

NUTRITION FACTS PER SERVING

Calories 237
Fat 9 g
Cholesterol 60 mg
Sodium 468 mg
Carbohydrates 17 g
Fiber 4 g
Protein 22 g

12 ounces boneless beef sirloin steak
⅔ cup bottled ginger vinaigrette salad dressing
3 cups fresh broccoli florets
8 cups mixed spring greens or baby salad greens
1 medium red sweet pepper, cut in bite-size strips

1. Trim fat from beef; thinly slice across the grain in bite-size strips. Set aside.

2. In a wok or large skillet heat 2 tablespoons of the salad dressing over medium-high heat. Add broccoli. Cook and stir for 3 minutes. Add meat to wok. Cook and stir for 2 to 3 minutes or until meat is slightly pink in center. Remove beef and broccoli from wok.

3. In large bowl toss together meat, broccoli, greens, and sweet pepper. Drizzle with remaining salad dressing; toss to coat.
MAKES 4 SERVINGS

Beefy Pasta Salad

START TO FINISH 30 minutes

NUTRITION FACTS
PER SERVING

Calories 322
Fat 12 g
Cholesterol 38 mg
Sodium 256 mg
Carbohydrates 27 g
Fiber 4 g
Protein 26 g

1   cup dried multigrain penne pasta (about 3½ ounces)
2   ears of corn, husks and silks removed
    Nonstick cooking spray
12 ounces boneless beef sirloin steak, trimmed of fat and cut in thin bite-size strips, or 2 cups shredded cooked beef pot roast (10 ounces)*
1   cup cherry tomatoes, halved
¼   cup shredded fresh basil
2   tablespoons finely shredded Parmesan cheese
1   recipe Vinegar and Oil Dressing
    Finely shredded Parmesan cheese (optional)

1. In a 4- to 6-quart Dutch oven cook pasta according to package directions, adding corn the last 3 minutes of cooking time. Using tongs, transfer corn to a large cutting board. Drain pasta. Rinse pasta with cold water; drain again. Set aside. Cool corn until easy to handle.

2. Meanwhile, coat a large unheated nonstick skillet with cooking spray. Preheat skillet over medium-high heat. Add beef strips. Cook for 4 to 6 minutes or until desired doneness, stirring occasionally. (If using shredded beef, cook until heated through.) Remove from heat and cool slightly.

3. On a cutting board, place an ear of corn pointed tip down. While holding corn firmly at stem end to keep in place, use a sharp knife to cut corn from cobs, cutting corn in planks; rotate cob to cut corn from all sides. In a large bowl combine pasta, beef, tomatoes, basil, and the 2 tablespoons Parmesan cheese.

4. Pour dressing over salad; toss gently to coat. Gently fold in corn planks or place planks on servings. Serve immediately. If desired, garnish with additional Parmesan cheese. MAKES 4 SERVINGS

Vinegar and Oil Dressing: In a screw-top jar combine 3 tablespoons white wine vinegar; 2 tablespoons olive oil; 1 clove garlic, minced; ¼ teaspoon salt; and ⅛ teaspoon black pepper. Cover and shake well.

***Tip:** If you have leftover beef pot roast, use it in this pasta salad. Simply shred the meat and use 2 cups in the salad.

Taco Salad Bowls

PREP 35 minutes
BAKE 10 minutes
OVEN 350°F

NUTRITION FACTS PER SERVING

Calories 297
Fat 13 g
Cholesterol 59 mg
Sodium 575 mg
Carbohydrates 23 g
Fiber 3 g
Protein 22 g

4   6- to 8-inch whole wheat or
    plain flour tortillas
    Nonstick cooking spray
12 ounces lean ground beef or
    uncooked ground turkey
½   cup chopped onion (1 medium)
1   clove garlic, minced
1   8-ounce can tomato sauce
1   tablespoon cider vinegar
½   teaspoon ground cumin
¼   teaspoon crushed red pepper
4   cups shredded lettuce
¼   cup shredded reduced-fat
    cheddar cheese (1 ounce)
¼   cup chopped green or red
    sweet pepper (optional)
12 cherry tomatoes, quartered

1. Preheat oven to 350°F. For tortilla bowls, wrap tortillas in foil. Heat in oven for 10 minutes. Coat four 10-ounce custard cups with cooking spray. Carefully press one tortilla into each cup. Bake for 10 to 15 minutes or until golden and crisp. Cool in custard cups on wire rack; remove bowls from custard cups. Set aside.

2. Meanwhile, in a large skillet cook ground beef, onion, and garlic until meat is brown and onion is tender. Drain off fat.

3. Stir tomato sauce, vinegar, cumin, and crushed red pepper into meat mixture in skillet. Bring to boiling; reduce heat. Simmer, uncovered, for 10 minutes.

4. Place tortilla bowls on four dinner plates. Line tortilla bowls with lettuce. Fill with meat mixture then top with cheese, sweet pepper (if desired), and cherry tomatoes. MAKES 4 SERVINGS

Tip: To make tortilla bowls ahead, prepare and cool as directed in Step 1. Place in large freezer container with paper towels between bowls and crumpled around the sides of bowls for protection. Seal, label, and freeze up to 1 month.

Asian Pork and Cabbage Salad

PREP 20 minutes
COOK 5 minutes

NUTRITION FACTS PER SERVING

Calories 242
Fat 10 g
Cholesterol 59 mg
Sodium 352 mg
Carbohydrates 16 g
Fiber 3 g
Protein 23 g

¼   cup low-sugar orange marmalade or low-sugar apricot preserves
2   tablespoons reduced-sodium soy sauce
2   tablespoons rice vinegar
1   tablespoon toasted sesame oil
1   clove garlic, minced
    Nonstick cooking spray
12 ounces boneless pork loin chops, trimmed of fat and cut in bite-size pieces
1   medium red or yellow sweet pepper, seeded and cut in thin bite-size strips
6   cups shredded napa cabbage
1   cup chopped cucumber
4   green onions, bias-sliced in 1-inch pieces
¼   cup slivered almonds, toasted*

1. For dressing, in a small bowl stir together orange marmalade, soy sauce, vinegar, toasted sesame oil, and garlic. Set aside.

2. Lightly coat an unheated wok or large nonstick skillet with cooking spray. Add pork and cook over medium-high heat for 2 minutes. Add sweet pepper strips to the pan; cook about 3 minutes or until pork is no longer pink and sweet pepper is crisp-tender, stirring occasionally. Add one-fourth of the dressing to pan; stir until well coated. Remove pan from heat.

3. In a large bowl toss cabbage with remaining dressing. On a serving platter layer cabbage, pork mixture, and cucumber. Sprinkle with green onions and almonds. Serve immediately.
MAKES 4 SERVINGS

*Tip: To toast nuts, spread them in a shallow pan. Bake in a 350°F oven for 5 to 7 minutes or until toasted, stirring once or twice. Watch closely to avoid burning.

Blackberry Salad with Pork

PREP 25 minutes
ROAST 25 minutes
STAND 5 minutes
OVEN 425°F

NUTRITION FACTS PER SERVING

Calories 277
Fat 12 g
Cholesterol 46 mg
Sodium 198 mg
Carbohydrates 27 g
Fiber 6 g
Protein 18 g

1   10- to 12-ounce pork
    tenderloin
¼   teaspoon salt
¼   teaspoon black pepper
2½ cup blackberries and/or
    raspberries
¼   cup lemon juice
3   tablespoons olive oil
3   tablespoons honey
6   cups packaged mixed baby
    greens (spring mix)
1   cup grape tomatoes, halved
2   tablespoons pine nuts, toasted
    (see tip, page 80) (optional)

1. Preheat oven to 425°F. Place pork on a rack in a shallow roasting pan. Sprinkle with ⅛ teaspoon of the salt and ⅛ teaspoon of the pepper. Roast, uncovered, for 25 to 35 minutes or until an instant-read thermometer inserted in center registers 155°F. Remove from oven. Cover roast with foil and let stand for 5 minutes until thermometer registers 160°F. Cool slightly. Slice pork ¼ inch thick.

2. For blackberry vinaigrette, in a blender or food processor combine ½ cup of the berries, the lemon juice, oil, honey, and the remaining salt and black pepper. Cover and blend or process until smooth. Strain dressing through a sieve; discard seeds.

3. To serve, divide greens among four salad bowls or dinner plates; top with the remaining 2 cups berries, tomatoes, pine nuts (if desired), and pork slices. Drizzle with blackberry vinaigrette. Serve immediately. **MAKES 4 SERVINGS**

Pork and Noodle Salad

PREP 25 minutes
CHILL 2 to 24 hours

NUTRITION FACTS
PER SERVING

Calories 328
Fat 12 g
Cholesterol 76 mg
Sodium 974 mg
Carbohydrates 31 g
Fiber 2 g
Protein 24 g

4 ounces dried Chinese egg noodles or fine noodles, broken in half
12 ounces fresh asparagus, trimmed and cut in 2-inch pieces, or one 10-ounce package frozen cut asparagus
8 ounces cooked lean pork, cut in thin strips
2 medium carrots, cut in thin strips
1 recipe Soy-Sesame Vinaigrette
   Sliced green onions (optional)
   Sesame seeds (optional)

1. Cook noodles according to package directions; drain.

2. If using fresh asparagus, cook in a covered saucepan in a small amount of boiling, lightly salted water for 4 to 6 minutes or until crisp-tender. (If using frozen asparagus, cook according to package directions.) Drain well.

3. In a large bowl combine noodles, asparagus, pork, and carrots. Cover and refrigerate for 2 to 24 hours.

4. To serve, drizzle Soy-Sesame Vinaigrette over salad; toss gently to coat. If desired, sprinkle salad with green onions and sesame seeds. **MAKES 4 SERVINGS**

Soy-Sesame Vinaigrette: In a screw-top jar combine ¼ cup reduced-sodium soy sauce, 2 tablespoons rice vinegar or vinegar, 1 tablespoon salad oil, 1 tablespoon honey, and 1 teaspoon sesame oil. Cover and shake well to mix. Chill for 2 to 24 hours.

Mexican Chicken Salad Stacks

PREP 30 minutes
BROIL 6 minutes

NUTRITION FACTS PER SERVING

Calories 276
Fat 11 g
Cholesterol 68 mg
Sodium 153 mg
Carbohydrates 16 g
Fiber 6 g
Protein 30 g

4   small skinless, boneless chicken breast halves (1 to 1¼ pounds total)
1   teaspoon ancho chile powder or chili powder
½   teaspoon dried oregano, crushed
½   teaspoon dried thyme, crushed
⅛   teaspoon salt
⅛   teaspoon black pepper
2   tablespoons orange juice
1   tablespoon olive oil
1   tablespoon white wine vinegar
1   teaspoon honey
4   cups shredded romaine lettuce
1   small avocado, halved, seeded, peeled, and sliced
2   oranges, peeled and sectioned
¼   cup crumbled queso fresco cheese or shredded reduced-fat Monterey Jack cheese (1 ounce)

1. Place each chicken breast half between two pieces of plastic wrap. Using the flat side of a meat mallet, pound chicken to about ½ inch thick. Remove plastic wrap.

2. Preheat broiler. In a small bowl stir together chile powder, oregano, thyme, salt, and black pepper. Sprinkle spice mixture evenly over chicken pieces; rub in with your fingers.

3. Place chicken on the unheated rack of a broiler pan. Broil 4 to 5 inches from heat for 6 to 8 minutes or until chicken is tender and no longer pink (170°F), turning once halfway through broiling. Slice chicken.

4. Meanwhile, in a medium bowl whisk together orange juice, olive oil, vinegar, and honey. Add lettuce; toss to coat.

5. To assemble, divide lettuce among four dinner plates. Top with sliced chicken, avocado, and orange sections. Sprinkle with cheese. **MAKES 4 SERVINGS**

Curried Chicken Salad with Jicama

PREP 30 minutes
CHILL 1 hour

NUTRITION FACTS PER SERVING

Calories 231
Fat 9 g
Cholesterol 71 mg
Sodium 246 mg
Carbohydrates 13 g
Fiber 1 g
Protein 23 g

1   orange
3   cups cubed cooked chicken or turkey (about 1 pound)
1½ cups seedless red grapes, halved
½   cup chopped jicama
1   cup thinly sliced celery
¼   cup light mayonnaise dressing or salad dressing
¼   cup lemon-flavor low-fat yogurt
2   teaspoons soy sauce
1   teaspoon curry powder
3   small papayas, peeled, bias-sliced in half lengthwise, and seeded (optional)
    Fresh chives (optional)

1. Peel and segment orange; halve or quarter each segment. In a large mixing bowl combine orange, chicken, grapes, jicama, and celery.

2. For dressing, in a small bowl stir together light mayonnaise dressing, yogurt, soy sauce, and curry powder. Pour dressing over chicken mixture; toss lightly to coat. Cover and refrigerate for 1 to 24 hours. If desired, serve in papaya halves and garnish with fresh chives. **MAKES 6 SERVINGS**

Mediterranean Chicken Salad

START TO FINISH 20 minutes

NUTRITION FACTS
PER SERVING

Calories 252
Fat 9 g
Cholesterol 41 mg
Sodium 422 mg
Carbohydrates 24 g
Fiber 5 g
Protein 19 g

⅓ cup lemon juice
2   tablespoons snipped fresh mint
2   tablespoons snipped fresh basil
2   tablespoons olive oil
1   tablespoon honey
¼   teaspoon black pepper
5   cups shredded romaine lettuce
2   cups cut-up cooked chicken breast (10 ounces)
2   plum tomatoes, cut in wedges
1   15-ounce can garbanzo beans (chickpeas), rinsed and drained
2   tablespoons pitted kalamata olives, quartered
2   tablespoons crumbled reduced-fat feta cheese
12 whole kalamata olives

1. For dressing, in a screw-top jar combine lemon juice, mint, basil, olive oil, honey, and pepper. Cover and shake well.

2. Place lettuce on a large platter. Top with chicken, tomatoes, beans, the quartered olives, and the cheese. Drizzle with dressing. Garnish with whole olives.
MAKES 6 SERVINGS

Mexican Grilled Chicken Salad

PREP 15 minutes
CHILL 1 hour
GRILL 8 minutes

NUTRITION FACTS PER SERVING

Calories 290
Fat 17 g
Cholesterol 45 mg
Sodium 309 mg
Carbohydrates 15 g
Fiber 5 g
Protein 21 g

6   tablespoons olive oil
¼   cup lime juice
¼   cup chopped cilantro
2   minced garlic cloves
1   minced shallot
¾   teaspoon sugar
½   teaspoon ground cumin
1   pound thinly sliced chicken cutlets
3   hearts of romaine, chopped (10 cups)
3   plum tomatoes, seeded and chopped
1   15.5-ounce can black beans, drained and rinsed
1   cup shredded pepper Jack cheese
1   cup frozen corn

1. In small bowl whisk together olive oil, lime juice, chopped cilantro, minced garlic, minced shallot, sugar, and cumin. Place 4 tablespoons in a large resealable plastic bag; set remaining dressing aside.

2. Add chicken cutlets to bag; seal and squeeze to coat chicken. Refrigerate at least 1 hour.

3. In very large serving bowl combine romaine, plum tomatoes, black beans, pepper Jack cheese, and corn.

4. Heat grill to medium-high. Grill chicken for 3 to 4 minutes per side or until done; discard marinade. Chop chicken in 1-inch pieces; add to serving bowl. Drizzle with reserved dressing and toss well to combine. **MAKES 8 SERVINGS**

Sweet-and-Sour Chicken Bowl

START TO FINISH 20 minutes

NUTRITION FACTS
PER SERVING

Calories 285
Fat 10 g
Cholesterol 72 mg
Sodium 81 mg
Carbohydrates 21 g
Fiber 3 g
Protein 28 g

2½ cups shredded or chopped cooked chicken breast (about 12 ounces)
4 cups packaged shredded cabbage with carrots (coleslaw mix)
1 cup fresh snow pea pods, trimmed and halved crosswise
¼ cup raspberry or strawberry spreadable fruit
2 tablespoons canola oil
4 teaspoons cider vinegar
⅔ cup chopped red apple (1 medium)

1. In a large bowl combine chicken, coleslaw mix, and pea pods; set aside.

2. For dressing, in a small bowl stir together spreadable fruit, oil, and vinegar; stir in apple. Pour dressing over coleslaw mixture; toss gently to coat. If desired, cover and chill up to 1 hour before serving. **MAKES 4 SERVINGS**

Parisian Chicken Salad

PREP 25 minutes
MARINATE 6 hours
BROIL 12 minutes

NUTRITION FACTS
PER SERVING

Calories 305
Fat 17 g
Cholesterol 59 mg
Sodium 261 mg
Carbohydrates 16 g
Fiber 1 g
Protein 23 g

4   medium skinless, boneless chicken breast halves (about 1 pound)
2   teaspoons finely shredded orange peel
⅓   cup orange juice
4   cloves garlic, minced
2   tablespoons honey
1½ teaspoons dried thyme, crushed
½   teaspoon salt
¼   teaspoon black pepper
¼   cup olive oil
2   tablespoons white wine vinegar
2   tablespoons orange juice
2   cloves garlic, minced
1½ teaspoons finely chopped shallots
4   cups torn baby salad greens
1   medium yellow sweet pepper, thinly sliced
2   medium oranges, peeled and sectioned

1. Place chicken in a large, heavy self-sealing plastic bag set in a shallow dish. For marinade, in a bowl combine orange peel, the ⅓ cup orange juice, the 4 cloves garlic, the honey, and thyme. Pour over chicken. Seal bag; turn to coat chicken. Marinate in the refrigerator at least 6 hours or up to 8 hours, turning bag occasionally.

2. Drain chicken, discarding marinade. Place chicken on the unheated rack of a broiler pan. Season with half the salt and half the pepper. Broil 4 to 5 inches from heat for 12 to 15 minutes or until tender and no longer pink, turning once halfway through broiling.

3. Meanwhile, for dressing, in a screw-top jar combine olive oil, vinegar, the 2 tablespoons orange juice, the 2 cloves garlic, shallots, remaining salt, and remaining pepper. Cover; shake well.

4. Divide greens among four dinner plates. Top with pepper slices. Cut chicken in ½-inch slices. Arrange chicken and orange sections on salads. Drizzle with the dressing. **MAKES 4 SERVINGS**

Chicken, Pear, and Parmesan Salad

START TO FINISH 25 minutes

NUTRITION FACTS PER SERVING

Calories 275
Fat 8 g
Cholesterol 64 mg
Sodium 343 mg
Carbohydrates 26 g
Fiber 4 g
Protein 26 g

2   tablespoons cider vinegar or white wine vinegar
2   tablespoons olive oil or canola oil
1   tablespoon honey
¼   teaspoon salt
¼   teaspoon black pepper
5   cups torn fresh spinach leaves
2   cups shredded or chopped cooked chicken breast (10 ounces)
2   medium pears, cored and cut in cubes
½   of a small red onion, thinly sliced
¼   cup dried cranberries or raisins
1   ounce Parmesan cheese, shaved

1. For dressing, in a small screw-top jar combine vinegar, olive oil, honey, salt, and pepper. Cover and shake well.

2. In a large salad bowl combine spinach, chicken, pears, onion, and cranberries. Drizzle with dressing; toss to coat evenly. Top with shaved cheese. **MAKES 4 SERVINGS**

Bruschetta Chicken-Stuffed Tomatoes

START TO FINISH 25 minutes

NUTRITION FACTS PER SERVING

Calories 249
Fat 14 g
Cholesterol 64 mg
Sodium 509 mg
Carbohydrates 16 g
Fiber 4 g
Protein 17 g

1 2- to 2½-pound whole roasted chicken
1 cup coarsely chopped fresh spinach leaves
¼ cup thinly sliced green onions (2)
¼ cup snipped fresh basil or 2 teaspoons dried basil, crushed
2 tablespoons white balsamic vinegar or regular balsamic vinegar
1 tablespoon olive oil
2 cloves garlic, minced
4 large tomatoes (8 to 10 ounces each)
2 very thin slices firm-texture whole wheat bread, toasted and cut in cubes
2 tablespoons shredded Parmesan cheese

1. Remove and discard skin and bones from chicken. Chop enough meat to measure 2 cups; save the remaining chicken for another use. In a medium bowl combine the 2 cups chicken, the spinach, green onions, basil, vinegar, olive oil, and garlic. Toss to evenly coat.

2. Cut a ¼-inch slice from the stem end of each tomato; discard slices. Using a spoon, carefully scoop out the tomato pulp and seeds, leaving a ¼- to ½-inch-thick shell. Place tomatoes on serving plate(s). Discard tomato seeds. Chop enough of the tomato pulp to measure ½ cup; discard remaining pulp. Stir the ½ cup tomato pulp into chicken mixture.

3. Divide chicken mixture among tomato shells. Top with bread cubes and cheese. MAKES 4 SERVINGS

Turkey Salad with Oranges

START TO FINISH 30 minutes

NUTRITION FACTS PER SERVING

Calories 338
Fat 8 g
Cholesterol 71 mg
Sodium 150 mg
Carbohydrates 39 g
Fiber 5 g
Protein 29 g

1   5-ounce package arugula or fresh baby spinach
2½ cups chopped roasted turkey (about 12 ounces)
1   medium red sweet pepper, seeded and cut in strips
¼   cup snipped fresh cilantro
2   tablespoons peanut oil or canola oil
¼   cup orange juice
¼   cup honey
3   tablespoons lemon juice
1   tablespoon Dijon mustard
1   teaspoon ground cumin
¼   teaspoon black pepper
4   medium oranges, peeled and sectioned

1. In a large bowl combine arugula, turkey, sweet pepper strips, and cilantro.

2. For dressing, in a screw-top jar combine oil, orange juice, honey, lemon juice, mustard, cumin, and black pepper. Cover and shake well.

3. To serve, add orange sections to arugula mixture. Shake dressing. Drizzle some dressing over salad; toss gently to coat. Cover and chill any remaining dressing for another use. **MAKES 4 SERVINGS**

Cobb Salad

PREP 20 minutes

NUTRITION FACTS PER SERVING

Calories 176
Fat 8 g
Cholesterol 71 mg
Sodium 699 mg
Carbohydrates 14 g
Fiber 8 g
Protein 14 g

1 large head romaine lettuce
1 large head chicory
1 small avocado, halved, pitted, peeled, and cut lengthwise in thin wedges
½ cup crumbled blue cheese (2 ounces)
1 cup cherry tomatoes, halved
2 hard-cooked eggs, quartered
6 strips turkey bacon, cooked and crumbled
4 ounces cooked turkey breast, cut in matchstick-size pieces (¾ cup)
1 recipe Cran-Raspberry Vinaigrette

1. Tear romaine and chicory in bite-size pieces. Place greens in a large shallow bowl. Arrange avocado, blue cheese, tomatoes, eggs, bacon, and turkey on the greens. Serve with Cran-Raspberry Vinaigrette.
MAKES 8 SERVINGS

Cran-Raspberry Vinaigrette: For raspberry puree, place ¾ cup raspberries in a sieve over a bowl. Press to remove seeds; discard seeds. In a food processor or blender combine puree, ½ cup cranberry juice, ½ cup red wine vinegar, ¼ cup hot water, 1 tablespoon olive oil, ¾ teaspoon salt, and ¼ teaspoon sugar. Process until smooth.

Grilled Salmon Salad Niçoise

PREP 20 minutes
COOK 15 minutes
GRILL 4 to 6 minutes per
½-inch thickness

**NUTRITION FACTS
PER SERVING**

Calories 279
Fat 18 g
Cholesterol 162 mg
Sodium 222 mg
Carbohydrates 16 g
Fiber 4 g
Protein 14 g

2 4- to 5-ounce fresh or frozen
   skinless salmon fillets
8 ounces tiny new potatoes
8 ounces fresh green beans,
   trimmed
¼ teaspoon lemon-pepper
   seasoning
   Nonstick cooking spray
6 cups torn mixed salad greens
12 grape tomatoes or cherry
   tomatoes, halved
½ cup snipped fresh chives
4 hard-cooked eggs, cut in
   wedges
¼ cup niçoise olives, pitted,
   and/or other pitted olives
1 recipe Lemon Vinaigrette

1. Thaw salmon, if frozen. Rinse salmon; pat dry with paper towels. Set aside. Peel a strip around the center of each potato. In a large covered saucepan cook potatoes in enough lightly salted boiling water to cover for 10 minutes. Add green beans. Return to boiling; reduce heat. Cover and simmer about 5 minutes or until potatoes and beans are tender. Drain. Rinse with cold water to cool quickly; drain again. Set aside.

2. Meanwhile, measure thickness of salmon fillets. Sprinkle salmon with lemon-pepper seasoning. Lightly coat both sides of salmon fillets with cooking spray.

3. For a charcoal grill, place salmon on the rack of an uncovered grill directly over medium coals. Grill for 4 to 6 minutes per ½-inch thickness or until fish flakes easily

when tested with a fork, turning once halfway through grilling if fish is more than ¾ inch thick. (For a gas grill, preheat grill. Reduce heat to medium. Place salmon on grill rack over heat. Cover and grill as above.) Cut salmon in serving-size pieces.

4. Line six dinner plates with salad greens. Arrange salmon, potatoes, green beans, tomatoes, chives, eggs, and olives on greens. Drizzle with Lemon Vinaigrette.
MAKES 6 SERVINGS

Lemon Vinaigrette: In a screw-top jar combine ½ teaspoon finely shredded lemon peel; ¼ cup lemon juice; 3 tablespoons olive oil; 1 clove garlic, minced; ⅛ teaspoon salt; and ⅛ teaspoon black pepper. Cover and shake well.

Citrus Tuna Pasta Salad

PREP 30 minutes
CHILL 1 hour

NUTRITION FACTS PER SERVING

Calories 389
Fat 11 g
Cholesterol 22 mg
Sodium 369 mg
Carbohydrates 49 g
Fiber 5 g
Protein 27 g

6	ounces dried mafalda pasta or medium shell macaroni
1	9-ounce package frozen artichoke hearts, thawed
1	9¼-ounce can chunk white tuna (water pack), drained and broken in chunks
1	cup sliced fresh mushrooms
1	cup chopped yellow sweet pepper
¼	cup sliced pitted ripe olives
1	recipe Lemon Dressing
1	cup cherry tomatoes, halved
2	tablespoons finely shredded Parmesan cheese

1. Cook pasta according to package directions, except omit any oil or salt. Add artichoke hearts to pasta the last 5 minutes of cooking. Drain in colander. Rinse with cold water; drain again. Halve any large artichoke hearts.

2. Transfer pasta mixture to a large bowl. Gently stir in tuna, mushrooms, sweet pepper, and olives. Prepare Lemon Dressing. Pour dressing over pasta mixture; toss to coat. Cover; refrigerate at least 1 hour. Gently stir in tomatoes. Sprinkle with Parmesan cheese. **MAKES 4 SERVINGS**

Lemon Dressing: In a small bowl whisk together 1 teaspoon finely shredded lemon peel; 3 tablespoons lemon juice; 3 tablespoons rice vinegar or white wine vinegar; 2 tablespoons salad oil; 1 tablespoon snipped fresh thyme or basil or 1 teaspoon dried thyme or basil, crushed; 2 cloves garlic; ½ teaspoon sugar; and ¼ teaspoon black pepper.

Iceberg Wedges with Shrimp and Blue Cheese Dressing

START TO FINISH 35 minutes

NUTRITION FACTS PER SERVING

Calories 190
Fat 10 g
Cholesterol 129 mg
Sodium 360 mg
Carbohydrates 8 g
Fiber 1 g
Protein 18 g

1½ pounds fresh or frozen large shrimp in shells
2 tablespoons lemon juice
⅛ teaspoon black pepper
1 recipe Blue Cheese Dressing
  Nonstick cooking spray
1 large head iceberg lettuce, cut in 12 wedges
1 large tomato, chopped
⅓ cup thinly sliced, quartered red onion
2 slices turkey bacon, cooked and crumbled

1. Thaw shrimp, if frozen. Peel and devein shrimp, leaving tails intact if desired. Rinse shrimp; pat dry with paper towels. In a medium bowl combine shrimp, lemon juice, and pepper. Toss to coat; set aside. Prepare Blue Cheese Dressing; set aside.

2. Coat an unheated grill pan with cooking spray. Preheat grill pan over medium-high heat. Thread shrimp onto six 10- to 12-inch skewers.* Place kabobs on grill pan. Cook for 3 to 5 minutes or until shrimp are opaque, turning once halfway through cooking. (If necessary, cook shrimp kabobs half at a time.)

3. Place two lettuce wedges on each of six serving plates. Top with shrimp, tomato, red onion, and bacon. Serve with dressing.
MAKES 6 SERVINGS

Blue Cheese Dressing: In a small bowl combine ½ cup light mayonnaise or salad dressing, 1 tablespoon lemon juice, ¼ to ½ teaspoon bottled hot pepper sauce, and ⅛ teaspoon black pepper. Stir in 2 tablespoons crumbled blue cheese. Stir in 3 to 4 tablespoons fat-free milk to make desired consistency.

***Tip:** If using wooden skewers, soak in enough water to cover for at least 30 minutes before using.

Lemon Shrimp Salad

START TO FINISH 20 minutes

NUTRITION FACTS PER SERVING

Calories 148
Fat 6 g
Cholesterol 171 mg
Sodium 310 mg
Carbohydrates 5 g
Fiber 0 g
Protein 19 g

12 ounces fresh or frozen peeled, cooked shrimp with tails
1   5-ounce package mixed baby salad greens
½   of a small red onion, thinly sliced
¼   cup light mayonnaise or salad dressing
2   tablespoons lemon juice
1   tablespoon water
¼   to ½ teaspoon Cajun seasoning
    Lemon slices (optional)

1. Thaw shrimp, if frozen. Rinse shrimp; pat dry with paper towels. In a large bowl combine shrimp, greens, and onion.

2. For dressing, in a small bowl stir together mayonnaise, lemon juice, the water, and Cajun seasoning. Pour dressing over greens; toss gently to coat. If desired, garnish with lemon slices.
MAKES 4 SERVINGS

CHAPTER 6

Soups & Stews

Beef Stew with Red Wine Gravy

PREP 30 minutes
COOK 12 hours (low) or
6 hours (high)

NUTRITION FACTS PER SERVING

Calories 215
Fat 4 g
Cholesterol 64 mg
Sodium 405 mg
Carbohydrates 7 g
Fiber 1 g
Protein 26 g

¼ cup all-purpose flour
2 teaspoons dried Italian seasoning
1 teaspoon salt
½ teaspoon black pepper
2 pounds boneless beef chuck roast, cut in 1-inch cubes
2 tablespoons olive oil
2 large onions, cut in thin wedges
8 ounces parsnips, quartered lengthwise and halved
8 ounces carrots, quartered lengthwise and halved
8 ounces Jerusalem artichoke (sunchokes), peeled and coarsely chopped
1 cup red wine (such as Cabernet Sauvignon) or beef broth
½ cup beef broth
¼ cup tomato paste
   Chopped plum tomatoes, golden raisins, and/or red wine vinegar or balsamic vinegar (optional)
   Crusty bread (optional)

1. In a resealable plastic bag combine flour, Italian seasoning, salt, and pepper. Add meat cubes, a few at a time, shaking to coat. In a large skillet heat olive oil over medium-high heat. Brown meat, half at a time, in the hot oil. Drain off fat.

2. In a 4½- to 6-quart slow cooker combine onions, parsnips, carrots, and artichokes; top with meat cubes. Pour wine and broth over meat in cooker.

3. Cover and cook on low-heat setting for 12 to 14 hours or on high-heat setting for 6 to 7 hours. Stir in tomato paste. If desired, top servings with tomatoes, raisins, and/or vinegar. Serve with crusty bread. **MAKES 6 SERVINGS**

Hearty Beef Chili

PREP 20 minutes
COOK 9 hours (low) or
4½ hours (high)

NUTRITION FACTS
PER SERVING

Calories 226
Fat 4 g
Cholesterol 50 mg
Sodium 467 mg
Carbohydrates 27 g
Fiber 8 g
Protein 26 g

1½ pounds beef chuck pot roast, cut in 1-inch cubes

2 cups low-sodium vegetable juice or tomato juice

2 cups chopped onions (2 large)

2 15- to 16-ounce cans black beans, red kidney beans, and/or garbanzo beans (chickpeas), rinsed and drained

1 14.5-ounce can no-salt-added diced tomatoes, undrained

1½ cups chopped green sweet peppers (2 medium)

1 10-ounce can diced tomatoes with green chile peppers, undrained

1 teaspoon ground chipotle chile pepper

1 teaspoon ground cumin

1 teaspoon dried oregano, crushed

3 cloves garlic, minced

1. In a 4½- or 6-quart slow cooker combine meat, vegetable juice, onions, beans, undrained tomatoes, sweet peppers, undrained tomatoes with chile peppers, ground chipotle chile pepper, cumin, oregano, and garlic.

2. Cover and cook on low-heat setting for 9 to 10 hours or on high-heat setting for 4½ to 5 hours.
MAKES 8 TO 10 SERVINGS

Pumpkin-Cider Stew

PREP 30 minutes
COOK 1 hour 45 minutes

NUTRITION FACTS PER SERVING

Calories 279
Fat 8 g
Cholesterol 67 mg
Sodium 247 mg
Carbohydrates 26 g
Fiber 3 g
Protein 26 g

3 tablespoons all-purpose flour
2 teaspoons fennel seeds, crushed
¼ teaspoon salt
¼ teaspoon black pepper
2 pounds boneless beef chuck roast, cut in 1-inch cubes
2 tablespoons olive oil
2 medium onions, halved and thinly sliced
1 14.5-ounce can lower-sodium beef broth
1½ cups apple cider
¼ cup cider vinegar
1 2- to 3-pound pie pumpkin or 2 pounds potatoes
4 medium parsnips and/or carrots, peeled and cut in 1-inch pieces
2 red apples, cored and cut in wedges

1. In a resealable plastic bag combine flour, fennel seeds, salt, and pepper. Add meat cubes, a few at a time, shaking to coat. In a 5-quart Dutch oven heat 1 tablespoon of the olive oil over medium heat. Cook half of the meat and half the onions in the hot oil until meat is brown. Using a slotted spoon, remove beef and onions from pan; set aside. Heat the remaining 1 tablespoon oil in the Dutch oven. Add the remaining meat and onions and cook until meat is brown. Return all the beef and onions to the Dutch oven. Add broth, apple cider, and vinegar. Bring to boiling; reduce heat. Simmer, covered, for 1¼ hours.

2. Meanwhile, if using pie pumpkin, peel, seed, and remove strings from pumpkin. Cut pumpkin in 1- to 2-inch chunks. If using potatoes, peel and cut potatoes in wedges.

3. Add pumpkin or potatoes and parsnips to beef mixture. Return to boiling; reduce heat. Simmer, covered, for 25 minutes. Add apples; cover and simmer for 5 to 10 minutes more or until vegetables and apples are tender.
MAKES 8 SERVINGS

French Beef Stew

PREP 25 minutes
COOK 1 hour 45 minutes

NUTRITION FACTS PER SERVING

Calories 289
Fat 8 g
Cholesterol 65 mg
Sodium 399 mg
Carbohydrates 17 g
Fiber 4 g
Protein 28 g

1 tablespoon olive oil

1 pound boneless beef round, cut in 1-inch cubes

⅓ cup chopped onion (1 small)

1 cup dry white wine

1 teaspoon dried herbes de Provence, crushed

¼ teaspoon salt

¼ teaspoon black pepper

2 cups water

8 small new potatoes (about 6 ounces)

8 pearl onions, peeled

⅔ cup chopped, seeded, peeled tomato (1 large)

¼ cup Niçoise olives, pitted, or pitted kalamata olives

2 tablespoons drained capers

8 ounces haricots verts or small green beans, trimmed and cut in 3-inch lengths

1 tablespoon snipped fresh Italian (flat-leaf) parsley

1. In a 4- to 5-quart Dutch oven heat olive oil over medium heat. Brown half the meat in the hot oil. Using a slotted spoon, remove meat from pan; set aside. Add remaining meat and the chopped onion to drippings in Dutch oven. Cook for 3 to 5 minutes or until meat is brown and onion is tender. Drain off any fat. Return all the meat to the Dutch oven. Add wine, stirring to loosen any browned bits from pan. Add herbes de Provence, salt, pepper, and the water. Bring to boiling; reduce heat. Simmer, covered, for 1¼ hours or until meat is nearly tender.

2. Add potatoes and pearl onions to meat mixture. Return to boiling; reduce heat. Simmer, covered, about 30 minutes or until meat and vegetables are tender. Stir in tomato, olives, and capers; heat through.

3. Meanwhile, in a medium saucepan cook haricots verts, covered, in a small amount of boiling water for 5 to 7 minutes or until tender. To serve, divide the stew among four bowls. Serve with haricots verts and garnish with parsley. **MAKES 4 SERVINGS**

Hearty Bavarian Soup

PREP 25 minutes
COOK 1 hour 15 minutes

NUTRITION FACTS
PER SERVING

Calories 244
Fat 9 g
Cholesterol 42 mg
Sodium 996 mg
Carbohydrates 19 g
Fiber 3 g
Protein 21 g

1   pound boneless beef top round
2   tablespoons vegetable oil
½   cup chopped onion
    (1 medium)
2   tablespoons all-purpose flour
1   tablespoon Hungarian paprika
2   cloves garlic, minced
3   14.5-ounce cans chicken broth
1   14.5-ounce can diced
    tomatoes, undrained
1½ cups sliced carrots
    (3 medium)
2   tablespoons tomato paste
1   bay leaf
½   teaspoon dried marjoram,
    crushed
½   teaspoon caraway seeds,
    crushed
½   teaspoon black pepper
2   cups cubed, peeled potatoes
    (2 medium)
    Light sour cream (optional)

1. Trim fat from meat. Cut meat in ½-inch pieces. In a 4- to 5-quart Dutch oven heat oil over medium-high heat. Cook meat and onion in hot oil about 5 minutes or until meat is browned and onion is tender.

2. Add flour, paprika, and garlic; cook and stir for 3 minutes. Stir in broth, undrained tomatoes, carrots, tomato paste, bay leaf, marjoram, caraway seeds, and pepper. Bring to boiling; reduce heat. Simmer, covered, for 50 minutes, stirring occasionally.

3. Stir in potatoes. Simmer, covered, for 25 to 30 minutes or until meat and potatoes are tender. Remove and discard bay leaf. If desired, top servings with sour cream. **MAKES 6 TO 8 SERVINGS**

Barley-Beef Soup

PREP 25 minutes
COOK 1 hour 45 minutes

NUTRITION FACTS PER SERVING

Calories 188
Fat 5 g
Cholesterol 20 mg
Sodium 492 mg
Carbohydrates 23 g
Fiber 5 g
Protein 14 g

1   tablespoon vegetable oil
12 ounces beef stew meat, cut in 1-inch cubes
4   14.5-ounce cans lower-sodium beef broth
1   cup chopped onion (1 large)
½   cup chopped celery (1 stalk)
1   teaspoon dried oregano or basil, crushed
2   cloves garlic, minced
¼   teaspoon black pepper
1   bay leaf
1   cup frozen mixed vegetables
1   14.5-ounce can diced tomatoes, undrained
1   cup ½-inch slices peeled parsnips or ½-inch cubes peeled potatoes
⅔   cup quick-cooking barley

1. In a 5- to 6-quart Dutch oven heat oil over medium-high heat. Brown meat in hot oil. Stir in broth, onion, celery, oregano, garlic, pepper, and bay leaf. Bring to boiling; reduce heat. Simmer, covered, for 1½ hours.

2. Stir in frozen vegetables, undrained tomatoes, parsnips, and barley. Return to boiling; reduce heat. Simmer, covered, about 15 minutes or until meat and vegetables are tender. Remove and discard bay leaf. **MAKES 8 SERVINGS**

Slow-Cooker Directions:
Brown meat as directed. Drain off fat. In a 5- or 6-quart slow cooker combine meat and remaining ingredients, substituting regular barley for quick-cooking barley. Cover and cook on low-heat setting for 8 to 10 hours or on high-heat setting for 4 to 5 hours.

Southwest Pork Salsa Stew

START TO FINISH **25 minutes**

NUTRITION FACTS PER SERVING

Calories 243
Fat 7 g
Cholesterol 47 mg
Sodium 594 mg
Carbohydrates 19 g
Fiber 6 g
Protein 26 g

Nonstick cooking spray
12 ounces boneless pork loin or sirloin, cut in bite-size strips
1 14.5-ounce can reduced-sodium chicken broth
½ cup bottled cilantro-flavor salsa*
1 6-ounce can no-salt-added tomato paste
½ teaspoon ground cumin
1 medium zucchini, halved lengthwise and thinly sliced (2 cups)
1 cup frozen edamame (green soybeans) or baby lima beans
½ cup chopped peeled mango (1 small)

1. Lightly coat a large saucepan with cooking spray. Cook and stir pork in hot pan over medium-high heat about 2 minutes or until browned. Stir in broth, salsa, tomato paste, and cumin. Stir in zucchini and edamame. Bring to boiling; reduce heat. Simmer, covered, about 10 minutes or until vegetables are tender. Top servings with chopped mango.

MAKES 4 SERVINGS

*Tip: If you can't find cilantro-flavor salsa, use regular salsa and stir in 2 tablespoons snipped fresh cilantro.

Italian Pork and Pepper Soup

PREP 20 minutes
COOK 6 hours (low) or
3 hours (high) + 15 minutes
(high)

NUTRITION FACTS PER SERVING

Calories 217
Fat 7 g
Cholesterol 73 mg
Sodium 943 mg
Carbohydrates 12 g
Fiber 1 g
Protein 25 g

1½ pounds boneless pork
    shoulder
2   14.5-ounce cans beef broth
1   14.5-ounce can diced
    tomatoes with basil, garlic,
    and oregano, undrained
1   cup bottled roasted red sweet
    peppers, drained and cut in
    bite-size strips
½   cup chopped onion
    (1 medium)
2   tablespoons balsamic vinegar
¼   teaspoon black pepper
2   cups sliced zucchini (2 small)
    Finely shredded Parmesan
    cheese (optional)

1. Trim fat from meat. Cut meat in 1-inch pieces. In a 3½- or 4-quart slow cooker combine meat, broth, undrained tomatoes, roasted sweet peppers, onion, vinegar, and black pepper.

2. Cover and cook on low-heat setting for 6 to 8 hours or on high-heat setting for 3 to 4 hours.

3. If using low-heat setting, turn to high-heat setting. Stir in zucchini. Cover and cook about 15 minutes more or until zucchini is crisp-tender. If desired, sprinkle servings with cheese.
MAKES 6 SERVINGS

Range-Top Method: Trim fat from meat. Cut meat in 1-inch pieces. In a 4-quart Dutch oven heat 2 tablespoons vegetable oil over medium-high heat. Cook half the meat at a time in the hot oil until brown, adding onion with the second batch of meat. Drain off fat. Return all the meat to Dutch oven. Stir in broth, undrained tomatoes, roasted sweet peppers, vinegar, and black pepper. Bring to boiling; reduce heat. Simmer, covered, for 50 minutes. Stir in zucchini. Return to boiling; reduce heat. Simmer, covered, about 15 minutes or until meat and zucchini are tender. Serve as directed.

Pineapple Pork Chili

START TO FINISH 20 minutes

NUTRITION FACTS PER SERVING

Calories 329
Fat 9 g
Cholesterol 53 mg
Sodium 852 mg
Carbohydrates 44 g
Fiber 11 g
Protein 22 g

1 pound ground pork or beef
1 16-ounce jar pineapple salsa*
1 15-ounce can red kidney beans, rinsed and drained
1 8-ounce can tomato sauce
1 tablespoon chili powder
Pineapple slices (optional)

1. In a large saucepan cook meat over medium heat until browned. Drain off fat. Stir in salsa, beans, tomato sauce, and chili powder. Bring to boiling; reduce heat. Simmer, uncovered, for 10 minutes. Serve with pineapple slices.

MAKES 4 SERVINGS

*Tip: If you can't find pineapple salsa, use regular salsa and stir in ⅓ to ½ cup canned crushed pineapple.

Cuban Black Bean Soup

START TO FINISH **25 minutes**

**NUTRITION FACTS
PER SERVING**

Calories 175
Fat 6 g
Cholesterol 12 mg
Sodium 1,359 mg
Carbohydrates 26 g
Fiber 8 g
Protein 10 g

1 16-ounce jar mild or medium thick and chunky salsa or salsa with lime and garlic
1 14.5-ounce can chicken broth
1¾ cups water
1 15- to 16-ounce can black beans, rinsed and drained
1½ cups cubed cooked ham (8 ounces)
1 teaspoon ground cumin
½ cup sour cream
¼ cup salsa verde (optional) Crushed lime-flavor tortilla chips (optional)

1. In a large saucepan or Dutch oven combine salsa, broth, the water, beans, ham, and cumin. Bring to boiling; reduce heat. Simmer, covered, for 10 minutes.

2. Top each serving with 2 tablespoons sour cream. If desired, top with salsa verde and crushed tortilla chips.
MAKES 4 SERVINGS

Cuban Black Bean Soup with Peppers: Prepare as above, except substitute 2 cups frozen (yellow, green, and red) peppers and onion stir-fry vegetables for the ham.

Country Captain Soup

PREP 10 minutes
COOK 20 minutes

NUTRITION FACTS PER SERVING

Calories 225
Fat 11 g
Cholesterol 67 mg
Sodium 909 mg
Carbohydrates 11 g
Fiber 2 g
Protein 20 g

2 teaspoons olive oil
¾ cup chopped green sweet pepper (1 medium)
½ cup chopped onion (1 medium)
⅔ cup chopped peeled Granny Smith apple (1 medium)
2 cloves garlic, minced
1 tablespoon curry powder
1 teaspoon grated fresh ginger
1¼ pounds boneless, skinless chicken thighs, cut into 1-inch pieces
2 14.5-ounce cans reduced-sodium chicken broth
1 14.5-ounce can diced tomatoes with jalapeños, undrained

1. In a large saucepan heat olive oil over medium heat. Cook sweet pepper, onion, apple, and garlic in hot oil about 4 minutes or until tender. Add curry powder and ginger; cook and stir for 1 minute.

2. Add chicken, broth, and undrained tomatoes. Bring to boiling; reduce heat. Simmer, covered, about 15 minutes or until chicken is no longer pink.
MAKES 6 SERVINGS

Moroccan Chicken Stew

START TO FINISH **30 minutes**

NUTRITION FACTS PER SERVING

Calories 363
Fat 7 g
Cholesterol 45 mg
Sodium 496 mg
Carbohydrates 51 g
Fiber 9 g
Protein 24 g

1 cup dried couscous
1 tablespoon olive oil
12 ounces skinless, boneless chicken thighs or breast halves, cut in 1-inch pieces
⅓ cup sliced shallots (2 large)
3 cloves garlic, minced
½ teaspoon salt
½ teaspoon paprika
½ teaspoon ground cumin
¼ teaspoon ground cinnamon
¼ teaspoon ground saffron or ground turmeric
⅛ teaspoon cayenne pepper
6 ounces baby pattypan squash or 1½ cups sliced zucchini
1 cup slender baby carrots, tops trimmed, or packaged peeled baby carrots
1 cup reduced-sodium chicken broth
¼ cup golden or dark raisins
   Fresh mint (optional)

1. Cook couscous according to package directions, except omit the oil and salt; set aside and keep warm.

2. Meanwhile, in a large nonstick skillet heat oil over medium-high heat. Add chicken, shallots, and garlic; cook for 2 minutes. In a small bowl stir together salt, paprika, cumin, cinnamon, saffron, and cayenne pepper; sprinkle evenly over chicken mixture in skillet. Cook and stir for 2 minutes.

3. Cut any large pieces of squash and carrots in half; add to skillet. Stir in broth and raisins. Bring to boiling; reduce heat. Simmer, covered, for 6 to 8 minutes or until chicken is no longer pink and vegetables are crisp-tender. Serve stew over couscous. If desired, garnish with fresh mint.
MAKES 4 SERVINGS

Easy Cassoulet Soup

PREP 20 minutes
COOK 7 hours (low) or
3½ hours (high)

NUTRITION FACTS
PER SERVING

Calories 248
Fat 6 g
Cholesterol 55 mg
Sodium 969 mg
Carbohydrates 31 g
Fiber 9 g
Protein 23 g

2 medium carrots, cut in ½-inch pieces
1 cup chopped onion (1 large)
1 medium red or green sweet pepper, seeded and cut in ½-inch pieces
3 cloves garlic, minced
2 15-ounce cans cannellini (white kidney) beans or Great Northern beans, rinsed and drained
1 14.5-ounce can Italian-style stewed tomatoes, undrained
8 ounces skinless, boneless chicken thighs, cut in 1-inch pieces
8 ounces cooked smoked turkey sausage, halved lengthwise and cut in ½-inch slices
1½ cups chicken broth
½ cup dry white wine or chicken broth
1 tablespoon snipped fresh parsley
1 bay leaf
1 teaspoon dried thyme, crushed
⅛ to ¼ teaspoon cayenne pepper

1. In a 3½- or 5-quart slow cooker combine carrots, onion, sweet pepper, and garlic. Add beans, undrained tomatoes, chicken, and sausage. Add broth, wine, parsley, bay leaf, thyme, and cayenne pepper.

2. Cover and cook on low-heat setting for 7 to 8 hours or on high-heat setting for 3½ to 4 hours. Remove and discard bay leaf. **MAKES 6 TO 8 SERVINGS**

Chicken Stew with Tortellini

START TO FINISH **35 minutes**

NUTRITION FACTS PER SERVING

Calories 219
Fat 6 g
Cholesterol 52 mg
Sodium 761 mg
Carbohydrates 17 g
Fiber 2 g
Protein 23 g

2 14.5-ounce cans reduced-sodium chicken broth
1½ cups water
1 medium yellow summer squash, halved lengthwise and cut in ½-inch slices
1 cup dried cheese-filled tortellini
1 cup sliced carrots (2 medium)
1 medium onion, cut in thin wedges
¾ cup coarsely chopped green sweet pepper (1 medium)
½ teaspoon salt
¼ teaspoon garlic-pepper seasoning
2½ cups chopped cooked chicken (about 12 ounces)
2 cups torn fresh spinach leaves
2 tablespoons snipped fresh basil
   Fresh parsley sprigs (optional)

1. In a 4- to 5-quart Dutch oven bring broth and the water to boiling. Stir in squash, tortellini, carrots, onion, sweet pepper, salt, and garlic-pepper seasoning.

2. Return to boiling; reduce heat. Simmer, covered, about 15 minutes or until tortellini and vegetables are nearly tender.

3. Stir in chicken and spinach. Cook, covered, about 5 minutes or until tortellini and vegetables are tender. Stir in basil. If desired, garnish servings with parsley. **MAKES 6 SERVINGS**

Tuscan Ravioli Stew

START TO FINISH 20 minutes

NUTRITION FACTS
PER SERVING

Calories 320
Fat 13 g
Cholesterol 65 mg
Sodium 704 mg
Carbohydrates 38 g
Fiber 5 g
Protein 15 g

1   tablespoon olive oil
½   cup thinly sliced leek (1 large)
3   cloves garlic, minced
1   14.5-ounce can beef broth
¾   cup water
¼   teaspoon crushed red pepper
    (optional)
5   cups coarsely chopped
    broccoli rabe (6 ounces)
1   14.5-ounce can no-salt-added
    stewed tomatoes, undrained
1   9-ounce package refrigerated
    chicken-filled or cheese-filled
    ravioli
1   tablespoon snipped fresh
    rosemary or 1 teaspoon dried
    rosemary, crushed
¼   cup grated Asiago cheese
    Fresh rosemary (optional)

1. In a large saucepan heat olive oil over medium heat. Add leek and garlic; cook for 5 minutes. Stir in broth, the water, and, if desired, red pepper. Bring to boiling. Stir in broccoli rabe, undrained tomatoes, ravioli, and the 1 tablespoon rosemary. Return to boiling; reduce heat. Simmer, covered, for 7 to 8 minutes or until broccoli rabe and ravioli are tender.

2. Ladle stew into shallow bowls. Top with cheese. If desired, garnish with rosemary.
MAKES 4 SERVINGS

Turkey Onion Soup

PREP 45 minutes
COOK 1 hour

NUTRITION FACTS PER SERVING

Calories 227
Fat 5 g
Cholesterol 80 mg
Sodium 522 mg
Carbohydrates 12 g
Fiber 3 g
Protein 33 g

1   tablespoon vegetable oil
1½ cups chopped onions
      (3 medium)
1½ cups sliced carrots (3 medium)
1½ cups sliced celery (3 stalks)
1   cup sliced green onions (8)
1   cup chopped leeks (3 medium)
⅓   cup finely chopped shallots
      (3 medium)
1   2½-pound turkey breast
      portion with bone, skinned
5½ cups water
½   cup snipped fresh parsley
1½ teaspoons dried oregano,
      crushed
1½ teaspoons dried Greek
      seasoning
1   teaspoon salt
1   teaspoon fennel seeds, crushed
½   teaspoon freshly ground black
      pepper
2   bay leaves

1. In a 4- to 5-quart Dutch oven heat oil over medium-high heat. Add onions, carrots, celery, green onions, leeks, and shallots; cook for 7 to 10 minutes or until vegetables are tender. Add turkey, the water, ¼ cup of the parsley, the oregano, Greek seasoning, salt, fennel seeds, pepper, and bay leaves. Bring to boiling; reduce heat. Simmer, covered, for 1 to 2 hours or until turkey is tender.

2. Remove turkey from Dutch oven; cool slightly. When cool enough to handle, remove meat from bones; discard bones. Chop meat and return to Dutch oven. Remove and discard bay leaves. If necessary, reheat soup. Ladle soup into bowls; sprinkle servings with the remaining ¼ cup parsley.
MAKES 6 SERVINGS

Turkey and New Potato Soup

PREP 15 minutes
COOK 20 minutes

NUTRITION FACTS PER SERVING

Calories 243
Fat 8 g
Cholesterol 57 mg
Sodium 1,297 mg
Carbohydrates 23 g
Fiber 3 g
Protein 19 g

1½ pounds tiny new potatoes (15 to 18 potatoes)
1 pound smoked turkey breast or chicken breast, shredded
2 14.5-ounce cans reduced-sodium chicken broth
⅓ cup sliced leek (1 medium)
⅓ cup whipping cream
3 tablespoons Dijon mustard
1 tablespoon snipped fresh lemon thyme or thyme
1½ cups coarsely shredded napa cabbage

1. Cut any large potatoes in half. In a 4-quart Dutch oven combine potatoes, turkey, broth, and leek. Bring to boiling; reduce heat. Simmer, covered, for 15 minutes.

2. In a small bowl stir together whipping cream and mustard. Stir cream mixture and thyme into turkey mixture. Simmer, uncovered, about 5 minutes more or until potatoes are tender, stirring occasionally. Ladle soup into bowls. Top servings with cabbage. **MAKES 6 SERVINGS**

Spiced Seafood Stew

PREP 30 minutes
COOK 6 minutes
STAND 45 minutes

NUTRITION FACTS PER SERVING

Calories 187
Fat 6 g
Cholesterol 116 mg
Sodium 503 mg
Carbohydrates 12 g
Fiber 1 g
Protein 23 g

8 ounces fresh or frozen medium shrimp in shells
8 ounces fresh or frozen scallops
8 ounces (8 to 12) fresh mussels in shells
1 tablespoon olive oil
1 cup finely chopped onions (2 medium)
4 cloves garlic, minced
1 teaspoon ground cumin
½ teaspoon ground cinnamon
¼ teaspoon cayenne pepper
1 cup fish or vegetable broth
1 cup finely chopped tomatoes (2 medium)
¼ teaspoon salt
⅛ teaspoon ground saffron
  Hot cooked couscous (optional)
  Italian (flat-leaf) parsley (optional)

1. Thaw shrimp and scallops, if frozen. Peel and devein shrimp, leaving tails intact. Rinse shrimp and scallops; pat dry with paper towels. Set aside. Scrub mussels; remove beards. In a large bowl combine 2 cups water and 3 tablespoons salt; soak mussels in salt water for 15 minutes. Drain; rinse. Repeat twice. Set aside.

2. In a large saucepan heat olive oil over medium heat. Add onions and garlic; cook until tender. Stir in cumin, cinnamon, and cayenne pepper; cook and stir for 1 minute. Stir in broth, tomatoes, the ¼ teaspoon salt, and the saffron. Bring to boiling; add shrimp, scallops, and mussels. Return to boiling; reduce heat. Simmer, covered, about 5 minutes or until mussel shells open. If desired, serve over couscous and garnish with parsley. **MAKES 4 SERVINGS**

Creamy Carrot and Pasta Soup

START TO FINISH **30 minutes**

NUTRITION FACTS PER SERVING

Calories 351
Fat 4 g
Cholesterol 7 mg
Sodium 937 mg
Carbohydrates 67 g
Fiber 3 g
Protein 14 g

2   14.5-ounce cans vegetable broth or chicken broth
2   cups sliced carrots (4 medium)
1   cup chopped peeled potato (1 large)
1   cup chopped onion (1 large)
1   tablespoon grated fresh ginger
½   teaspoon Jamaican jerk seasoning
8   ounces dried radiatore or rotini pasta
1½ cups milk
    Fresh chives (optional)

1. In a large saucepan combine broth, carrots, potato, onion, ginger, and jerk seasoning. Bring to boiling; reduce heat. Simmer, covered, for 15 to 20 minutes or until vegetables are very tender. Cool slightly.

2. Meanwhile, cook pasta according to package directions; drain.

3. Place one-fourth of the vegetables at a time in a food processor. Cover and process until smooth. Transfer puree to a bowl. Return all the pureed vegetables to a saucepan. Stir in cooked pasta and milk; heat through. If desired, top servings with chives.
MAKES 4 SERVINGS

Hearty Garlic and Snap Pea Soup

PREP **30 minutes**
COOK **19 minutes**

NUTRITION FACTS
PER SIDE-DISH SERVING

Calories 102
Fat 3 g
Cholesterol 0 mg
Sodium 404 mg
Carbohydrates 15 g
Fiber 3 g
Protein 3 g

2   tablespoons olive oil
4   cloves garlic, chopped
¼   cup chopped onion
1   pound Yukon Gold potatoes, quartered
2   14.5-ounce cans reduced-sodium chicken broth
1¾ cups water
1   medium fennel bulb, thinly slivered (fronds reserved)
1½ cups sugar snap peas, trimmed
½   teaspoon salt
¼   teaspoon black pepper
1   tablespoon fresh snipped fennel fronds
    Plain yogurt (optional)
    Olive oil (optional)

1. In a large saucepan heat the 2 tablespoons oil over medium heat. Add garlic; cook for 1 minute. Add onion; cook until tender. Add potatoes, broth, and the water. Bring to boiling; reduce heat. Simmer, covered, for 15 to 18 minutes or until the potatoes are tender.

2. Place one-third of the potato mixture at a time in a food processor or blender. Cover and process until smooth. Return all of the potato puree to saucepan. Add slivered fennel and sugar snap peas. Bring to boiling; reduce heat. Simmer, uncovered, for 3 minutes.

3. Stir in salt and pepper. Ladle soup into bowls. Top with fennel fronds. If desired, top with yogurt and drizzle with olive oil.
**MAKES 8 SIDE-DISH SERVINGS OR
4 MAIN-DISH SERVINGS**

Vegetable Soup with Corn Bread Croutons

Prep 40 minutes
Bake 12 minutes
Oven 350°F Cook 15 minutes

NUTRITION FACTS PER SERVING

Calories 345
Fat 11 g
Cholesterol 42 mg
Sodium 933 mg
Carbohydrates 52 g
Fiber 6 g
Protein 15 g

1   recipe Corn Bread Croutons (see below)
1   28-ounce can whole Italian-style tomatoes
2   medium leeks, sliced or 1 medium onion, chopped (½ cup)
1   tablespoon olive oil or cooking oil
1   8-ounce package fresh mushrooms, quartered
1   large yellow or red sweet pepper, coarsely chopped
4   cloves garlic, minced
3   cups water
1   15 to 19-ounce can cannellini beans (white kidney beans), rinsed and drained
1   teaspoon coarse sea salt or ½ teaspoon salt
¼   teaspoon freshly ground black pepper
8   ounces spinach leaves (about 4 cups)

1. Prepare Corn Bread Croutons; set aside to cool.

2. Remove tomatoes from can, reserving liquid. Coarsely chop tomatoes. In a 4-quart Dutch oven cook leeks in hot oil over medium heat until tender, stirring occasionally. Add mushrooms, sweet pepper, and garlic; cook 5 minutes more, stirring occasionally. Add water, tomatoes and canning liquid, cannellini beans, salt, and black pepper. Bring to boiling; reduce heat. Simmer, uncovered, for 5 minutes. Stir in spinach; serve with Corn Bread Croutons. **MAKES 6 TO 8 SERVINGS (ABOUT 10 CUPS TOTAL SOUP)**

Corn Bread Croutons

Preheat oven to 350°F. Grease 2 large baking sheets; set aside. In a medium bowl lightly beat 1 egg. Add one 8.5-ounce package corn muffin mix, ⅔ cup finely shredded Romano or Parmesan cheese, and 2 tablespoons milk. Drop into small mounds by scant teaspoonfuls onto prepared baking sheet(s). Lightly sprinkle with a dash of freshly ground black pepper and, if desired, coarse sea salt. Bake for 12 to 14 minutes or until golden. Remove from baking sheet; let cool completely on a wire rack. Store Corn Bread Croutons in an airtight container at room temperature up to 1 day or in the refrigerator up to 3 days (let stand 30 minutes at room temperature before serving). **MAKES ABOUT 28**

Caramelized Ginger-Carrot Soup

PREP 30 minutes
COOK 50 minutes

NUTRITION FACTS
PER SERVING

Calories 105
Fat 5 g
Cholesterol 9 mg
Sodium 524 mg
Carbohydrates 13 g
Fiber 2 g
Protein 2 g

2   tablespoons vegetable oil
3   cups thinly sliced onions
     (3 large)
2   tablespoons sugar
⅛   teaspoon freshly ground
     black pepper
2   tablespoons grated fresh
     ginger
8   carrots (about 1¼ pounds)
1   medium sweet potato
6   cups chicken broth
1   cup half-and-half or light cream
     Salt and freshly ground black
     pepper

1. For caramelized onions, in a large skillet heat oil over medium heat. Add onion slices, sugar, and the ⅛ teaspoon pepper; reduce heat to low and cook, covered, for 30 minutes, stirring twice. Add ginger; cook, uncovered, 20 to 30 minutes more or until onions are golden brown, stirring occasionally. Divide in half.

2. Meanwhile, peel carrots and sweet potato and cut in 1-inch pieces. In a large saucepan or Dutch oven combine broth, carrots, and sweet potato. Bring to boiling; reduce heat. Simmer, covered, for 40 minutes or until very tender. Add half the caramelized onions. Puree until nearly smooth with a handheld blender or process 2 cups at a time in a food processor. Add cream; heat through. If desired, season with salt and freshly ground black pepper. Garnish with remaining caramelized onions.

MAKES 12 SIDE-DISH SERVINGS OR 4 MAIN-DISH SERVINGS

Avocado Soup

PREP 20 minutes
CHILL 1 to 24 hours

NUTRITION FACTS PER SERVING

Calories 92
Fat 7 g
Cholesterol 0 mg
Sodium 322 mg
Carbohydrates 6 g
Fiber 4 g
Protein 3 g

2   ripe medium avocados, seeded, peeled, and cut up
½   cup chopped peeled cucumber
⅓   cup chopped onion (1 small)
¼   cup shredded carrot
1   clove garlic, minced
2   14.5-ounce cans reduced-sodium chicken broth
    Several dashes bottled hot pepper sauce
1½ teaspoons paprika
⅓   cup bottled salsa (optional)

1. In a blender or food processor combine avocados, cucumber, onion, carrot, and garlic. Add 1 can of the broth. Cover and blend or process until nearly smooth.

2. Add the remaining can of broth and pepper sauce. Cover and blend or process until smooth. Pour puree/soup into a bowl. Cover surface with plastic wrap and chill for 1 to 24 hours.

3. To serve, ladle into chilled soup bowls. Sprinkle with paprika. If desired, top with salsa.
MAKES 6 SIDE-DISH OR APPETIZER SERVINGS

CHAPTER 7

Beef & Lamb

Best-Ever Roast Beef

PREP **15 minutes**
ROAST **1 hour 15 minutes**
STAND **15 minutes**
OVEN **400°F**

NUTRITION FACTS PER SERVING

Calories 251
Fat 12 g
Cholesterol 60 mg
Sodium 457 mg
Carbohydrates 7 g
Fiber 1 g
Protein 24 g

Nonstick cooking spray
2 large onions, cut in ¼-inch slices and separated in rings
1 cup dry red wine
1 3-pound beef eye of round roast
¼ cup ketchup
2 tablespoons bottled teriyaki sauce
2 tablespoons Dijon mustard
1 tablespoon balsamic vinegar*
½ cup water
3 tablespoons all-purpose flour
2 cups beef broth

1. Preheat oven to 400°F. Coat a roasting pan with cooking spray. Scatter onion rings in pan. Pour red wine into the pan. Place roast on onion rings. Set aside.

2. In a small bowl stir together ketchup, teriyaki sauce, mustard, and balsamic vinegar. Reserve 2 tablespoons of the ketchup mixture for gravy; brush some of the remaining ketchup mixture on the top and sides of the roast.

3. Roast, uncovered, about 1¼ hours or until a meat thermometer registers 135°F. Transfer meat to a cutting board. Cover and let stand for 15 minutes before slicing. The temperature of the meat after standing should be 145°F. Transfer onions to a serving bowl; cover and keep warm.

4. For gravy, add the water to reserved 2 tablespoons ketchup mixture; whisk in flour until smooth. Set aside. Place roasting pan on stovetop over medium-high heat. Add broth; cook for 2 minutes, stirring and scraping up any browned bits from bottom of pan. Slowly whisk in flour mixture; cook and stir about 3 minutes or until thickened and bubbly. Thinly slice roast. Serve meat with onions and gravy. **MAKES 12 SERVINGS**

*Tip: While there's no true substitute for the rich, complex flavor of balsamic vinegar, in a pinch, you can use 1 tablespoon cider vinegar or red-wine vinegar plus ½ teaspoon sugar for each tablespoon of balsamic vinegar called for in a recipe.

Beef and Sweet Potato Pan Roast

PREP 25 minutes
ROAST 30 minutes
STAND 10 minutes
OVEN 425°F

NUTRITION FACTS PER SERVING

Calories 362
Fat 14 g
Cholesterol 65 mg
Sodium 587 mg
Carbohydrates 32 g
Fiber 5 g
Protein 26 g

1 tablespoon dried Italian seasoning
6 cloves garlic, minced
1 teaspoon salt
½ teaspoon crushed red pepper
3 tablespoons olive oil
2 pounds sweet potatoes and/ or russet potatoes, peeled and cut in 1-inch wedges
4 6- to 8-ounce beef shoulder petite tenders or one 1½- to 2-pound beef tenderloin roast*
1 cup cherry tomatoes
1 recipe Chopped Parsley Topping

1. Preheat oven to 425°F. In a small bowl stir together Italian seasoning, garlic, salt, and crushed red pepper. Stir in olive oil. Divide seasoning mixture between two large resealable plastic bags. Place sweet potatoes in one bag. Seal bag and shake to coat potatoes. Spread potatoes in a single layer in a greased shallow roasting pan. Roast, uncovered, for 15 minutes.

2. Meanwhile, place meat in the second bag. Seal bag and shake to coat meat. Remove meat from bag. In a large skillet brown meat over medium-high heat.

3. Stir sweet potatoes in roasting pan and push to edges of pan. Place meat in center of pan. Roast, uncovered, for 5 minutes. Add tomatoes; roast for 10 to 15 minutes more or until meat is desired doneness (145°F for medium rare to 160°F for medium). Cover and let stand for 10 minutes before slicing. Cut meat in serving-size pieces. Serve with Chopped Parsley Topping. **MAKES 6 SERVINGS**

Chopped Parsley Topping: In a small bowl stir together ¼ cup snipped fresh parsley; 2 teaspoons finely shredded orange peel; 2 cloves garlic, minced; and ⅛ teaspoon salt.

*Tip: To substitute beef tenderloin for shoulder petite tenders, prepare potatoes and meat as directed, except do not roast potatoes before adding meat. Place browned tenderloin in center of greased roasting pan. Place potato wedges around pan edges. Roast, uncovered, for 30 to 45 minutes or until desired doneness (145°F for medium-rare to 160°F for medium), adding tomatoes during the last 10 to 15 minutes of roasting. Let stand for 5 minutes before slicing.

Beef with Portobello Relish

PREP 15 minutes
GRILL 15 minutes
STAND 5 minutes

NUTRITION FACTS PER SERVING

Calories 329
Fat 18 g
Cholesterol 87 mg
Sodium 617 mg
Carbohydrates 9 g
Fiber 2 g
Protein 33 g

4   beef tenderloin steaks, cut 1-inch thick (about 1¼ pounds total)
     Kosher salt and cracked black pepper
1   medium onion, cut in ½-inch slices
8   ounces portobello mushrooms, stems removed
4   plum tomatoes, halved lengthwise
3   tablespoons snipped fresh basil
6   large cloves garlic, minced (2 tablespoons)
2   tablespoons olive oil
1   teaspoon kosher salt
1   teaspoon cracked black pepper

1. Trim fat from steaks. Season steaks with salt and pepper. For a charcoal grill, grill steaks, onion slices, mushrooms, and tomatoes on the rack of an uncovered grill directly over medium coals until steaks are desired doneness and vegetables are tender, turning once halfway through grilling. For steaks, allow 10 to 12 minutes for medium rare (145°F) or 12 to 15 minutes for medium (160°F). For vegetables, allow 15 minutes for onion and 10 minutes for mushrooms and tomatoes. (For a gas grill, preheat grill. Reduce heat to medium. Place steaks and vegetables on grill rack over heat. Cover and grill as above.) Cover steaks with foil; let stand for 5 minutes before serving.

2. Meanwhile, for relish, cut grilled onion, mushrooms, and tomatoes in 1-inch pieces. In a medium bowl stir together basil, garlic, oil, the 1 teaspoon kosher salt, and the 1 teaspoon cracked black pepper. Add vegetables to basil mixture; toss to coat. To serve, spoon warm relish around steaks. **MAKES 4 SERVINGS**

Steaks with Tomato Salsa

START TO FINISH 25 minutes

NUTRITION FACTS PER SERVING

Calories 267
Fat 14 g
Cholesterol 54 mg
Sodium 451 mg
Carbohydrates 8 g
Fiber 2 g
Protein 26 g

¾ teaspoon kosher salt or ½ teaspoon regular salt
½ teaspoon ground cumin
½ teaspoon chili powder
½ teaspoon dried oregano, crushed
½ teaspoon packed brown sugar
2 8-ounce boneless beef ribeye steaks, cut ½ to ¾ inch thick
    Nonstick cooking spray
2 tablespoons olive oil
½ cup chopped onion (1 medium)
2 cloves garlic, minced
2 cups red and/or yellow cherry or pear tomatoes, halved
1 canned chipotle pepper in adobo sauce, drained and finely chopped (see tip, page 63)
2 tablespoons lime juice
¼ cup snipped fresh cilantro

1. In a small bowl stir together ½ teaspoon of the kosher salt or ¼ teaspoon of the regular salt, the cumin, chili powder, dried oregano, and brown sugar. Sprinkle on both sides of steaks; rub in with your fingers.

2. Lightly coat a grill pan with cooking spray. Preheat pan over medium-high heat. Add steaks. Reduce heat to medium. Cook for 8 to 10 minutes for medium-rare (145°F) to medium (160°F), turning occasionally. Cover steaks with foil; let stand for 5 minutes before serving.

3. Meanwhile, for salsa, in a large skillet heat oil over medium heat. Add onion and garlic; cook and stir until tender. Stir in tomatoes, chipotle pepper, lime juice, and the remaining salt. Cook and stir for 1 minute. Transfer to a bowl; stir in cilantro.

4. Cut each steak in half; serve with salsa. **MAKES 4 SERVINGS**

Tip: If you like, cook the steaks on an outdoor grill. For a charcoal grill, grill steaks on the rack of an uncovered grill directly over medium coals until desired doneness. Allow 8 to 10 minutes for medium rare (145°F) or 10 to 12 minutes for medium (160°F). (For a gas grill, preheat grill. Reduce heat to medium. Place steaks on grill rack over heat. Cover and grill as above.)

Bail-Out Beef Stroganoff

START TO FINISH **30 minutes**

NUTRITION FACTS PER SERVING

Calories 413
Fat 16 g
Cholesterol 103 mg
Sodium 504 mg
Carbohydrates 33 g
Fiber 3 g
Protein 33 g

3   cups dried wide noodles
3   cups broccoli florets
    (12 ounces)
½   cup light sour cream
1½ teaspoons prepared
    horseradish
½   teaspoon fresh dill
1   pound beef ribeye steak
1   tablespoon vegetable oil
1   small onion, cut in ½-inch
    slices
1   clove garlic, minced
4   teaspoons all-purpose flour
½   teaspoon black pepper
1   14.5-ounce can beef broth
3   tablespoons tomato paste
1   teaspoon Worcestershire
    sauce

1. Cook noodles according to package directions, adding broccoli for the last 5 minutes of cooking. Drain. Return pasta mixture to hot pan; cover to keep warm.

2. Meanwhile, in a small serving bowl stir together the sour cream, horseradish, and dill; cover and chill until serving time.

3. Trim fat from meat. Cut meat in bite-size strips. In a large skillet heat oil over medium heat. Add half the meat, the onion, and garlic; cook and stir until onion is tender and meat is desired doneness. Remove meat mixture from skillet. Add remaining meat to skillet; cook and stir until meat is desired doneness. Return meat mixture to the skillet; sprinkle flour and pepper over all. Stir to coat.

4. Stir in broth, tomato paste, and Worcestershire sauce. Cook and stir until thickened and bubbly. Cook and stir for 1 minute more. Divide noodles among four bowls. Spoon meat on noodles. Top with the sour cream. **MAKES 4 SERVINGS**

Sirloin with Mustard and Chives

START TO FINISH 20 minutes

NUTRITION FACTS PER SERVING

Calories 164
Fat 5 g
Cholesterol 59 mg
Sodium 265 mg
Carbohydrates 2 g
Fiber 0 g
Protein 26 g

1   to 1¼ pounds boneless beef sirloin or ribeye steaks, cut ¾-inch thick
2   teaspoons garlic-pepper seasoning
½   cup light sour cream
2   tablespoons Dijon mustard
1   tablespoon snipped fresh chives

1. If necessary, cut steaks in four serving-size pieces. Evenly sprinkle both sides of steaks with 1½ teaspoons of the garlic-pepper seasoning. For a charcoal grill, grill steaks on the rack of an uncovered grill directly over medium coals to desired doneness, turning once halfway through grilling. Allow 9 to 11 minutes for medium rare (145°F) and 11 to 13 minutes for medium (160°F). (For a gas grill, preheat grill. Reduce heat to medium. Place steaks on grill rack over heat. Cover and grill as above.) Cover steaks with foil; let stand for 5 minutes before serving.

2. Meanwhile, in a small bowl stir together sour cream, mustard, chives, and the remaining ½ teaspoon garlic-pepper seasoning. Spoon sour cream mixture on steaks.
MAKES 4 SERVINGS

Steak and Potato Kabobs

PREP **30 minutes**
MARINATE **4 to 6 hours**
GRILL **12 minutes**

NUTRITION FACTS
PER SERVING

Calories 289
Fat 10 g
Cholesterol 69 mg
Sodium 401 mg
Carbohydrates 22 g
Fiber 3 g
Protein 26 g

1   pound boneless beef sirloin steak, cut 1 inch thick
¼   cup bottled red wine vinaigrette salad dressing
2   tablespoons snipped fresh thyme or 2 teaspoons dried thyme, crushed
2   tablespoons Worcestershire sauce
¼   teaspoon garlic powder
12 ounces tiny new potatoes, halved or quartered
2   medium green and/or yellow sweet peppers, seeded and cut in 1-inch squares
1   medium red onion, cut in wedges

1. Trim fat from meat. Cut meat in 1-inch cubes. Place meat cubes in a resealable plastic bag set in a shallow dish. For marinade, in a small bowl combine salad dressing, thyme, Worcestershire sauce, and garlic powder. Pour marinade over meat. Seal bag; turn to coat meat. Marinate in the refrigerator for 4 to 6 hours, turning bag occasionally.

2. Meanwhile, place twelve 10-inch wooden skewers in a shallow dish; add enough water to cover. Soak for 1 hour; drain. In a large covered saucepan cook potatoes in enough lightly salted boiling water to cover for 7 minutes; drain and cool.

3. Drain steak, reserving marinade. On skewers, alternately thread meat, sweet peppers, onion, and potatoes, leaving a ¼-inch space between pieces.

4. For a charcoal grill, grill kabobs on the rack of an uncovered grill directly over medium coals until meat is desired doneness, turning once and brushing occasionally with reserved marinade up to the last 5 minutes of grilling. Allow 12 to 14 minutes for medium (160°F). Discard any remaining marinade. (For a gas grill, preheat grill. Reduce heat to medium. Place skewers on grill rack over heat. Cover and grill as above.)
MAKES 4 SERVINGS

Lemony Flank Steak

PREP 15 minutes
MARINATE 2 to 24 hours
BROIL 17 minutes

NUTRITION FACTS
PER SERVING

Calories 301
Fat 12 g
Cholesterol 68 mg
Sodium 378 mg
Carbohydrates 9 g
Fiber 0 g
Protein 38 g

1   1½-pound beef flank steak or boneless beef sirloin steak, cut 1 inch thick
1   teaspoon finely shredded lemon peel
½   cup lemon juice
2   tablespoons sugar
2   tablespoons reduced-sodium soy sauce
2   teaspoons snipped fresh oregano or ½ teaspoon dried oregano, crushed
⅛   teaspoon black pepper
    Lemon slices (optional)
    Fresh oregano sprigs (optional)

1. Score both sides of steak in a diamond pattern by making shallow diagonal cuts at 1-inch intervals. Place meat in a resealable plastic bag set in a shallow dish. For marinade, in a small bowl stir together lemon peel, lemon juice, sugar, soy sauce, oregano, and pepper. Pour marinade over meat; seal bag. Turn to coat meat. Marinate in the refrigerator for 2 to 24 hours, turning bag occasionally.

2. Drain steak, reserving marinade. Pat steak dry with paper towels. Preheat broiler. Place steak on the unheated rack of a broiler pan. Broil 3 to 4 inches from the heat for 17 to 22 minutes or until medium doneness (160°F), turning and brushing once with reserved marinade halfway through broiling. Discard any remaining marinade.

3. To serve, thinly slice meat diagonally across the grain. If desired, garnish with lemon slices and fresh oregano sprigs.
MAKES 4 SERVINGS

Flank Steak with Mushrooms

PREP 25 minutes
MARINATE 1 hour
BROIL 17 minutes

NUTRITION FACTS PER SERVING

Calories 240
Fat 9 g
Cholesterol 53 mg
Sodium 291 mg
Carbohydrates 6 g
Fiber 1 g
Protein 27 g

1 1½-pound beef flank steak
¾ cup dry red wine
1 tablespoon sherry vinegar or red wine vinegar
1 tablespoon finely shredded orange peel
¼ teaspoon fennel seeds, crushed
1 tablespoon butter
¼ cup chopped shallots (2 medium)
2 cloves garlic, minced
3 cups sliced fresh cremini, oyster, and/or button mushrooms (8 ounces)
1 tablespoon cornstarch
¾ cup beef broth
   Salt and black pepper

1. Trim fat from meat. Score both sides of meat in a diamond pattern by making shallow diagonal cuts at 1-inch intervals. Place meat in a resealable plastic bag set in a shallow dish. For marinade, in a small bowl combine wine, vinegar, orange peel, and crushed fennel seeds. Pour marinade over meat. Seal bag; turn to coat meat. Marinate in the refrigerator for 1 hour, turning bag once or twice.

2. Preheat broiler. Drain meat, reserving ⅓ cup of the marinade. Place meat on the unheated rack of a broiler pan. Broil 3 to 4 inches from the heat for 17 to 21 minutes or until medium doneness (160°F), turning once halfway through broiling.

3. Meanwhile, for mushroom sauce, in a medium saucepan melt butter over medium heat. Add shallots and garlic; cook for 2 minutes, stirring occasionally. Add mushrooms; cook and stir until tender. In a small bowl combine the ⅓ cup reserved marinade and cornstarch; stir into mushroom mixture. Add broth. Cook and stir until thickened and bubbly. Cook and stir for 2 minutes more. Season with salt and pepper.

4. Thinly slice meat diagonally across the grain. Serve with mushroom sauce. **MAKES 6 SERVINGS**

Steak with Sweet Potato-Mango Chutney

START TO FINISH **20 minutes**

NUTRITION FACTS
PER SERVING

Calories 344
Fat 5 g
Cholesterol 70 mg
Sodium 418 mg
Carbohydrates 32 g
Fiber 4 g
Protein 40 g

1   large sweet potato (12 ounces),
    peeled and diced
4   boneless beef eye round
    steaks, about ¾ inch thick
    Salt
    Steak seasoning
⅓   cup mango chutney
¼   cup dried cranberries
    Rosemary sprigs (optional)

1. In a medium saucepan bring lightly salted water to boiling. Add sweet potato; simmer, covered, for 8 to 10 minutes or until tender. Drain and keep warm.

2. Meanwhile, sprinkle steaks lightly with salt and steak seasoning. In a large nonstick skillet cook meat over medium heat to desired doneness, turning once. Allow 8 to 10 minutes for medium rare (145°F) to medium (160°F). Transfer to serving plates; cover to keep warm.

3. For sweet potato-mango chutney, add sweet potatoes to skillet; cook and stir for 2 minutes. Add chutney and cranberries to skillet; stir gently to heat through. Season with additional salt and steak seasoning. Serve chutney with steaks. If desired, garnish with rosemary. **MAKES 4 SERVINGS**

Szechwan Beef Stir-Fry

START TO FINISH **40 minutes**

NUTRITION FACTS PER SERVING

Calories 317
Fat 7 g
Cholesterol 48 mg
Sodium 859 mg
Carbohydrates 35 g
Fiber 3 g
Protein 24 g

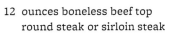
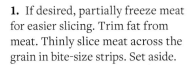

12 ounces boneless beef top round steak or sirloin steak
3 tablespoons dry sherry or orange juice
3 tablespoons soy sauce
2 tablespoons water
2 tablespoons bottled hoisin sauce
1 tablespoon grated fresh ginger or ½ teaspoon ground ginger
2 teaspoons cornstarch
1 teaspoon sugar
2 cloves garlic, minced
¼ to ½ teaspoon crushed red pepper (optional)
1 tablespoon vegetable oil
1 cup thinly bias-sliced carrots (2 medium)
1 14-ounce can whole baby corn, drained
1 medium red sweet pepper, seeded and cut in 1-inch pieces
2 cups hot cooked rice
Thinly sliced green onions (optional)

1. If desired, partially freeze meat for easier slicing. Trim fat from meat. Thinly slice meat across the grain in bite-size strips. Set aside.

2. For sauce, in a small bowl stir together sherry, soy sauce, the water, hoisin sauce, ginger, cornstarch, sugar, garlic, and, if desired, crushed red pepper; set aside.

3. In a wok or large skillet heat oil over medium-high heat. (Add more oil if necessary during cooking.) Add carrots; cook and stir for 2 minutes. Add baby corn and sweet pepper. Cook and stir for 1 to 2 minutes or until vegetables are crisp-tender. Remove vegetables from wok.

4. Add meat to wok. Cook and stir for 2 to 3 minutes or until meat is slightly pink in center. Push meat from center of wok.

5. Stir sauce. Add sauce to center of wok. Cook and stir until thickened and bubbly. Return cooked vegetables to wok. Stir all ingredients together to coat with sauce. Cook and stir for 1 to 2 minutes more or until heated through. Serve with hot cooked rice. If desired, sprinkle with sliced green onions. **MAKES 4 SERVINGS**

Beefy Italian Skillet

PREP 35 minutes
COOK 1 hour 15 minutes

NUTRITION FACTS PER SERVING

Calories 438
Fat 8 g
Cholesterol 56 mg
Sodium 273 mg
Carbohydrates 55 g
Fiber 4 g
Protein 37 g

1   pound boneless beef round steak
    Nonstick cooking spray
2   cups sliced fresh mushrooms
1   cup chopped onion (1 large)
1   cup coarsely chopped green sweet pepper (1 large)
½   cup chopped celery (1 stalk)
2   cloves garlic, minced
1   14.5-ounce can diced tomatoes, undrained
½   teaspoon dried basil, crushed
¼   teaspoon dried oregano, crushed
¼   teaspoon crushed red pepper (optional)
8   ounces dried spaghetti
2   tablespoons grated Parmesan cheese (optional)

1. Trim fat from meat. Cut meat in four serving-size pieces. Lightly coat an unheated large skillet with cooking spray. Heat skillet over medium heat. Brown meat on both sides in hot skillet; remove meat from skillet.

2. Add mushrooms, onion, sweet pepper, celery, and garlic to the skillet. Cook until vegetables are nearly tender, stirring occasionally. Stir in undrained tomatoes, the basil, oregano, and, if desired, crushed red pepper. Add meat to skillet; spoon vegetable mixture over the meat. Reduce heat to medium-low. Simmer, covered, about 1¼ hours or until meat is tender, stirring occasionally.

3. Meanwhile, cook spaghetti according to package directions. Transfer meat to a serving platter. Spoon vegetable mixture over meat. Serve with spaghetti. If desired, sprinkle with Parmesan cheese. **MAKES 4 SERVINGS**

Swiss Steak

PREP 25 minutes
COOK 1 hour 15 minutes

NUTRITION FACTS PER SERVING

Calories 340
Fat 9 g
Cholesterol 82 mg
Sodium 459 mg
Carbohydrates 35 g
Fiber 3 g
Protein 28 g

1 pound boneless beef round steak, cut ¾ inch thick
2 tablespoons all-purpose flour
¼ teaspoon salt
¼ teaspoon black pepper
1 tablespoon vegetable oil
1 14.5-ounce can diced tomatoes with basil, oregano, and garlic, undrained
1 small onion, sliced and separated in rings
½ cup sliced celery (1 stalk)
½ cup sliced carrot (1 medium)
2 cups hot cooked noodles or mashed potatoes

1. Trim fat from meat. Cut in four serving-size pieces. In a small bowl combine flour, salt, and pepper. With the notched side of a meat mallet pound flour mixture into meat.

2. In a large skillet heat oil over medium heat. Brown meat on both sides in hot oil. Drain off fat. Add undrained tomatoes, onion, celery, and carrot. Bring to boiling; reduce heat. Simmer, covered, about 1¼ hours or until meat is tender. Skim off fat. Serve with noodles.
MAKES 4 SERVINGS

Oven Directions: Preheat oven to 350°F. Prepare and brown meat in skillet as directed. Transfer meat to a 2-quart square baking dish. In the same skillet combine undrained tomatoes, onion, celery, and carrot. Bring to boiling, scraping up any browned bits on bottom of skillet. Pour over meat. Cover and bake about 1 hour or until meat is tender. Serve with noodles.

Beef and Noodles

PREP 30 minutes
COOK 1 hour 40 minutes

NUTRITION FACTS PER SERVING

Calories 351
Fat 12 g
Cholesterol 94 mg
Sodium 677 mg
Carbohydrates 29 g
Fiber 1 g
Protein 31 g

1   pound boneless beef round steak or chuck roast
¼   cup all-purpose flour
1   tablespoon vegetable oil
½   cup chopped onion (1 medium)
2   cloves garlic, minced
3   cups beef broth
1   teaspoon dried marjoram or basil, crushed
¼   teaspoon black pepper
8   ounces frozen noodles
2   tablespoons snipped fresh parsley (optional)

1. Trim fat from meat. Cut meat in ¾-inch cubes. Place flour in a large resealable plastic bag. Add meat to bag. Seal bag; shake to coat meat with the flour. In a large saucepan heat oil over medium heat; cook half the meat in the hot oil until browned. Remove meat from saucepan. Add the remaining meat, onion, and garlic to pan. Cook until meat is browned and onion is tender, adding more oil if necessary. Drain off fat. Return all meat to the saucepan.

2. Stir in broth, marjoram, and pepper. Bring to boiling; reduce heat. Simmer, covered, for 1¼ to 1½ hours or until meat is tender.

3. Stir noodles into broth mixture. Bring to boiling; reduce heat. Cook, uncovered, for 25 to 30 minutes or until noodles are tender. Serve in bowls; sprinkle with parsley, if desired.
MAKES 4 SERVINGS

Ketchup-Glazed Meat Loaves

PREP 20 minutes
BAKE 30 minutes
STAND 10 minutes
OVEN 350°F

NUTRITION FACTS PER SERVING

Calories 271
Fat 13 g
Cholesterol 142 mg
Sodium 928 mg
Carbohydrates 14 g
Fiber 0 g
Protein 24 g

1½ pounds lean ground beef or ground pork
2 eggs
1 envelope (½ of a 2-ounce package) onion soup mix
⅔ cup ketchup or hot-style ketchup
⅓ cup fine dry bread crumbs
3 cloves garlic, minced

1. Preheat oven to 350°F. In a large resealable plastic bag combine meat, eggs, dry onion soup mix, ⅓ cup of the ketchup, the bread crumbs, and garlic; seal bag. Use your hands to knead until well mixed. Form mixture in six mini loaves, each about 4 inches long and 2½ inches wide.* Arrange loaves in a foil-lined 15×10×1-inch baking pan.

2. Bake, uncovered, about 30 minutes or until internal temperature of each loaf registers 160°F** on an instant-read thermometer. Remove from oven. Spoon about 1 tablespoon of the remaining ketchup over each meat loaf. Let stand for 10 minutes before serving. **MAKES 6 SERVINGS**

*Tip: To shape loaves, shape meat in a 5-inch square on the foil-lined baking pan. Use a knife to cut square in six equal portions then shape in individual loaves.

**Tip: The internal color of meat loaf is not a reliable doneness indicator. Meat loaf cooked to 160°F is safe, regardless of color. To measure the doneness, insert an instant-read thermometer into the center of the loaf.

Tip: To make one large meat loaf, prepare as directed, except lightly pat into an 8×4×2-inch loaf pan. Bake, uncovered, for 1 to 1¼ hours or until internal temperature registers 160°F on an instant-read thermometer. Remove from oven. Carefully drain off excess fat. Spoon the remaining ⅓ cup ketchup over meat loaf. Let stand for 10 minutes before carefully lifting from pan.

Make-Ahead Baked Penne with Meat Sauce

PREP 30 minutes
BAKE 1 hour 15 minutes
OVEN 350°F

NUTRITION FACTS PER SERVING

Calories 342
Fat 10 g
Cholesterol 51 mg
Sodium 465 mg
Carbohydrates 37 g
Fiber 2 g
Protein 22 g

8 ounces dried penne pasta
1 14.5-ounce can diced tomatoes, undrained
½ of a 6-ounce can (⅓ cup) Italian-style tomato paste
⅓ cup dry red wine or tomato juice
⅓ cup water
½ teaspoon sugar
2 teaspoons snipped fresh oregano or ½ teaspoon dried oregano, crushed
¼ teaspoon salt
¼ teaspoon black pepper
1 pound lean ground beef
½ cup chopped onion (1 medium)
¼ cup sliced pitted ripe olives
1 cup shredded reduced-fat mozzarella cheese (4 ounces)

1. Cook pasta according to package directions; drain.

2. In a medium bowl stir together tomatoes, tomato paste, wine, the water, sugar, dried oregano (if using), salt, and pepper.

3. In a large skillet cook meat and onion over medium heat until meat is browned and onion is tender. Drain off fat. Stir in tomato mixture. Bring to boiling; reduce heat. Simmer, covered, for 10 minutes. Stir in pasta, fresh oregano (if using), and olives.

4. Divide the pasta mixture among six 10- to 12-ounce individual casseroles (or one 3-quart rectangular baking dish*.) Cover with freezer wrap, label, and freeze up to 1 month.

5. To serve, preheat oven to 350°F. Remove freezer wrap; cover each casserole with foil. Bake about 70 minutes or until heated

through. Sprinkle with mozzarella cheese. Bake, uncovered, about 5 minutes more or until cheese is melted. (Or thaw overnight in the refrigerator. Remove freezer wrap; cover each casserole with foil. Bake in preheated 350°F oven about 45 minutes or until heated through. Sprinkle with cheese and bake about 5 minutes more or until cheese is melted.) **MAKES 6 SERVINGS**

*Tip: If using a 3-quart baking dish, remove freezer wrap; cover dish with foil. Bake in a 350°F oven about 1½ hours or until heated through, stirring carefully once. Sprinkle with mozzarella cheese. Bake, uncovered, about 5 minutes more or until cheese is melted. (Or thaw overnight in the refrigerator. Remove freezer wrap; cover baking dish with foil. Bake in a 350°F oven 55 minutes or until heated through, stirring once. Sprinkle with cheese and bake 5 minutes more or until cheese is melted.)

Cheesy Polenta with Meat Sauce

PREP 15 minutes
BAKE 30 minutes
OVEN 350°F

NUTRITION FACTS PER SERVING

Calories 184
Fat 10 g
Cholesterol 39 mg
Sodium 458 mg
Carbohydrates 10 g
Fiber 0 g
Protein 13 g

Nonstick cooking spray
8 ounces lean ground beef
1 15-ounce container refrigerated marinara sauce
1 16-ounce tube refrigerated cooked plain polenta
¾ cup shredded Italian 4-cheese blend (3 ounces)

1. Preheat oven to 350°F. Lightly coat a 2-quart square baking dish with cooking spray. Set aside. In a large skillet cook ground beef over medium-high heat until browned. Drain off fat. Stir in marinara sauce; set aside.

2. Cut polenta in ½-inch slices. Arrange polenta slices in the prepared baking dish. Sprinkle with ½ cup of the cheese. Spoon meat sauce evenly over polenta. Cover with foil. Bake, covered, about 30 minutes or until heated through. Sprinkle with the remaining ¼ cup cheese. Let stand for 1 to 2 minutes or until cheese is melted. **MAKES 6 SERVINGS**

Spaghetti Squash with Chili

PREP 30 minutes
BAKE 45 minutes
OVEN 350°F

1 2-pound spaghetti squash
8 ounces lean ground beef
½ cup chopped onion
   (1 medium)
1 clove garlic, minced
1 14.5-ounce can diced
   tomatoes and green chiles,
   undrained
1 11-ounce can no-salt-added
   corn, drained
1 8-ounce can no-salt-added
   tomato sauce
2 tablespoons no-salt-added
   tomato paste
2 teaspoons chili powder
½ teaspoon dried oregano,
   crushed
   Fresh oregano leaves
   (optional)

1. Preheat oven to 350°F. Halve the spaghetti squash lengthwise and remove seeds and membranes. Place squash halves, cut sides down, on a baking sheet. Bake for 45 to 50 minutes or until tender.* Cool slightly. Using a fork, shred and separate the spaghetti squash into strands.

2. Meanwhile, for sauce, in a medium saucepan cook ground beef, onion, and garlic until meat is browned and onion is tender. Drain off fat.

3. Stir undrained tomatoes and green chiles, drained corn, tomato sauce, tomato paste, chili powder, and dried oregano into meat mixture in saucepan. Bring to boiling; reduce heat. Simmer, uncovered, about 10 minutes or until desired consistency.

4. Serve meat sauce with spaghetti squash. If desired, sprinkle with fresh oregano. **MAKES 4 SERVINGS**

*Tip: To cook the squash in the microwave, place one squash half at a time, cut side down, in a microwave-safe baking dish with ¼ cup water. Cover and microwave on high for 5 to 8 minutes or until tender; remove and keep warm. Continue with recipes as directed.

Mexican Beef and Veggies

START TO FINISH **30 minutes**

NUTRITION FACTS PER SERVING

Calories 313
Fat 9 g
Cholesterol 54 mg
Sodium 504 mg
Carbohydrates 39 g
Fiber 3 g
Protein 20 g

12 ounces lean ground beef
1   medium (1¼ pounds) butternut squash, peeled, seeded, and cubed (about 3 cups)
2   cloves garlic, minced
1   teaspoon ground cumin
½   teaspoon salt
⅛   teaspoon ground cinnamon
1   14.5-ounce can diced tomatoes, undrained
1   medium zucchini, halved lengthwise and sliced ¼-inch thick
¼   cup water
¼   cup snipped fresh cilantro
2   to 3 cups hot cooked white or brown rice
    Bottled hot pepper sauce (optional)

1. In a large skillet cook ground beef, squash, garlic, cumin, salt, and cinnamon over medium heat until meat is browned. Drain off fat.

2. Stir in undrained tomatoes. Bring to boiling; reduce heat. Simmer, covered, about 8 minutes or just until squash is tender. Stir in zucchini and the water. Simmer, covered, about 4 minutes or until zucchini is tender. Stir in cilantro. Serve over hot cooked rice. If desired, season with bottled hot pepper sauce. **MAKES 4 TO 6 SERVINGS**

Taco Lover's Pasta

START TO FINISH 35 minutes

NUTRITION FACTS PER SERVING

Calories 325
Fat 7 g
Cholesterol 32 mg
Sodium 562 mg
Carbohydrates 47 g
Fiber 3 g
Protein 17 g

8	ounces lean ground beef
1	cup chopped onion (1 large)
¾	cup chopped green, red, or yellow sweet pepper (1 medium)
2	cloves garlic, minced
1	15-ounce can tomato sauce
1	14.5-ounce can diced tomatoes, undrained
1½	teaspoons chili powder
¼	teaspoon ground cumin Salt and black pepper
10	ounces dried pasta
2	tablespoons snipped fresh cilantro
½	cup shredded Monterey Jack or cheddar cheese (2 ounces)

1. In a large saucepan cook ground beef, onion, sweet pepper, and garlic over medium heat until meat is browned. Drain off fat. Stir in tomato sauce, undrained tomatoes, chili powder, and cumin. Bring to boiling; reduce heat. Simmer, uncovered, for 10 to 15 minutes or until desired consistency, stirring occasionally. Season with salt and black pepper.

2. Meanwhile, cook pasta according to package directions; drain. Just before serving, stir cilantro into meat. Serve over hot cooked pasta. Sprinkle with cheese. **MAKES 6 SERVINGS**

Greek-Style Beef and Vegetables

PREP 15 minutes
COOK 6 hours (low) or
3 hours (high) + 30 minutes
(high)

NUTRITION FACTS PER SERVING

Calories 446
Fat 16 g
Cholesterol 64 mg
Sodium 539 mg
Carbohydrates 46 g
Fiber 5 g
Protein 28 g

1   pound ground beef
1   cup chopped onion (1 large)
3   cloves garlic, minced
1   14.5-ounce can beef broth
3   cups frozen mixed vegetables
1   14.5-ounce can diced
    tomatoes, undrained
3   tablespoons tomato paste
1   teaspoon dried oregano,
    crushed
⅛   teaspoon ground cinnamon
⅛   teaspoon ground nutmeg
2   cups dried medium shell
    macaroni
1   cup shredded Monterey Jack
    or crumbled feta cheese
    (4 ounces)

1. In a large skillet cook ground beef, onion, and garlic over medium heat until meat is browned and onion is tender. Drain off fat. Place meat mixture in a 3½- or 4-quart slow cooker. Stir in broth, frozen vegetables, undrained tomatoes, tomato paste, oregano, cinnamon, and nutmeg.

2. Cover and cook on low-heat setting for 6 to 8 hours or on high-heat setting for 3 to 4 hours. If using low-heat setting, turn to high-heat setting. Add pasta. Cover and cook about 30 minutes more or until pasta is tender. Top servings with cheese. **MAKES 6 SERVINGS**

Mexican Beef and Tortillas

START TO FINISH **20 minutes**

NUTRITION FACTS PER SERVING

Calories 319
Fat 10 g
Cholesterol 64 mg
Sodium 857 mg
Carbohydrates 34 g
Fiber 5 g
Protein 27 g

8   6-inch corn tortillas
1   17-ounce package refrigerated beef pot roast with juices
1   14.5-ounce can diced tomatoes with green chiles, undrained
1   medium green sweet pepper, seeded and cut in strips
1   lime, cut in wedges
    Light sour cream (optional)
    Fresh cilantro sprigs (optional)

1. Wrap tortillas in paper towels. Microwave on high for 45 to 60 seconds or until warm. Keep warm.

2. Microwave beef according to package directions. Meanwhile, place undrained tomatoes in a small saucepan; heat through.

3. Transfer meat to a cutting board, reserving juices. Slice meat across grain. Serve meat on warm tortillas with tomatoes and green pepper strips. Drizzle with reserved juices. Pass lime wedges and, if desired, sour cream and cilantro. **MAKES 4 SERVINGS**

Mediterranean Lamb Chops

START TO FINISH 30 minutes

NUTRITION FACTS PER SERVING

Calories 410
Fat 11 g
Cholesterol 40 mg
Sodium 798 mg
Carbohydrates 58 g
Fiber .9 g
Protein 22 g

6   lamb loin chops, cut
     1½ inches thick
2   teaspoons vegetable oil
2   medium red onions, cut in
     thin wedges
1   26- to 28-ounce jar garlic and
     onion pasta sauce
1   19-ounce can cannellini beans
     (white kidney beans), rinsed
     and drained
½   cup pitted kalamata olives,
     halved
½   cup bottled roasted red sweet
     peppers, cut in strips
2   tablespoons balsamic vinegar
2   teaspoons snipped fresh
     rosemary
     Hot cooked orzo pasta or rice

1. Trim fat from chops. In a large skillet heat oil over medium-high heat. Cook chops in hot oil for 11 to 13 minutes or until medium doneness (160°F), turning once halfway through cooking. Transfer chops to a large bowl or platter; cover with foil to keep warm.

2. In the same skillet cook onions in drippings over medium heat until tender. Add pasta sauce, beans, olives, roasted peppers, balsamic vinegar, and rosemary. Cook and stir over medium heat until heated through. Add chops to skillet; cover and heat through for 3 minutes.

3. Serve lamb chops and sauce over hot cooked orzo.
MAKES 6 SERVINGS

Slow Cooker Directions:
Arrange lamb chops in a 4- or 5-quart slow cooker. In a medium bowl combine pasta sauce, beans, red onion, olives, roasted peppers, balsamic vinegar, and rosemary. Pour over lamb chops in slow cooker. Cover and cook on low-heat setting for 5 to 6 hours or on high-heat setting for 2½ to 3 hours. Serve as directed.

Lamb Chops with Tomatoes

START TO FINISH **20 minutes**

NUTRITION FACTS PER SERVING

Calories 273
Fat 7 g
Cholesterol 70 mg
Sodium 153 mg
Carbohydrates 26 g
Fiber 3 g
Protein 25 g

8 lamb loin chops, cut 1-inch thick
   Salt and black pepper
1 8.8-ounce pouch cooked long grain rice
4 medium plum tomatoes, chopped
4 green onions, sliced
1 tablespoon snipped fresh oregano
1 tablespoon balsamic vinegar

1. Sprinkle chops with salt and pepper. For a charcoal grill, place chops on the rack of an uncovered grill directly over medium coals. Grill to desired doneness, turning once halfway through grilling. Allow 12 to 14 minutes for medium-rare (145°F) and 15 to 17 minutes for medium (160°F). (For a gas grill, preheat grill. Reduce heat to medium. Place chops on grill rack over heat. Cover and grill as above.)

2. Meanwhile, cook rice in the microwave according to package directions. In a medium bowl combine tomatoes, green onions, and oregano. Stir in vinegar. Season with salt and pepper. Spoon rice onto a serving platter; arrange chops on rice. Top with tomato mixture. **MAKES 4 SERVINGS**

Moroccan Lamb

PREP 25 minutes
COOK 8 hours (low)
to 4 hours (high)

NUTRITION FACTS
PER SERVING

Calories 472
Fat 12 g
Cholesterol 95 mg
Sodium 505 mg
Carbohydrates 58 g
Fiber 5 g
Protein 37 g

2   pounds boneless lamb
    shoulder roast
2   tablespoons olive oil
½   cup chopped onion (1 medium)
2   cloves garlic, minced
1   tablespoon grated fresh
    ginger
1   6-ounce package long grain
    and wild rice mix
1   cup dried apricots
½   cup raisins
½   cup dried tart cherries
2   medium yellow summer
    squash, cut in 1-inch pieces
    (2½ cups)
8   ounces fresh mushrooms,
    halved or quartered
½   teaspoon coarsely ground
    black pepper
¼   teaspoon ground cinnamon
⅛   to ¼ teaspoon cayenne pepper
1½ cups water

1. Trim fat from meat. Cut meat in 1-inch pieces. In a large skillet heat oil over medium-high heat. Cook meat, half at a time, in hot oil until browned. Transfer meat to a 4½- or 5-quart slow cooker. Add onion, garlic, ginger, rice mix, contents of seasoning packet, dried apricots, raisins, and dried cherries. Top with squash and mushrooms. Sprinkle with black pepper, cinnamon, and cayenne pepper. Pour the water over all in cooker.

2. Cover and cook on low-heat setting for 8 to 9 hours or on high-heat setting for 4 to 4½ hours. Stir gently before serving.
MAKES 6 SERVINGS

CHAPTER 8

Pork

Plum and Rosemary Pork Roast

PREP **35 minutes**
ROAST **40 minutes**
STAND **15 minutes**
OVEN **300°F**

NUTRITION FACTS PER SERVING

Calories 367
Fat 10 g
Cholesterol 83 mg
Sodium 249 mg
Carbohydrates 19 g
Fiber 2 g
Protein 34 g

1   2-pound boneless pork top
    loin roast (single loin)
    Kosher salt and freshly
    ground black pepper
1   tablespoon olive oil
½   cup chopped onion (1 medium)
½   cup chopped carrot
    (1 medium)
2   tablespoons snipped fresh
    rosemary
2   cloves garlic, minced
1½ cups port wine
¼   cup reduced-sodium chicken
    broth
6   fresh plums, pitted and
    quartered
    Fresh rosemary sprigs
    (optional)

1. Preheat oven to 300°F. Sprinkle meat with kosher salt and pepper. In a 4- to 5-quart oven-going Dutch oven heat oil over medium heat. Add meat; cook for 5 to 8 minutes or until browned, turning to brown evenly on all sides. Remove meat from Dutch oven; set aside.

2. Add onion and carrot to Dutch oven. Cook about 5 minutes or until onion is golden brown, stirring frequently. Stir in the 2 tablespoons snipped rosemary and the garlic; cook and stir for 1 minute more. Add port wine and broth. Return meat to the Dutch oven. Heat just until boiling.

3. Roast, covered, for 20 minutes. Add plums to Dutch oven. Roast, covered, for 20 to 25 minutes more or until internal temperature of meat registers 150°F on an instant-read thermometer.

4. Transfer meat to a cutting board; cover with foil and let stand for 15 minutes. The temperature of the meat after standing should be 160°F.

5. Meanwhile, using a slotted spoon, transfer plums to a serving platter. For sauce, place Dutch oven over medium-high heat on the stovetop. Reduce heat; boil gently, uncovered, about 10 minutes or until sauce is reduced to about ¾ cup.

6. To serve, thinly slice meat. Arrange meat slices on platter with plums. Serve with sauce. If desired, garnish with fresh rosemary sprigs. **MAKES 6 SERVINGS**

Mushroom-Tomato-Stuffed Pork Loin

PREP 40 minutes
ROAST 40 minutes
STAND 15 minutes
OVEN 350°F

NUTRITION FACTS PER SERVING

Calories 209
Fat 6 g
Cholesterol 71 mg
Sodium 153 mg
Carbohydrates 10 g
Fiber 1 g
Protein 28 g

1   large portobello mushroom (about 6 ounces) or 2 cups button mushrooms
2   teaspoons olive oil
½   of a medium fresh poblano chile, seeded and chopped (about ½ cup) (see tip, page 63)
½   cup chopped onion (1 medium)
3   cloves garlic, minced
¾   cup reduced-sodium chicken broth
¼   cup quick-cooking (hominy) grits
2   tablespoons snipped dried tomatoes (not oil-pack)
1   1½- to 2-pound boneless pork loin roast
¼   teaspoon black pepper

1. Remove stem from portobello mushroom; scrape out scales. Chop mushroom. (Or if using button mushrooms, chop mushrooms.) In a large nonstick skillet heat oil over medium heat. Add chopped mushrooms, poblano chile, onion, and garlic; cook for 5 to 8 minutes or until tender, stirring occasionally. Remove mushroom mixture from skillet; set aside.

2. In the same skillet bring broth to boiling. Gradually stir in grits; stir in tomatoes. Reduce heat to low. Cook, uncovered, for 2 to 3 minutes or until thick, stirring often. Remove from heat; stir in mushroom mixture. Set aside.

3. Preheat oven to 350°F. Trim fat from roast. Place roast on cutting board with one end toward you. Using a long sharp knife, make a lengthwise cut 1 inch in from the left side of the roast, cutting down to about 1 inch from the bottom of the roast. Turn the knife and cut to the right, as if forming the letter L; stop when you get to about 1 inch from the right side of the roast.

4. Open up the roast so it lies nearly flat on the cutting board.

Place a large piece of plastic wrap over the roast. Using the flat side of a meat mallet, pound meat to ¼- to ½-inch thickness. Discard plastic wrap. Spread mushroom mixture on meat, leaving a 1-inch border around the edge. Starting from one of the long sides, roll meat around filling. Using 100%-cotton kitchen string, tie roast securely at 1½-inch intervals. Sprinkle meat with black pepper. Place on a rack in a shallow roasting pan.

5. Insert an oven-going meat thermometer into center of meat. Roast, uncovered, for 40 to 45 minutes or until thermometer registers 150°F. Cover meat tightly with foil and let stand for 15 minutes before serving. The temperature of the meat should be 160°F after standing. Remove string and slice meat to serve.
MAKES 6 SERVINGS

Pork Loin with Parsnips and Pears

START TO FINISH **25 minutes**

NUTRITION FACTS PER SERVING

Calories 311
Fat 11 g
Cholesterol 62 mg
Sodium 293 mg
Carbohydrates 28 g
Fiber 4 g
Protein 26 g

1   pound boneless pork top loin roast
¼   teaspoon salt
¼   teaspoon black pepper
3   tablespoons Pickapeppa sauce or Worcestershire sauce
1   tablespoon olive oil
3   or 4 small parsnips, peeled and sliced
2   pears, cored and sliced and/or chopped
½   cup pear nectar or apple juice
    Snipped fresh Italian (flat-leaf) parsley (optional)
    Fresh pear cut in narrow wedges (optional)

1. Trim fat from meat. Cut meat into ½-inch slices; sprinkle lightly with salt and black pepper. Brush with some of the Pickapeppa sauce.

2. In a 12-inch skillet heat oil over medium heat. Cook meat in hot oil until browned on both sides. Transfer meat to a plate, reserving drippings in skillet. Cover meat and keep warm.

3. Add parsnips and the 2 chopped or sliced pears to the reserved drippings. Cook about 5 minutes or until parsnips are crisp-tender, stirring occasionally. Stir in the remaining Pickapeppa sauce and the pear nectar; return meat to skillet. Cook about 5 minutes or until meat is slightly pink in center (160°F). Divide meat, parsnips, and pears among dinner plates.

4. For sauce, bring nectar mixture to boiling; reduce heat. Boil gently, uncovered, until slightly thickened. Pour sauce over meat, parsnips, and pears. If desired, sprinkle with parsley and garnish with pear wedges. **MAKES 4 SERVINGS**

Cajun Pork

PREP 20 minutes
COOK 7 hours (low) or
3½ hours (high) + 30 minutes
(high)

NUTRITION FACTS PER SERVING

Calories 233
Fat 8 g
Cholesterol 77 mg
Sodium 444 mg
Carbohydrates 15 g
Fiber 4 g
Protein 25 g

2½ to 3 pounds boneless pork shoulder
Nonstick cooking spray
2 medium yellow sweet peppers, seeded and cut in 1-inch pieces
1 tablespoon Cajun seasoning
1 14.5-ounce can diced tomatoes with green pepper and onion, undrained
1 16-ounce package frozen cut okra
1 6-ounce package quick-cooking brown rice
Bottled hot pepper sauce (optional)

1. Trim fat from meat. Cut meat in 1-inch pieces. Lightly coat a large skillet with cooking spray. In hot skillet cook meat, half at a time, over medium heat until browned. Drain off fat.

2. Transfer meat to a 3½- or 4-quart slow cooker. Add sweet peppers to cooker. Sprinkle with Cajun seasoning and top with undrained tomatoes.

3. Cover and cook on low-heat setting for 7 to 8 hours or on high-heat setting for 3½ to 4 hours.

4. If using low-heat setting, turn to high-heat setting. Stir in frozen okra. Cover and cook for 30 minutes more. Meanwhile, cook rice according to package directions. Serve pork over rice. If desired, pass hot pepper sauce.
MAKES 6 TO 8 SERVINGS

Lime-Jerked Pork with Salsa

PREP 30 minutes
MARINATE 1 hour
GRILL 30 minutes
STAND 10 minutes

NUTRITION FACTS PER SERVING

Calories 167
Fat 5 g
Cholesterol 55 mg
Sodium 64 mg
Carbohydrates 13 g
Fiber 1 g
Protein 18 g

2   tablespoons finely shredded lime peel
⅓   cup lime juice
2   tablespoons packed brown sugar
1   tablespoon canola oil
1   tablespoon Jamaican jerk seasoning
2   cloves garlic, minced
¼   teaspoon cayenne pepper
2   pork tenderloins (about ¾ pound each)
1   recipe Salsa (see below)

1. For marinade, in a bowl combine all ingredients except pork and Salsa. Place pork in a large self-sealing plastic bag set in a shallow dish. Pour marinade over pork. Seal bag. Marinate in refrigerator 1 hour; turn bag occasionally. Drain pork; discard marinade.

2. For a charcoal grill, arrange hot coals around a drip pan. Test for medium-hot heat above pan. Place meat on grill rack over the drip pan. Cover and grill for 30 to 35 minutes or until an instant-read thermometer inserted in meat registers 155°F. (For a gas grill, preheat grill. Reduce heat to medium-high. Adjust for indirect cooking. Place meat on rack in a roasting pan, place on grill rack, and grill as above.) Let stand 10 minutes. Slice tenderloins and serve with Salsa. **MAKES 8 SERVINGS**

Salsa: In a small bowl combine 1 cup chopped banana; ⅓ cup raisins; 2 medium fresh jalapeno chile peppers, seeded and finely chopped (see tip, page 63); 3 tablespoons lime juice; 2 tablespoons finely chopped red onion; 1 tablespoon canola oil; 1 tablespoon frozen orange juice concentrate, thawed; 2 teaspoons snipped fresh cilantro; 1 teaspoon ground coriander; 1 teaspoon honey; and 1 teaspoon grated fresh ginger. **MAKES 1½ CUPS**

Pork Tenderloin with Pears and Barley

PREP 25 minutes
ROAST 25 minutes
STAND 15 minutes
OVEN 425°F

NUTRITION FACTS PER SERVING

Calories 434
Fat 4 g
Cholesterol 73 mg
Sodium 499 mg
Carbohydrates 71 g
Fiber 9 g
Protein 29 g

1   1-pound pork tenderloin
2   tablespoons snipped fresh sage
2   cloves garlic, minced
¼   teaspoon salt
¼   teaspoon black pepper
6   ounces red boiling onions (about 6), peeled and halved
2   medium red and/or yellow sweet peppers, seeded and cut in bite-size pieces
¼   cup balsamic vinegar
1   29-ounce can pear halves in light syrup
1   cup quick-cooking barley
2   teaspoons snipped fresh sage
½   teaspoon salt

1. Preheat oven to 425°F. Starting on a long side, split pork tenderloin in half lengthwise, cutting almost to the opposite side. In a small bowl combine the 2 tablespoons sage, the garlic, the ¼ teaspoon salt, and the black pepper. Sprinkle mixture on cut surfaces of pork; pat in with your fingers. Fold cut sides together; place meat in a 13×9×2-inch baking pan. Arrange onions and sweet peppers around pork.

2. Drizzle vinegar over pork and vegetables. Roast for 15 minutes. Meanwhile, drain pears, reserving syrup. Halve each pear half; add pears to roasting pan with vegetables. Stir gently to coat with vinegar. Roast for 10 to 20 minutes more or until internal temperature of tenderloin registers 155°F on an instant-read thermometer. Cover with foil and let stand for 15 minutes. The temperature of the meat after standing should be 160°F.

3. Meanwhile, add enough water to the reserved pear syrup to measure 2 cups total liquid. In a medium saucepan combine syrup mixture, barley, the 2 teaspoons sage, and the ½ teaspoon salt. Bring to boiling; reduce heat. Simmer, covered, for 10 to 12 minutes or until barley is tender and most of the liquid is absorbed. Spoon barley onto a serving platter. Slice meat; arrange on barley. Using a slotted spoon, transfer vegetables and pears to platter. Serve with pan juices. **MAKES 4 SERVINGS**

Cornmeal-Crusted Pork

START TO FINISH **20 minutes**

NUTRITION FACTS PER SERVING

Calories 310
Fat 13 g
Cholesterol 127 mg
Sodium 385 mg
Carbohydrates 21 g
Fiber 5 g
Protein 29 g

1   1-pound pork tenderloin
½   cup yellow cornmeal
½   teaspoon salt
½   teaspoon black pepper
1   egg, lightly beaten
1   tablespoon water
2   tablespoons olive oil
12 ounces fresh green beans
2½ cups thinly bias-sliced zucchini and/or yellow summer squash (2 medium)
2   tablespoons fresh oregano leaves

1. Trim fat from meat. Cut meat crosswise in ½-inch slices; set aside. In a shallow dish stir together cornmeal, salt, and pepper. In another shallow dish combine egg and the water. Dip pork in egg mixture, then coat with cornmeal mixture.

2. In a 12-inch skillet heat oil over medium-high heat. Add pork slices; cook for 4 to 5 minutes or until meat is slightly pink in center, turning once. Transfer pork to a serving platter; keep warm.

3. Add beans and zucchini to skillet; cook and stir for 6 to 8 minutes or until crisp-tender. Season with additional salt and pepper. Serve vegetables with pork. Sprinkle with oregano.
MAKES 4 SERVINGS

Pork Tenderloin with Cranberry Chutney

PREP 30 minutes
ROAST 25 minutes
COOK 20 minutes
OVEN 425°F

NUTRITION FACTS PER SERVING

Calories 277
Fat 7 g
Cholesterol 76 mg
Sodium 260 mg
Carbohydrates 30 g
Fiber 2 g
Protein 24 g

1   tablespoon ground allspice
2   to 3 teaspoons cracked black pepper
1   teaspoon salt
3   1-pound pork tenderloins
2   tablespoons vegetable oil
1   tablespoon butter
1   large onion, cut in quarters and thinly sliced
1   12-ounce package cranberries
1   10-ounce jar currant jelly
1   cup cranberry juice
¼   cup packed brown sugar
3   tablespoons cider vinegar
1   tablespoon grated fresh ginger or ½ teaspoon ground ginger
½   teaspoon curry powder
2   bunches watercress

1. Preheat oven to 425°F. In a small bowl combine allspice, pepper, and salt. Sprinkle on all sides of tenderloins; rub in with your fingers.

2. In a very large skillet heat oil over medium heat. Brown tenderloins on all sides in the hot oil. Transfer tenderloins to a shallow roasting pan. Insert an oven-going meat thermometer into center of one tenderloin. Roast for 25 minutes or until meat thermometer registers 155°F. Remove from oven. Cover with foil and let stand for 15 minutes. The temperature of the meat after standing should be 160°F.

3. Meanwhile, for chutney, in the same skillet melt butter over medium heat. Add onion; cook about 5 minutes or until nearly tender, stirring occasionally. Add cranberries, jelly, cranberry juice, brown sugar, vinegar, ginger, and curry powder to skillet. Bring to boiling; reduce heat. Boil gently, uncovered, for 20 to 25 minutes or until thickened to desired consistency and reduced to about 3 cups.

4. To serve, slice pork and arrange on a platter. Sprinkle with watercress. Serve chutney on the side. **MAKES 12 TO 16 SERVINGS**

Make-Ahead Directions:
Prepare pork and cranberry chutney as directed; allow pork and chutney to cool for 30 minutes. Cover and refrigerate pork up to 3 days and chutney up to 1 week. Warm pork in a 350°F oven for 20 to 25 minutes or until heated through. Heat cranberry chutney in a saucepan over medium-low heat until heated through, stirring occasionally. Serve as above.

Chipotle Baby Back Ribs

PREP **20 minutes**
BROIL **10 minutes**
COOK **6 hours (low) or**
3 hours (high) + 15 minutes
(high)

NUTRITION FACTS PER SERVING

Calories 286
Fat 8 g
Cholesterol 91 mg
Sodium 526 mg
Carbohydrates 10 g
Fiber 1 g
Protein 40 g

3 pounds pork loin back ribs or meaty pork spareribs
¾ cup no-salt-added tomato sauce
½ cup barbecue sauce
2 canned chipotle peppers in adobo sauce, seeded and finely chopped (see tip, page 63)
2 tablespoons cornstarch
2 tablespoons water
   Shredded cabbage with carrot (coleslaw mix) and/or thinly sliced fresh jalapeños (see tip, page 63) (optional)

1. Preheat broiler. Cut ribs in two-rib portions. Place ribs on the unheated rack of a broiler pan. Broil 6 inches from the heat about 10 minutes or until brown, turning once.* Transfer ribs to a 4- or 5-quart slow cooker.

2. In a medium bowl combine tomato sauce, barbecue sauce, and chipotle peppers. Pour over ribs in cooker.

3. Cover and cook on low-heat setting for 6 to 7 hours or on high-heat setting for 3 to 3½ hours.

4. Transfer ribs to a serving platter, reserving cooking liquid. Cover ribs to keep warm. Skim the fat from the cooking liquid.

5. If using low-heat setting, turn to high-heat setting. For sauce, in a small bowl combine cornstarch and the water. Stir into liquid in cooker. Cover and cook about 15 minutes or until thickened. Serve ribs with sauce. If desired, serve ribs over coleslaw mix and/or thinly sliced jalapeños.
MAKES 8 SERVINGS

***Tip:** Broiling reduces the fat on the ribs so there will be less fat to skim from the slow cooker. You may omit this step, if desired.

Floribbean Ribs

PREP 20 minutes
BAKE 2 hours
GRILL 10 minutes
OVEN 350° F

NUTRITION FACTS PER SERVING

Calories 239
Fat 7 g
Cholesterol 84 mg
Sodium 454 mg
Carbohydrates 20 g
Fiber 2 g
Protein 25 g

1   tablespoon whole allspice
1   tablespoon cumin seeds
2   teaspoons fennel seeds
1   teaspoon mustard seeds
1   teaspoon salt
4   to 5 pounds meaty pork spareribs or pork loin back ribs
2   cups hickory or oak wood chips
2   medium mangoes, seeded, peeled, and chopped
2   tablespoons honey
2   tablespoons grated fresh ginger
2   tablespoons key lime juice or lime juice
2   tablespoons bourbon (optional)
¼   cup chopped green onions (2)
1   fresh jalapeño, seeded and finely chopped (see tip, page 63)

1. Preheat oven to 350°F. Heat a medium skillet over medium heat. Add allspice, cumin seeds, fennel seeds, and mustard seeds to hot skillet. Cook about 3 minutes or until seeds are fragrant, stirring occasionally. Crush seeds with a mortar and pestle or in a clean coffee grinder. Stir in salt.

2. Trim fat from ribs. Place ribs in a shallow roasting pan. Generously sprinkle allspice mixture evenly on both sides of ribs; rub in with your fingers. Bake, covered, for 2 to 2½ hours or until ribs are very tender. Drain off fat.

3. At least 1 hour before grilling, soak wood chips in enough water to cover. Drain before using.

4. For mango mojo, in a food processor or blender combine mangoes, honey, ginger, lime juice, and, if desired, bourbon. Cover and process until smooth. Stir in green onions and jalapeño.

5. For a charcoal grill with a cover, sprinkle wood chips on medium coals. Place ribs on grill rack directly over coals. Cover and grill about 10 minutes or until ribs are browned, turning once halfway through grilling and brushing occasionally with some of the mango mojo. (For a gas grill, preheat grill. Reduce heat to medium. Add wood chips according to the manufacturer's directions. Place ribs on grill rack over heat. Cover and grill as above.) Drizzle ribs with the remaining mango mojo.
MAKES 6 SERVINGS

Ribs and Kraut

PREP 20 minutes
COOK 7 hours (low) or
3½ hours (high)

NUTRITION FACTS PER SERVING

Calories 312
Fat 12 g
Cholesterol 96 mg
Sodium 541 mg
Carbohydrates 19 g
Fiber 4 g
Protein 30 g

1 14-ounce can sauerkraut, rinsed and drained
2 cups sliced sweet onion (1 large)
2 cups sliced peeled tart cooking apples (2 medium)
2 pounds boneless pork country-style ribs
1 cup apple juice
   Snipped fresh chives (optional)

1. In a 4- or 4½-quart slow cooker combine sauerkraut, onion, and apples. Top with ribs. Pour apple juice over all in cooker.

2. Cover and cook on low-heat setting for 7 to 8 hours or on high-heat setting for 3½ to 4 hours. Using a slotted spoon, transfer ribs, sauerkraut, onion, and apples to serving platter. If desired, sprinkle with chives.
MAKES 6 TO 8 SERVINGS

Corn Bread-Stuffed Pork Chops

PREP 25 minutes
BAKE 25 minutes
OVEN 375°F

NUTRITION FACTS PER SERVING

Calories 341
Fat 9 g
Cholesterol 139 mg
Sodium 248 mg
Carbohydrates 12 g
Fiber 1 g
Protein 49 g

2   teaspoons canola oil
¼   cup chopped onion
1   clove garlic, minced
½   cup corn bread stuffing mix
¼   cup snipped dried apricots
2   teaspoons snipped fresh sage
      or ½ teaspoon dried sage,
      crushed
½   teaspoon ground coriander
½   teaspoon ground cumin
¼   teaspoon paprika
1   tablespoon water
4   bone-in pork rib chops, cut
      1 inch thick (2¼ pounds total)
⅛   teaspoon salt
      Nonstick cooking spray

1. Preheat oven to 375°F. For stuffing, in a small saucepan heat oil over medium heat. Add onion and garlic; cook for 3 to 4 minutes or until onion is tender, stirring occasionally. Remove from heat. Stir in stuffing mix, dried apricots, and sage. In a small bowl combine coriander, cumin, and paprika. Stir half the coriander mixture into the apricot mixture. Drizzle with the 1 tablespoon water; toss gently to moisten.

2. Trim fat from chops. Using a knife, cut a pocket in each chop by cutting horizontally from the meaty side almost to the bone. Spoon stuffing evenly into pockets.* Secure with wooden toothpicks. Sprinkle tops of chops with salt and the remaining coriander mixture.

3. Coat an unheated 12-inch oven-going skillet with cooking spray; heat skillet over medium-high heat. Cook chops, seasoned sides down, in skillet about 2 minutes or until bottoms are browned on bottom/underside. Turn chops over and place skillet in oven.

4. Bake chops for 25 to 30 minutes or until pork juices run clear (160°F). Remove toothpicks before serving. **MAKES 4 SERVINGS**

*Tip: When stuffing each chop, hold it upright with the bone side down so it is easy to reach the opening in the pocket.

Caramelized Pork with Melon

START TO FINISH **22 minutes**

NUTRITION FACTS PER SERVING

Calories 327
Fat 10 g
Cholesterol 117 mg
Sodium 452 mg
Carbohydrates 19 g
Fiber 2 g
Protein 39 g

1   small cantaloupe
¼   cup orange juice
3   tablespoons hoisin sauce
4   center cut pork chops, cut
    ½-inch thick
    Salt and black pepper
1   tablespoon vegetable oil
3   green onions, thinly sliced
    Shredded Napa cabbage
    (optional)

1. Remove and discard rind and seeds from the cantaloupe; chop melon. Measure 2 cups of the chopped melon; set remaining melon side. In a food processor combine the 2 cups melon and the orange juice. Process until smooth. Transfer ½ cup of the pureed melon to a small bowl; stir in hoisin sauce. Strain the remaining puree. Set aside the juice; discard solids.

2. Trim fat from chops. Sprinkle chops lightly with salt and pepper; brush generously with the melon-hoisin mixture. In a 12-inch skillet heat oil over medium heat. Add chops to skillet and cook for 3 to 4 minutes on each side or until well browned and only a trace of pink remains (160°F).

3. Remove chops from skillet; add remaining pureed melon to skillet. Cook and stir until heated through. Spoon onto serving plates. Top each with a chop. Add the reserved chopped melon, strained juice, and the green onions to the skillet; warm slightly. Spoon over chops. If desired, serve with shredded Napa cabbage. **MAKES 4 SERVINGS**

Pork Chops with Chili-Apricot Glaze

PREP 10 minutes
BROIL 9 minutes

NUTRITION FACTS PER SERVING

Calories 307
Fat 8 g
Cholesterol 106 mg
Sodium 331 mg
Carbohydrates 17 g
Fiber 1 g
Protein 38 g

¼ cup apricot jam or preserves
¼ cup chili sauce
1 tablespoon sweet-hot mustard or brown mustard
1 tablespoon water
4 boneless pork loin chops, cut 1-inch thick

1. Preheat broiler. Cut up any large pieces of fruit in jam. For the glaze, in a small saucepan combine jam, chili sauce, mustard, and the water. Cook and stir over medium-low heat until heated through. Remove from heat.

2. Trim fat from chops. Place chops on the unheated rack of a broiler pan. Broil 3 to 4 inches from heat for 9 to 11 minutes or until juices run clear (160°F), turning once halfway through broiling and brushing generously with glaze during the last 2 to 3 minutes of broiling. Spoon any remaining glaze over chops before serving. **MAKES 4 SERVINGS**

Apple-Pecan Pork Chops

START TO FINISH **20 minutes**

NUTRITION FACTS PER SERVING

Calories 250
Fat 13 g
Cholesterol 66 mg
Sodium 360 mg
Carbohydrates 12 g
Fiber 1 g
Protein 22 g

4	boneless pork loin chops cut ¾ to 1 inch thick
	Salt and black pepper
2	tablespoons butter
1	medium red apple, cored and thinly sliced
¼	cup pecan halves
2	tablespoons packed brown sugar

1. Trim fat from chops. Sprinkle with salt and pepper. Set aside.

2. In a large skillet melt butter over medium heat. Add apple slices; cook and stir for 2 minutes. Push apple slices to side of skillet. Add pork chops; cook for 4 minutes. Turn chops, moving apple slices aside as needed. Spoon apple slices over chops. Sprinkle with pecans and brown sugar.

3. Cover and cook for 4 to 8 minutes more or until juices run clear (160°F). Serve apples, pecans, and cooking juices over chops. **MAKES 4 SERVINGS**

Grilled Peppered Pork Chops with Mediterranean Relish

PREP 25 minutes
MARINATE 15 minutes
GRILL 7 minutes

NUTRITION FACTS PER SERVING

Calories 215
Fat 6 g
Cholesterol 83 mg
Sodium 390 mg
Carbohydrates 6 g
Fiber 1 g
Protein 35 g

6   boneless pork top loin chops, cut ¾ inch thick (about 2 pounds total)
1   6.5-ounce jar marinated artichoke hearts
1   teaspoon bottled hot pepper sauce
1½ cups chopped tomatoes (3 medium)
½   cup bottled roasted red sweet peppers, drained and chopped
¼   cup pitted ripe olives, sliced
1   small fresh jalapeño, seeded and finely chopped (see tip, page 63) (optional)
    Fresh oregano (optional)

1. Trim fat from chops. Place chops in large resealable plastic bag. Drain artichokes, reserving marinade. Add hot pepper sauce to reserved marinade; pour over chops. Seal bag; turn to coat chops. Place in a shallow dish; marinate in the refrigerator for 15 to 30 minutes.

2. For relish, coarsely chop artichoke hearts. In a medium bowl combine the chopped artichokes, tomatoes, roasted red peppers, olives, and, if desired, jalapeño.

3. Drain chops, discarding marinade. For a charcoal grill, grill chops on rack of an uncovered grill directly over medium coals for 7 to 9 minutes or until chops are slightly pink in the center and juices run clear (160°F), turning once halfway through grilling. (For a gas grill; preheat grill. Reduce heat to medium. Place chops on grill rack over heat. Cover and grill as above.)

4. Serve chops with relish. If desired, garnish with oregano.
MAKES 6 SERVINGS

Jamaican Pork Stir-Fry

START TO FINISH 20 minutes

NUTRITION FACTS PER SERVING

Calories 357
Fat 9 g
Cholesterol 54 mg
Sodium 405 mg
Carbohydrates 45 g
Fiber 2 g
Protein 22 g

1 tablespoon vegetable oil
1 16-ounce package frozen (yellow, green, and red) peppers and onion stir-fry vegetables
12 ounces pork strips for stir-frying*
2 to 3 teaspoons Jamaican jerk seasoning
½ cup bottled plum sauce
   Soy sauce (optional)
   Peanuts (optional)
2 cups hot cooked rice or pasta

1. In a wok or large skillet heat oil over medium-high heat. Add frozen vegetables; cook and stir for 5 to 7 minutes or until vegetables are crisp-tender. Remove from wok.

2. Toss pork with jerk seasoning; add to hot wok. Add more oil if necessary. Cook and stir for 2 to 5 minutes or until pork is no longer pink.

3. Return vegetables to wok; stir in plum sauce. Toss gently to coat meat and vegetables and to heat through. If desired, season with soy sauce and sprinkle with peanuts. Serve over rice.
MAKES 4 SERVINGS

***Tip:** If you can't find pork strips, cut them from a boneless pork loin.

Greens, Beans, and Ham

PREP 10 minutes
COOK 8 minutes

NUTRITION FACTS PER SERVING

Calories 353
Fat 6 g
Cholesterol 12 mg
Sodium 537 mg
Carbohydrates 51 g
Fiber 11 g
Protein 27 g

2 15-ounce cans Great Northern beans
1 tablespoon olive oil
6 cloves garlic, minced
2 cups cooked smoked ham, cut in bite-size strips
3 cups chopped fresh spinach or one 10-ounce package frozen spinach, thawed and well drained

1. Drain beans, reserving liquid. In a large nonstick skillet heat oil over medium heat. Add garlic; cook for 1 minute. Add beans and ham to skillet. Cook about 5 minutes or until heated through, stirring occasionally.

2. Stir spinach into bean mixture in skillet; cover and cook for 2 to 5 minutes or until fresh greens are wilted or frozen spinach is heated through. If desired, thin mixture with some of the reserved bean liquid. **MAKES 4 SERVINGS**

Quick Campanelle with Peas and Artichokes

START TO FINISH **25 minutes**

NUTRITION FACTS PER SERVING

Calories 341
Fat 9 g
Cholesterol 18 mg
Sodium 314 mg
Carbohydrates 50 g
Fiber 5 g
Protein 15 g

8 ounces dried campanelle, radiatore, or rotini pasta
1 cup frozen peas
½ cup frozen or canned artichoke hearts (rinsed if canned), coarsely chopped
2 cloves garlic, minced
½ cup chopped tomato (1 medium)
½ cup finely shredded Pecorino Romano or Parmesan cheese
2 tablespoons lemon juice
1 tablespoon olive oil
⅛ teaspoon black pepper
¼ cup slivered cooked Black Forest ham
Finely shredded Pecorino Romano or Parmesan cheese (optional)

1. Cook pasta according to package directions, adding frozen peas, frozen artichoke hearts (if using), and garlic during the last 3 minutes of cooking time. Drain, reserving ¼ cup of the pasta water.

2. In a large serving bowl toss together drained pasta mixture, the ¼ cup reserved pasta water, the canned artichoke hearts (if using), tomato, the ½ cup cheese, the lemon juice, olive oil, and pepper. Toss to combine. Sprinkle with ham and, if desired, additional shredded cheese. **MAKES 4 SERVINGS**

CHAPTER 9

Chicken & Turkey

Chicken in Shiitake Mushroom Sauce

PREP 20 minutes
COOK 40 minutes

NUTRITION FACTS PER SERVING

Calories 195
Fat 6 g
Cholesterol 69 mg
Sodium 350 mg
Carbohydrates 10 g
Fiber 2 g
Protein 24 g

3   pounds meaty chicken pieces (breast halves, thighs, and drumsticks), skinned
½   teaspoon salt
¼   teaspoon black pepper
    Nonstick cooking spray
8   ounces pearl onions
4   medium carrots, cut in 1-inch-long pieces
¼   cup dry vermouth
1   14-ounce can reduced-sodium chicken broth
3   tablespoons snipped fresh parsley
1   tablespoon snipped fresh thyme or 1 teaspoon dried thyme, crushed
1   tablespoon snipped fresh rosemary or 1 teaspoon dried rosemary, crushed
8   ounces fresh shiitake or button mushrooms, halved
    Fresh rosemary sprigs (optional)

1. Sprinkle chicken with salt and pepper. Coat a 12-inch nonstick skillet with cooking spray. Heat skillet over medium heat. Cook chicken in hot skillet about 10 minutes or until chicken is golden, turning to brown evenly. Remove chicken from skillet.

2. Add pearl onions and carrots to skillet. Cook about 5 minutes or until onions are golden, stirring occasionally. Add vermouth, scraping up any crusty browned bits from bottom of skillet. Return chicken to skillet. Pour broth over chicken; sprinkle with parsley, thyme, and the snipped rosemary.

3. Bring to boiling; reduce heat. Simmer, covered, about 40 minutes or until chicken is no longer pink (170°F for breasts; 180°F for thighs and drumsticks), adding mushrooms the last 10 minutes of cooking. If desired, garnish with rosemary sprigs. **MAKES 8 SERVINGS**

Spinach Chicken Breast Rolls

PREP **30 minutes**
BAKE **50 minutes**
STAND **10 minutes**
OVEN **375°F**

NUTRITION FACTS PER SERVING

Calories 292
Fat 7 g
Cholesterol 101 mg
Sodium 718 mg
Carbohydrates 10 g
Fiber 3 g
Protein 46 g

4   medium skinless, boneless chicken breast halves (about 1¼ pounds total)
½   of a 10-ounce package frozen chopped spinach, thawed and well drained
1   cup part-skim mozzarella cheese, shredded (4 ounces)
⅓   cup low-fat cottage cheese, drained
1   egg white
½   of a 26-ounce jar (1¼ cups) light spaghetti sauce with garlic and herbs
2   tablespoons tomato paste
6   ounces dried multigrain spaghetti or whole wheat spaghetti, cooked (optional)

1. Preheat oven to 375°F. Place each chicken breast half between two pieces of plastic wrap. Using the flat side of a meat mallet, lightly pound chicken to an even ¼-inch thickness. Set aside.

2. In a small bowl stir together spinach, ½ cup of the mozzarella cheese, the cottage cheese, and egg white. Spoon spinach mixture over chicken breast halves, leaving a ½-inch border around edges. Roll up breast halves from short ends. Place chicken rolls, seam sides down, in a 2-quart rectangular baking dish. In a small bowl stir together spaghetti sauce and tomato paste; spoon over chicken. Cover dish with foil.

3. Bake, covered, for 25 minutes. Uncover; sprinkle with the remaining ½ cup mozzarella cheese. Bake, uncovered, about 25 minutes more or until chicken is no longer pink (170°F). Let stand for 10 minutes before serving. If desired, serve with hot cooked spaghetti. **MAKES 4 SERVINGS**

Triple-Mango Chicken

START TO FINISH 20 minutes

NUTRITION FACTS PER SERVING

Calories 274
Fat 9 g
Cholesterol 66 mg
Sodium 277 mg
Carbohydrates 22 g
Fiber 2 g
Protein 28 g

1   tablespoon olive oil
4   medium skinless, boneless
     chicken breast halves (about
     1¼ pounds total)
1   cup cubed, peeled, and seeded
     mango (1 medium)
½   cup mango-blend fruit drink*
¼   cup mango chutney
2   medium zucchini, thinly
     sliced lengthwise
¼   cup water
     Salt
     Crushed red pepper

1. In 12-inch skillet heat oil over medium heat. Cook chicken in hot oil for 6 minutes; turn chicken. Add mango cubes, mango drink, and the chutney. Cook for 4 to 6 minutes more or until chicken is no longer pink (170°F), stirring mango mixture occasionally.

2. Meanwhile, place zucchini and the water in a microwave-safe 2-quart dish. Cover with vented plastic wrap. Microwave on high for 2 to 3 minutes or until crisp-tender, stirring once. Drain. Serve chicken and mango mixture on zucchini. Season with salt and crushed red pepper.
MAKES 4 SERVINGS

*****Tip:** Mango nectar, carrot juice, or orange juice may be substituted for the mango-blend drink.

Grilled Rosemary Chicken

PREP 15 minutes
MARINATE 1 hour
GRILL 12 minutes

NUTRITION FACTS PER SERVING

Calories 162
Fat 3 g
Cholesterol 77 mg
Sodium 135 mg
Carbohydrates 2 g
Fiber 0 g
Protein 31 g

6   medium skinless, boneless chicken breast halves (about 2 pounds total)
1   teaspoon finely shredded lime peel
½   cup lime juice
1   tablespoon snipped fresh rosemary
1   tablespoon olive oil
2   teaspoons sugar
2   cloves garlic, minced
¼   teaspoon salt
⅛   teaspoon black pepper

1. Place each chicken breast half between two pieces of plastic wrap. Using the flat side of a meat mallet, lightly pound chicken to an even ½-inch thickness. Place in a large resealable plastic bag set in a shallow dish.

2. In a small bowl stir together lime peel, lime juice, rosemary, olive oil, sugar, garlic, and salt. Pour over chicken in bag; seal bag. Turn to coat chicken. Marinate in the refrigerator for 1 to 4 hours, turning bag occasionally.

3. Remove chicken from marinade, discarding marinade. Sprinkle chicken with pepper. For a charcoal grill, grill chicken on the rack of an uncovered grill directly over medium coals for 12 to 15 minutes or until chicken is no longer pink (170°F), turning once halfway through grilling. (For a gas grill, preheat grill. Reduce heat to medium. Place chicken on grill rack over heat. Cover and grill as above.) **MAKES 6 SERVINGS**

Maple Chicken Fettuccine

START TO FINISH **25 minutes**

NUTRITION FACTS PER SERVING

Calories 466
Fat 6 g
Cholesterol 79 mg
Sodium 285 mg
Carbohydrates 60 g
Fiber 2 g
Protein 40 g

10	ounces dried fettuccine
5	medium skinless, boneless chicken breast halves (about 1½ pounds total)
	Salt and black pepper
1	tablespoon olive oil
1	16-ounce package frozen (yellow, green, and red) peppers and onion stir-fry vegetables
¾	cup chicken broth
1	tablespoon cornstarch
1	teaspoon snipped fresh rosemary
⅛	teaspoon black pepper
¼	cup maple syrup

1. Cook pasta according to package directions; keep warm.

2. Meanwhile, sprinkle chicken with salt and black pepper. In a 12-inch skillet heat olive oil over medium heat. Cook chicken in hot oil for 8 to 12 minutes or until chicken is no longer pink (170°F), turning once halfway through cooking. Remove chicken from skillet; cover and keep warm.

3. Increase heat to medium-high. Add the frozen vegetables to skillet; cook and stir for 6 to 8 minutes or until vegetables are crisp-tender.

4. In a small bowl stir together broth, cornstarch, rosemary, and the ⅛ teaspoon black pepper. Add to skillet. Cook and stir until thickened and bubbly. Cook and stir for 1 minute more. Stir in maple syrup.

5. To serve, place chicken on pasta. Spoon vegetables over chicken and pasta.
MAKES 5 SERVINGS

Chicken with Cherry-Ginger Chutney

START TO FINISH **20 minutes**

NUTRITION FACTS PER SERVING

Calories 364
Fat 12 g
Cholesterol 82 mg
Sodium 249 mg
Carbohydrates 30 g
Fiber 3 g
Protein 35 g

4   medium skinless, boneless chicken breast halves (about 1¼ pounds total)
    Salt and black pepper
½   teaspoon ground ginger
1   tablespoon olive oil
½   cup dried tart red cherries
1   large apple, thinly sliced horizontally, seeds removed
⅓   cup coarsely chopped walnuts
4   teaspoons packed brown sugar
¼   cup water
3   tablespoons cider vinegar

1. Cut chicken breast halves in quarters. Sprinkle chicken lightly with salt, pepper, and ¼ teaspoon of the ginger.

2. In a large skillet heat olive oil over medium heat. Cook chicken in hot oil for 8 to 12 minutes or until no longer pink (170°F), turning to cook evenly. Transfer chicken to a serving platter; cover and keep warm.

3. For chutney, add cherries, apple, and walnuts to skillet; cook and stir for 2 minutes. In a small bowl stir together brown sugar, the water, vinegar, and the remaining ¼ teaspoon ginger; add to skillet. Cook and stir for 1 minute. Serve chutney with chicken.
MAKES 4 SERVINGS

Rosemary Chicken with Vegetables

START TO FINISH 27 minutes

NUTRITION FACTS
PER SERVING

Calories 326
Fat 10 g
Cholesterol 95 mg
Sodium 247 mg
Carbohydrates 25 g
Fiber 2 g
Protein 33 g

4   medium skinless, boneless
     chicken breast halves (about
     1¼ pounds total)
½   teaspoon lemon-pepper
     seasoning
2   tablespoons olive oil
4   ounces refrigerated spinach
     or plain linguine or 1 cup
     quick-cooking couscous
2   cloves garlic, minced
2½   cups sliced zucchini and/or
     yellow summer squash
     (2 medium)
½   cup apple juice
2   teaspoons snipped fresh
     rosemary or ½ teaspoon dried
     rosemary, crushed
2   tablespoons dry white wine or
     chicken broth
2   teaspoons cornstarch
1   cup halved cherry or grape
     tomatoes
     Fresh rosemary sprigs
     (optional)

1. Sprinkle chicken with lemon-pepper seasoning. In a large skillet heat olive oil over medium heat. Cook chicken in hot oil for 8 to 12 minutes or until no longer pink (170°F), turning once halfway through cooking. Transfer chicken to a platter; cover and keep warm.

2. Meanwhile, cook linguine or couscous according to package directions; keep warm.

3. Add garlic to skillet; cook and stir for 15 seconds. Add zucchini, apple juice, and rosemary. Bring to boiling; reduce heat. Simmer, covered, for 2 minutes.

4. In a small bowl stir together wine and cornstarch; add to skillet. Cook and stir until thickened and bubbly. Cook and stir for 2 minutes more. Stir in tomatoes. Serve chicken on pasta with vegetables on the side. If desired, garnish with rosemary sprigs. **MAKES 4 SERVINGS**

Apricots, Chicken, and Orzo

START TO FINISH **20 minutes**

NUTRITION FACTS PER SERVING

Calories 458
Fat 9 g
Cholesterol 66 mg
Sodium 230 mg
Carbohydrates 59 g
Fiber 4 g
Protein 34 g

1¼ cups dried orzo (about 8 ounces)
1 15-ounce can unpeeled apricot halves in light syrup
4 medium skinless, boneless chicken breast halves (about 1¼ pounds total)
   Salt and black pepper
1½ teaspoons curry powder
2 tablespoons olive oil
6 green onions

1. Cook orzo according to package directions; drain. Drain apricot halves, reserving ½ cup syrup.

2. Meanwhile, sprinkle chicken with salt, pepper, and ½ teaspoon of the curry powder. In a large skillet heat olive oil over medium heat. Cook chicken in hot oil for 8 to 10 minutes or until no longer pink (170°F), turning once halfway through cooking, and adding apricots, cut sides down, the last 2 minutes of cooking. Transfer chicken and apricots to dinner plates.

3. Meanwhile, cut green tops of two green onions in wide diagonal slices; set aside. Chop remaining green onions.

4. Add chopped green onions and the remaining 1 teaspoon curry powder to skillet; cook and stir for 1 minute. Stir in the reserved apricot syrup and the cooked orzo. Spoon orzo onto plates with chicken and apricots. Sprinkle with green onion tops.
MAKES 4 SERVINGS

Chicken with Balsamic Succotash

PREP 10 minutes
COOK 30 minutes

NUTRITION FACTS
PER SERVING

Calories 446
Fat 10 g
Cholesterol 99 mg
Sodium 627 mg
Carbohydrates 42 g
Fiber 8 g
Protein 47 g

1 tablespoon chili powder
½ teaspoon salt
¼ teaspoon black pepper
4 medium skinless, boneless chicken breast halves (about 1¼ pounds total)
2 tablespoons olive oil
2 cloves garlic, minced
1 cup chopped sweet onion (1 large)
¾ cup coarsely chopped red sweet pepper (1 medium)
2 cups frozen corn, thawed
2 cups frozen lima beans, thawed
3 tablespoons balsamic vinegar
1 teaspoon chili powder
¼ cup chicken broth or water
1 tablespoon snipped parsley

1. In a small bowl stir together the 1 tablespoon of the chili powder, the salt, and black pepper. Sprinkle chicken with chili powder mixture; rub in with your fingers.

2. In a large nonstick skillet heat 1 tablespoon of the olive oil over medium heat. Cook chicken in hot oil for 8 to 12 minutes or until no longer pink (170°F), turning once halfway through cooking time. Remove chicken from skillet; cover and keep warm.

3. For succotash, in the same skillet heat the remaining 1 tablespoon oil. Add garlic; cook over low heat for 3 to 4 minutes or until garlic is soft. Increase heat to medium. Add onion and sweet pepper; cook for 5 minutes. Add corn, lima beans, vinegar, and the 1 teaspoon chili powder; cook for 5 minutes. Add broth and parsley; heat through. Serve chicken on succotash. **MAKES 4 SERVINGS**

Springtime Chicken and Pasta

START TO FINISH 30 minutes

NUTRITION FACTS PER SERVING

Calories 395
Fat 10 g
Cholesterol 74 mg
Sodium 248 mg
Carbohydrates 47 g
Fiber 3 g
Protein 30 g

1½ pounds skinless, boneless chicken breast halves
1 pound dried cavatappi or rotini pasta
1 pound fresh asparagus, trimmed and cut in 2-inch pieces
1 tablespoon olive oil
1 yellow sweet pepper, seeded and cut into thin strips
2 cups cherry tomatoes, halved
1 5.2-ounce package spreadable herb cheese (such as Boursin)
¼ teaspoon salt
¼ teaspoon black pepper

1. Cut chicken in 1-inch pieces; set aside. Cook pasta according to package directions, adding asparagus the last 2 minutes of cooking. Drain, reserving ¼ cup pasta water.

2. Meanwhile, in a large nonstick skillet heat olive oil over medium-high heat. Cook chicken in hot oil for 5 minutes, stirring occasionally.

Add sweet pepper; cook and stir for 1 minute more or until chicken is no longer pink. Remove from heat.

3. In large bowl combine hot pasta mixture, the chicken mixture, reserved pasta water, the tomatoes, cheese, salt, and black pepper. Toss until cheese is melted. Serve immediately. **MAKES 8 SERVINGS**

Thai-Spiced Chicken Kabobs

PREP 30 minutes
GRILL 12 minutes

**NUTRITION FACTS
PER SERVING**

Calories 285
Fat 5 g
Cholesterol 73 mg
Sodium 332 mg
Carbohydrates 34 g
Fiber 2 g
Protein 27 g

1 small fresh pineapple (3 to
   3½ pounds)
   Nonstick cooking spray
1 pound skinless, boneless
   chicken breast halves, cut in
   1-inch pieces
1 recipe Thai Brushing Sauce
1 tablespoon butter, melted
1 tablespoon packed brown
   sugar (optional)
   Hot cooked rice (optional)
   Fresh basil leaves (optional)
   Fresh whole red chile peppers
   (optional)

1. Cut off pineapple ends. Halve pineapple lengthwise; cut each half crosswise in 4 slices. Lightly coat pineapple slices with cooking spray. Set aside.

2. Thread chicken onto four long metal skewers, leaving ¼ inch between pieces. Set aside ¼ cup Thai Brushing Sauce; reserve remaining sauce.

3. For a charcoal grill, grill kabobs on the rack of an uncovered grill directly over medium coals for 7 minutes. Turn kabobs; brush with the ¼ cup Thai Brushing Sauce, discarding any sauce remaining from brushing. Arrange pineapple slices on grill rack directly over medium coals. Grill chicken and pineapple for 6 to 8 minutes or until chicken is no longer pink and pineapple is heated through, turning pineapple once. (For a gas grill, preheat grill. Reduce heat to medium. Place kabobs on grill rack

over heat. Cover and grill chicken and pineapple as directed.)

4. In a small bowl combine the reserved Thai Brushing Sauce, melted butter, and, if desired, brown sugar. Serve sauce with chicken and pineapple. If desired, serve with rice and garnish with basil and chile peppers.
MAKES 4 SERVINGS

Thai Brushing Sauce: In a small bowl combine ⅔ cup sweet-and-sour sauce, 2 tablespoons snipped fresh basil, 1 teaspoon Thai seasoning or five-spice powder, and 1 clove garlic, minced.

Make-Ahead Directions:
To make ahead, prepare Thai Brushing Sauce, cut pineapple in slices, and thread chicken onto skewers as directed. Cover and refrigerate separately in refrigerator up to 24 hours.

Garlic Chicken

PREP 20 minutes
MARINATE 30 minutes
COOK 6 minutes

NUTRITION FACTS PER SERVING

Calories 352
Fat 9 g
Cholesterol 66 mg
Sodium 555 mg
Carbohydrates 34 g
Fiber 3 g
Protein 32 g

1 pound skinless, boneless chicken breast halves
1 cup water
3 tablespoons reduced-sodium soy sauce
2 tablespoons chicken broth
1 tablespoon cornstarch
2 tablespoons vegetable oil
10 green onions, bias-sliced in 1-inch pieces
1 cup thinly sliced fresh mushrooms
12 cloves garlic, peeled and thinly sliced, or 2 tablespoons bottled minced garlic
½ cup sliced water chestnuts
2 cups hot cooked rice (optional)

1. Cut chicken in bite-size pieces. Place chicken in a resealable plastic bag set in a shallow bowl. In a small bowl stir together the water, the soy sauce, and broth. Pour over chicken in bag; seal bag. Turn bag to coat chicken. Marinate in the refrigerator for 30 minutes.

2. Drain chicken, reserving marinade. Stir cornstarch into the reserved marinade; set aside.

3. In a wok or large skillet heat oil over medium-high heat. Add green onions, mushrooms, and garlic; cook and stir for 1 to 2 minutes or until tender. Remove vegetables from wok. Add chicken to wok; cook and stir for 2 to 3 minutes or

until no longer pink, adding more oil if necessary. Push chicken from center of wok. Stir marinade; add to center of wok. Cook and stir until thickened and bubbly.

4. Return cooked vegetables to wok. Add water chestnuts. Cook and stir about 1 minute or until combined and heated through. Serve with rice. **MAKES 4 SERVINGS**

Garlic Chicken Stir-Fry with Cashews: Prepare as above, except stir ½ teaspoon crushed red pepper into marinade mixture. Add 1 cup roasted cashews with the water chestnuts.

Chicken, Long Bean, and Tomato Stir-Fry

START TO FINISH **30 minutes**

NUTRITION FACTS
PER SERVING

Calories 321
Fat 7 g
Cholesterol 49 mg
Sodium 284 mg
Carbohydrates 44 g
Fiber 3 g
Protein 21 g

6	ounces wide rice noodles or dried egg noodles
4	teaspoons vegetable oil
2	cloves garlic, minced
1	pound Chinese long beans or whole green beans, cut in 4-inch pieces
¼	cup water
12	ounces skinless, boneless chicken breast halves, cut in bite-size strips
1½	teaspoons Thai or other spicy seasoning blend
2	medium tomatoes, cut in wedges
2	tablespoons cider vinegar or seasoned rice vinegar

1. Cook rice noodles in boiling, lightly salted water for 3 to 5 minutes or until tender. (Or cook egg noodles according to package directions.) Drain noodles; return to pan. Cover and keep warm.

2. Meanwhile, in a large nonstick skillet heat 2 teaspoons of the oil. Add garlic; cook and stir for 15 seconds. Add beans; cook and stir for 2 minutes. Carefully add the water to skillet; reduce heat to low. Simmer, covered, for 5 to 7 minutes or until beans are crisp-tender. Remove beans from skillet.

3. Toss chicken with Thai seasoning. In the same skillet heat the remaining 2 teaspoons oil over medium-high heat. Add chicken; cook and stir for 3 to 4 minutes or until no longer pink. Add beans, noodles, tomatoes, and vinegar; heat through. Serve immediately.
MAKES 2 SERVINGS

Chicken with Pretzels and Couscous

PREP 15 minutes
BAKE 10 minutes
OVEN 425°F

NUTRITION FACTS PER SERVING

Calories 336
Fat 12 g
Cholesterol 39 mg
Sodium 344 mg
Carbohydrates 31 g
Fiber 4 g
Protein 26 g

Nonstick cooking spray
1   cup pretzel sticks
⅔   cup unsalted peanuts
¼   to ½ teaspoon crushed red
    pepper (optional)
½   cup refrigerated or frozen egg
    product, thawed
1   14- to 16-ounce package
    chicken breast tenderloins or
    1 pound skinless, boneless
    chicken breast halves, cut
    lengthwise in 1-inch strips
1   16-ounce package frozen
    (yellow, green, and red)
    peppers and onion stir-fry
    vegetables
½   cup reduced-sodium chicken
    broth
½   cup dried couscous
2   tablespoons seasoned rice
    vinegar
1   tablespoon vegetable oil
1   recipe Mustard Dipping Sauce
    (optional)

1. Preheat oven to 425°F. Line a 15×10×1-inch pan with foil; lightly coat foil with cooking spray. Set pan aside. In a food processor* combine pretzels, ½ cup of the peanuts, and the crushed red pepper. Cover and process until coarsely ground; transfer to a resealable plastic bag.

2. Place egg product in a shallow dish. Dip chicken in egg product, allowing excess to drip off. Transfer chicken, half at a time, to bag with crumb mixture; seal bag. Turn to coat chicken. Arrange chicken in the prepared pan. Bake for 10 to 12 minutes or until chicken is no longer pink.

3. Meanwhile, in a large saucepan combine stir-fry vegetables and broth. Bring to boiling. Stir in couscous; remove from heat. Cover and let stand for 5 minutes. Chop remaining peanuts. Stir peanuts, rice vinegar, and oil into couscous. Serve couscous with chicken. If desired, serve with Dipping Sauce.
MAKES 6 SERVINGS

*Tip: If you do not have a food processor, place pretzels in a large resealable plastic bag; seal bag and finely crush pretzels using a rolling pin or meat mallet. Finely chop ½ cup of the peanuts and add to pretzel crumbs in bag.

Mustard Dipping Sauce: In a small bowl stir together ⅓ cup plain yogurt, 2 tablespoons yellow mustard, and 2 teaspoons honey.

Peruvian-Style Chicken Tacos

START TO FINISH **30 minutes**
OVEN **350°F**

NUTRITION FACTS PER TACO

Calories 194
Fat 10 g
Cholesterol 9 mg
Sodium 328 mg
Carbohydrates 18 g
Fiber 3 g
Protein 11 g

1   pound ground uncooked chicken
½   cup chopped onion (1 medium)
2   teaspoons ground coriander
2   teaspoons ground cumin
1   teaspoon salt
1   14.5-ounce can diced tomatoes, undrained
1   cup finely chopped peeled potato (1 medium)
¼   cup snipped pitted dried plums
¼   cup chopped pimiento-stuffed green olives
12 6- to 7-inch corn or flour tortillas
1   to 1½ cups shredded Cotija or Monterey Jack cheese (4 to 6 ounces)
    Chopped onion (optional)
    Snipped fresh cilantro (optional)

1. Preheat oven to 350°F. In a large skillet cook chicken and the ½ cup onion over medium heat until chicken is no longer pink and onion is tender, stirring to break apart. If necessary, drain off fat. Add coriander, cumin, and salt; cook and stir for 1 to 2 minutes. Add undrained tomatoes, the potato, plums, and olives. Bring to boiling; reduce heat. Simmer, covered, for 12 to 15 minutes or until potato is tender. Uncover; cook about 5 minutes more or until most of the liquid has evaporated.

2. Meanwhile, wrap tortillas in foil; place in oven about 15 minutes or until heated. To assemble, place ⅓ cup chicken mixture in center of each tortilla. Top with cheese. If desired, sprinkle with additional chopped onion and snipped fresh cilantro. Roll up tortillas.
MAKES 12 TACOS

Chicken Caesar Lasagna

PREP 35 minutes
BAKE 50 minutes
STAND 15 minutes
OVEN 325°F

NUTRITION FACTS PER SERVING

Calories 268
Fat 10 g
Cholesterol 68 mg
Sodium 557 mg
Carbohydrates 20 g
Fiber 2 g
Protein 24 g

9   dried whole wheat or regular lasagna noodles
2   10-ounce containers refrigerated light Alfredo sauce
3   tablespoons lemon juice
½   teaspoon cracked black pepper
3   cups chopped cooked chicken breast*
1   10-ounce package frozen chopped spinach, thawed and well drained
1   cup bottled roasted red sweet peppers, drained and chopped
    Nonstick cooking spray
¾   cup shredded Italian blend cheeses (3 ounces)

1. Preheat oven to 325°F. Cook noodles according to package directions; drain. Rinse with cold water; drain again. Meanwhile, in a large bowl stir together Alfredo sauce, lemon juice, and black pepper. Stir in chicken, spinach, and sweet peppers.

2. Lightly coat a 3-quart rectangular baking dish with cooking spray. Lay 3 noodles in prepared dish. Top with one-third of the chicken mixture. Repeat layers twice. Cover with foil.

3. Bake, covered, for 45 to 55 minutes or until heated through. Uncover; sprinkle with cheese. Bake, uncovered, about 5 minutes more or until cheese is melted. Let stand for 15 minutes before serving. **MAKES 9 SERVINGS**

*Tip: For 3 cups chopped cooked chicken breast, sprinkle 2 pounds uncooked skinless, boneless chicken breast halves with ¼ teaspoon salt and ⅛ teaspoon black pepper. In a large skillet cook chicken in 1 tablespoon hot oil over medium heat for 8 to 12 minutes or until no longer pink (170°F), turning once. Cool chicken slightly before chopping.

Chicken Lasagna Rolls with Chive-Cream Sauce

PREP 40 minutes
BAKE 35 minutes
OVEN 350°F

NUTRITION FACTS PER SERVING

Calories 288
Fat 13 g
Cholesterol 65 mg
Sodium 412 mg
Carbohydrates 22 g
Fiber 2 g
Protein 19 g

6   dried lasagna noodles
1   8-ounce package reduced-fat cream cheese (Neufchâtel), softened
½   cup milk
¼   cup grated Romano or Parmesan cheese
1   tablespoon snipped fresh chives
1½ cups chopped cooked chicken (about 10 ounces)
½   of a 10-ounce package frozen chopped broccoli, thawed and drained (1 cup)
½   cup bottled roasted red sweet peppers, drained and sliced
⅛   teaspoon black pepper
1   cup purchased marinara or pasta sauce

1. Preheat oven to 350°F. Cook lasagna noodles according to package directions. Drain noodles; rinse with cold water. Drain again. Cut each in half crosswise; set aside.

2. Meanwhile, for chive-cream sauce, in a medium mixing bowl beat cream cheese with a mixer on medium to high for 30 seconds. Slowly add milk, beating until smooth. Stir in Romano cheese and chives.

3. For filling, in a medium bowl stir together ½ cup of the chive-cream sauce, the chicken, broccoli, roasted peppers, and black pepper. Place about ¼ cup filling at one end of each noodle half. Roll up noodles around filling. Arrange rolls, seam sides down, in a 3-quart rectangular baking dish.

4. Spoon the marinara sauce over the rolls. Cover with foil. Bake for 35 to 40 minutes or until heated through. Pass remaining chive-cream sauce. **MAKES 6 SERVINGS**

Chicken-Vegetable Ratatouille

START TO FINISH **30 minutes**

NUTRITION FACTS PER SERVING

Calories 442
Fat 9 g
Cholesterol 50 mg
Sodium 578 mg
Carbohydrates 64 g
Fiber 11 g
Protein 28 g

1 tablespoon olive oil
1 cup chopped onion (1 large)
2 cloves garlic, minced
1 medium eggplant, cut in 1-inch pieces
2 cups frozen zucchini, carrots, cauliflower, lima beans, and Italian beans
1 14.5-ounce can diced tomatoes, undrained
1 teaspoon dried Italian seasoning, crushed
¾ teaspoon seasoned salt
¼ teaspoon black pepper
2⅔ cups dried penne, ziti, or wagon wheel pasta (8 ounces)
1½ cups chopped cooked chicken (about 10 ounces)

1. In a 4-quart Dutch oven heat oil over medium heat. Add onion and garlic; cook for 2 minutes. Stir in eggplant, frozen vegetables, undrained tomatoes, Italian seasoning, seasoned salt, and pepper. Bring to boiling; reduce heat. Simmer, uncovered, for 10 to 12 minutes or until eggplant is tender.

2. Meanwhile, in a large saucepan cook pasta according to package directions; drain. Cover and keep warm.

3. Add chicken to vegetable mixture; heat through. Serve chicken and vegetables over pasta.
MAKES 4 TO 5 SERVINGS

Chicken and Melon-Stuffed Shells

START TO FINISH 25 minutes

NUTRITION FACTS PER SERVING

Calories 176
Fat 2 g
Cholesterol 26 mg
Sodium 55 mg
Carbohydrates 28 g
Fiber 2 g
Protein 14 g

½ of a medium cantaloupe, halved and seeded
4 dried jumbo macaroni shells
⅔ cup chopped cooked chicken breast
¼ cup finely chopped honeydew melon
2 tablespoons plain fat-free yogurt
1 tablespoon lemon juice
1½ teaspoons snipped fresh chives
½ teaspoon Dijon mustard
Fresh thyme sprigs (optional)

1. Cut the cantaloupe half in three wedges; cover and chill two of the wedges. Peel and finely chop the remaining wedge; set aside.

2. Cook pasta shells according to package directions; drain. Rinse with cold water; drain again. Set aside.

3. In a small bowl stir together chopped cantaloupe, chicken, honeydew, yogurt, lemon juice, chives, and mustard. Spoon about ¼ cup into each pasta shell. Arrange two filled shells and a chilled cantaloupe wedge on each of two serving plates. If desired, garnish with thyme sprigs.
MAKES 2 SERVINGS

Potluck Chicken Tetrazzini

PREP 30 minutes
BAKE 15 minutes
STAND 5 minutes
OVEN 350°F

NUTRITION FACTS PER SERVING

Calories 282
Fat 10 g
Cholesterol 48 mg
Sodium 258 mg
Carbohydrates 28 g
Fiber 2 g
Protein 20 g

1   2- to 2½-pound purchased roasted chicken
8   ounces dried spaghetti or linguine, broken
12 ounces fresh asparagus, trimmed and cut in 1-inch pieces
2   tablespoons butter
8   ounces small whole fresh mushrooms*
3   medium red and/or yellow sweet peppers, seeded and cut in 1-inch pieces
¼   cup all-purpose flour
⅛   teaspoon black pepper
1   14.5-ounce can chicken broth
¾   cup milk
½   cup shredded Swiss cheese (2 ounces)
1   tablespoon finely shredded lemon peel
2   slices sourdough bread, cut in cubes (about 1½ cups)
1   tablespoon olive oil
2   tablespoons snipped fresh parsley

1. Preheat oven to 350°F. Remove and discard skin and bones from chicken. Chop enough chicken to equal 3 cups. Save remaining chicken for another use.

2. Cook pasta according to package directions, adding asparagus the last 1 minute of cooking. Drain. Return to pan.

3. Meanwhile, in large skillet melt butter over medium heat. Cook mushrooms and sweet peppers in hot butter for 8 to 10 minutes or until mushrooms are tender, stirring occasionally. Stir in flour and black pepper. Add broth and milk all at once. Cook and stir until thickened and bubbly.

4. Add mushrooms, chicken, cheese, and half the lemon peel to pasta mixture in pan. Toss gently to combine. Spoon pasta into a 3-quart rectangular baking dish.

5. In a medium bowl toss together bread cubes, olive oil, and the remaining lemon peel. Spread on pasta.

6. Bake, uncovered, about 15 minutes or until heated through. Let stand for 5 minutes before serving. Sprinkle with parsley. **MAKES 10 SERVINGS**

*Tip: If mushrooms are large, cut them in halves or quarters, about 1- to 1½-inch pieces.

Teriyaki Turkey Tenderloins

PREP 25 minutes
MARINATE 1 hour
GRILL 16 minutes

NUTRITION FACTS PER SERVING

Calories 239
Fat 8 g
Cholesterol 68 mg
Sodium 557 mg
Carbohydrates 12 g
Fiber 2 g
Protein 29 g

2   turkey breast tenderloins (about 1 pound total)
¼   cup soy sauce
2   tablespoons packed brown sugar
2   tablespoons lemon juice
1   tablespoon vegetable oil
1   teaspoon grated fresh ginger
1   clove garlic, minced
1   recipe Hot Pineapple Slaw

1. Cut turkey tenderloins in half horizontally to make four portions. Place turkey in a resealable plastic bag set in a shallow dish. For marinade, in a small bowl combine soy sauce, brown sugar, lemon juice, oil, ginger, and garlic. Pour marinade over turkey; seal bag. Turn to coat turkey. Marinate in the refrigerator for 1 to 2 hours, turning bag once.

2. Drain turkey, reserving marinade. For a charcoal grill, grill turkey on the rack of an uncovered grill directly over medium coals for 16 to 20 minutes or until turkey is no longer pink (170°F), turning once and brushing with marinade halfway through cooking. Discard any remaining marinade. (For a gas grill, preheat grill. Reduce heat to medium. Place turkey on grill rack over heat. Cover and grill as above.)

3. Serve with Hot Pineapple Slaw.
MAKES 4 SERVINGS

Hot Pineapple Slaw: In a medium saucepan heat 1 tablespoon vegetable oil over medium heat. Add ¼ cup thinly sliced green onions (2) and ⅛ teaspoon crushed red pepper; cook and stir for 2 minutes. Stir in 2 cups shredded Napa cabbage, 1 cup bite-size fresh pineapple pieces, ¼ cup thin bite-size green sweet pepper strips, 1 teaspoon toasted sesame oil, and dash salt. Heat and stir just until cabbage is wilted.

Turkey Saltimbocca

START TO FINISH **20 minutes**

NUTRITION FACTS PER SERVING

Calories 244
Fat 8 g
Cholesterol 94 mg
Sodium 528 mg
Carbohydrates 9 g
Fiber 3 g
Protein 34 g

2   turkey breast tenderloins
¼   teaspoon coarsely ground
     black pepper
2   tablespoons butter
2   ounces thinly sliced deli ham
½   cup orange juice
2   9- to 10-ounce packages fresh
     spinach
     Salt and black pepper
     Orange wedges (optional)

1. Cut each tenderloin in half horizontally to make four portions. Sprinkle turkey with the ¼ teaspoon pepper. In a 12-inch skillet melt butter over medium-high heat. Cook turkey in hot butter about 12 minutes or until no longer pink (170°F), turning once halfway through cooking. Meanwhile, cut ham in bite-size strips.

2. Remove turkey from skillet; cover and keep warm. Add ham to skillet; cook and stir for 1 to 2 minutes or until ham is heated through and starts to crisp. Using a slotted spoon, remove ham from skillet. Add orange juice to skillet; bring to boiling. Add spinach, half at a time, to skillet; cook and stir about 1 minute or just until spinach starts to wilt.

3. Using tongs, transfer spinach to dinner plates. Sprinkle with salt and pepper. Top spinach with sliced turkey and the ham. Drizzle any remaining pan drippings over turkey. If desired, serve with orange wedges. **MAKES 4 SERVINGS**

Greek Meatballs and Orzo Pilaf

PREP 20 minutes
BAKE 40 minutes
COOK 22 minutes
OVEN 350°F

NUTRITION FACTS PER SERVING

Calories 342
Fat 13 g
Cholesterol 90 mg
Sodium 999 mg
Carbohydrates 28 g
Fiber 3 g
Protein 27 g

1   pound ground uncooked turkey
8   ounces fresh mushrooms, finely chopped
½   cup fat-free plain yogurt
5   tablespoons snipped fresh mint
1½ teaspoons dried oregano
¾   teaspoon lemon-pepper seasoning
1   teaspoon salt
1   tablespoon olive oil
2   tablespoons chopped onion
¾   cup uncooked orzo
2   cloves garlic, minced
1   14.5-ounce can chicken broth
⅛   teaspoon black pepper
1   6-ounce package fresh baby spinach
8   cherry tomatoes, cut in quarters
    Snipped fresh mint (optional)

1. Preheat oven to 350°F. Line a 15×11×1-inch baking pan with foil; set pan aside.

2. In a large bowl mix together turkey, mushrooms, yogurt, 3 tablespoons of the mint, the oregano, lemon-pepper seasoning, and ¾ teaspoon of the salt. Shape into 28 meatballs, using 1 slightly rounded tablespoon for each. Place meatballs in the prepared pan.

3. Bake about 40 minutes or until until done (165°F).*

4. Meanwhile, for orzo pilaf, in a medium saucepan heat olive oil over medium heat. Add onion; cook for 3 minutes. Add orzo and garlic; cook and stir for 3 minutes.

Add broth, the remaining ¼ teaspoon salt, and the black pepper. Simmer, covered, about 15 minutes or until orzo is tender. Stir in the spinach, tomatoes, and 2 tablespoons snipped mint. Cook about 1 minute or until spinach is wilted and tomatoes are heated through.

5. Serve meatballs with orzo pilaf. If desired, garnish with additional mint. **MAKES 4 SERVINGS**

*Tip The internal color of a meatball is not a reliable doneness indicator. A turkey or chicken meatball cooked to 165°F is safe, regardless of color. To measure doneness, insert an instant-read thermometer into a few of the meatballs.

CHAPTER 10

Fish & Seafood

Citrus-Glazed Salmon

PREP 20 minutes
BAKE 4 to 6 minutes per ½-inch thickness
OVEN 450°F

NUTRITION FACTS PER SERVING

Calories 227
Fat 6 g
Cholesterol 59 mg
Sodium 170 mg
Carbohydrates 21 g
Fiber 1 g
Protein 24 g

1   2-pound fresh or frozen salmon fillet, skin removed
     Salt and black pepper
¾   cup orange marmalade
¼   cup sliced green onions (2)
1   clove garlic, minced
2   teaspoons dry white wine
1   teaspoon grated fresh ginger
1   teaspoon Dijon mustard
¼   teaspoon cayenne pepper
⅛   teaspoon five-spice powder
3   tablespoons sliced almonds, toasted (see tip, page 80)
     Steamed asparagus (optional)

1. Thaw fish, if frozen. Rinse fish; pat dry with paper towels. Preheat oven to 450°F. Measure thickness of fish. Sprinkle fish with salt and black pepper. Place fish in a shallow baking pan; set aside.

2. For glaze, in a small bowl stir together orange marmalade, green onions, garlic, wine, ginger, mustard, cayenne pepper, and five-spice powder. Spoon marmalade mixture over salmon.

3. Bake, uncovered, until fish flakes easily when tested with a fork. Allow 4 to 6 minutes per ½-inch thickness of fish. Transfer fish and glaze to a serving dish. Sprinkle with almonds. If desired, serve with steamed asparagus. **MAKES 8 SERVINGS**

Salmon with Fruit Salsa

PREP 15 minutes
BROIL 8 minutes

NUTRITION FACTS PER SERVING

Calories 123
Fat 5 g
Cholesterol 18 mg
Sodium 95 mg
Carbohydrates 5 g
Fiber 1 g
Protein 15 g

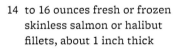

14 to 16 ounces fresh or frozen skinless salmon or halibut fillets, about 1 inch thick
1 teaspoon olive oil
¼ teaspoon lemon-pepper seasoning
¾ cup chopped fresh strawberries or chopped, peeled peaches or nectarines
⅓ cup chopped, peeled kiwifruit or fresh apricots
1 tablespoon snipped fresh cilantro
1 tablespoon orange juice or apple juice
1 fresh jalapeño, seeded and chopped (see tip, page 63)
Nonstick cooking spray
Fresh cilantro sprigs (optional)

1. Thaw fish, if frozen. Rinse fish; pat dry with paper towels. Preheat broiler. Cut fillets in four serving-size pieces, if necessary. Brush both sides of each fillet with olive oil. Sprinkle with lemon-pepper seasoning. Set aside.

2. For fruit salsa, in a medium bowl stir together strawberries, kiwifruit, the snipped cilantro, orange juice, and jalapeño. Set salsa aside.

3. Coat the unheated rack of a broiler pan with cooking spray. Place fish on broiler pan. Broil 4 inches from heat for 8 to 12 minutes or until fish flakes easily when tested with a fork, turning once halfway through broiling. Serve fish with fruit salsa. If desired, garnish with cilantro sprigs. **MAKES 4 SERVINGS**

Fish Tacos

PREP 20 minutes
MARINATE 15 minutes
GRILL 4 to 6 minutes per
½-inch thickness

NUTRITION FACTS
PER SERVING

Calories 380
Fat 17 g
Cholesterol 62 mg
Sodium 168 mg
Carbohydrates 30 g
Fiber 5 g
Protein 27 g

1   pound fresh or frozen skinless salmon or halibut fillets, ¾ to 1 inch thick
½   teaspoon finely shredded lime peel or lemon peel
1   fresh jalapeño or serrano chile, seeded and finely chopped (see tip, page 63)
2   cloves garlic, minced
½   teaspoon ground cumin
⅛   teaspoon salt
1   tablespoon lime juice or lemon juice
8   6-inch corn tortillas or 8-inch flour tortillas
1½ cups shredded lettuce
1   cup chopped red or green sweet pepper (1 large)
1   medium red onion, halved and thinly sliced
   Snipped fresh cilantro (optional)
   Mango or papaya slices (optional)
   Salsa (optional)
   Lime wedges (optional)

1. Thaw fish, if frozen. Rinse fish; pat dry with paper towels. Measure thickness of fish.

2. For marinade, in a small bowl combine lime peel, jalapeño, garlic, cumin, and salt. Brush fish with lime juice. Spread marinade evenly over fish. Cover and marinate in the refrigerator for 15 minutes. Meanwhile wrap tortillas tightly in foil.

3. For a charcoal grill, grill fish on the greased rack of an uncovered grill directly over medium coals for 4 to 6 minutes per ½-inch thickness of fish or until fish flakes easily when tested with a fork, turning once halfway through grilling. Place foil-wrapped tortillas on edge of the grill directly over medium coals for 8 to 10 minutes or until heated through, turning once. (For a gas grill, preheat grill. Reduce heat to medium. Place fish and foil-wrapped tortillas on the greased grill rack directly over heat. Cover and grill as above.)

4. Transfer fish to a cutting board. With a fork, break fish into bite-size pieces.

5. To serve, divide lettuce among warm tortillas. Top with fish, sweet pepper, and red onion. Fold tortillas in half over filling. If desired, serve with cilantro, mango slices, salsa, and lime wedges. **MAKES 4 SERVINGS**

Halibut with Eggplant Peperonata

START TO FINISH 45 minutes

NUTRITION FACTS
PER 1 HALIBUT STEAK

Calories 283
Fat 8 g
Cholesterol 36 mg
Sodium 507 mg
Carbohydrates 25 g
Fiber 5 g
Protein 28 g

4   4-ounce fresh or frozen halibut steaks
1   tablespoon olive oil
½   of a medium sweet onion, thinly sliced
1   small eggplant (about 10 ounces), cut in 1-inch pieces (3 cups)
1   large yellow or red sweet pepper, seeded and thinly sliced
4   cloves garlic, minced
1   teaspoon snipped fresh rosemary or ½ teaspoon dried rosemary, crushed
½   teaspoon salt
¼   teaspoon black pepper
4   cups fresh spinach
4   ounces whole grain baguette, sliced

1. Thaw fish, if frozen. Rinse fish; pat dry with paper towels. Set aside.

2. In a large skillet heat olive oil over medium heat. Add onion; cook for 5 minutes, stirring occasionally. Add eggplant, sweet pepper, garlic, rosemary, and ¼ teaspoon of the salt. Cook for 10 to 12 minutes or until vegetables are very tender, stirring occasionally. Remove from skillet and keep warm.

3. Add about 1 inch of water to the same skillet. Insert a steamer basket and bring water to boiling over high heat. Sprinkle halibut steaks with the remaining ¼ teaspoon salt and the black pepper. Place halibut in steamer basket. Cover and steam over medium heat for 6 to 8 minutes or until fish flakes easily when tested with a fork.

4. Line four plates with spinach. Place halibut and vegetables on spinach. Serve with bread.
MAKES 4 SERVINGS

Basil Halibut Steaks

PREP 25 minutes
BROIL 8 minutes

NUTRITION FACTS
PER SERVING

Calories 274
Fat 13 g
Cholesterol 61 mg
Sodium 273 mg
Carbohydrates 8 g
Fiber 2 g
Protein 31 g

4   5- to 6-ounce fresh or frozen
    halibut steaks, 1 inch thick
1   tablespoon olive oil
½   cup chopped onion (1 medium)
1   clove garlic, minced
2   cups chopped, seeded, and
    peeled tomatoes (4 medium)
¼   teaspoon salt
¼   teaspoon black pepper
4   tablespoons snipped fresh
    basil
2   tablespoons butter, melted
    Nonstick cooking spray
    Salt and black pepper

1. Thaw fish, if frozen. Rinse fish; pat dry with paper towels. Set aside. Preheat broiler. In a medium skillet heat olive oil over medium heat. Add onion and garlic; cook until tender, stirring occasionally. Stir in tomatoes, the ¼ teaspoon salt, and the ¼ teaspoon pepper. Bring to boiling; reduce heat. Simmer, uncovered, for 15 minutes. Stir in 2 tablespoons of the basil.

2. Meanwhile, combine melted butter and the remaining 2 tablespoons basil; brush on one side of the halibut steaks.

3. Lightly coat the unheated rack of a broiler pan with cooking spray. Place fish, brushed side up, on broiler pan. Broil 4 inches from heat for 8 to 12 minutes or until fish flakes easily when tested with a fork, turning once halfway through broiling.

4. Season with additional salt and pepper. Serve with tomato mixture. **MAKES 4 SERVINGS**

Halibut with Pepper Salsa

PREP 15 minutes
BROIL 4 to 6 minutes per ½-inch thickness
CHILL 1 hour

NUTRITION FACTS PER SERVING

Calories 150
Fat 3 g
Cholesterol 36 mg
Sodium 525 mg
Carbohydrates 3 g
Fiber 1 g
Protein 25 g

4   4-ounce fresh or frozen skinless halibut or swordfish steaks, ¾ to 1 inch thick
3   tablespoons rice vinegar
2   tablespoons soy sauce
½   teaspoon grated fresh ginger
⅛   teaspoon black pepper
¾   cup coarsely chopped red and/or yellow sweet pepper (1 medium)
½   cup chopped cucumber (½ of a small)
2   tablespoons thinly sliced green onion (1)
2   tablespoons snipped fresh cilantro
½   of a small fresh jalapeño, seeded and finely chopped (see tip, page 63)
1   teaspoon sesame seeds
    Napa cabbage leaves (optional)

1. Thaw fish, if frozen.

2. For pepper salsa, in a small bowl combine vinegar, soy sauce, and ginger. In another small bowl combine 2 tablespoons of the vinegar mixture and the black pepper; set aside. To the remaining vinegar mixture, add sweet pepper, cucumber, green onion, cilantro, and jalapeño; toss to coat. Cover and refrigerate salsa up to 1 hour.

3. Preheat broiler. Rinse fish steaks; pat dry with paper towels. Measure thickness of fish. Place fish on the greased unheated rack of a broiler pan. Brush fish with the reserved 2 tablespoons vinegar mixture. Sprinkle fish with sesame seeds.

4. Broil 4 inches from heat for 4 to 6 minutes per ½-inch thickness of fish or until fish flakes easily when tested with a fork, tuning once halfway through broiling if fish is 1 inch thick.

5. If desired, line four plates with Napa cabbage leaves. Place fish on plates and serve with pepper salsa.
MAKES 4 SERVINGS

Sesame-Crusted Cod

START TO FINISH: 30 minutes

NUTRITION FACTS
PER SERVING

Calories 240
Fat 12 g
Cholesterol 71 mg
Sodium 274 mg
Carbohydrates 12 g
Fiber 4 g
Protein 23 g

1   pound fresh or frozen skinless cod fillets, ¾ inch thick
    Salt and black pepper
3   tablespoons butter, melted
2   tablespoons sesame seeds
1   12-ounce package trimmed fresh tender young green beans
1   medium orange, halved and sliced
3   cloves garlic, thinly sliced

1. Thaw fish, if frozen. Rinse fish; pat dry with paper towels. Cut fish in four serving-size pieces, if necessary. Place fish on the unheated rack of a broiler pan. Sprinkle fish with salt and pepper.

2. In a small bowl stir together melted butter and sesame seeds. Reserve 1 tablespoon of the butter mixture to cook the green beans; set aside. Brush fish with half the remaining butter mixture.

3. Broil fish 5 to 6 inches from heat for 4 minutes; turn fish. Brush with remaining butter mixture. Broil for 5 to 6 minutes more or until fish flakes easily when tested with a fork.

4. Meanwhile, in a large skillet heat the reserved butter mixture over medium-high heat. Add green beans and orange slices. Cover and cook for 2 minutes. Uncover; add garlic. Cook, uncovered, for 5 to 6 minutes more or until beans are crisp-tender, stirring frequently. Serve beans with fish.
MAKES 4 SERVINGS

Baked Mediterranean Cod and Asparagus

PREP 15 minutes
BAKE 12 minutes
OVEN 475°F

NUTRITION FACTS PER SERVING

Calories 275
Fat 12 g
Cholesterol 73 mg
Sodium 738 mg
Carbohydrates 5 g
Fiber 3 g
Protein 32 g

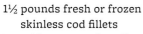

1½ pounds fresh or frozen skinless cod fillets
2 tablespoons olive oil
  Salt and black pepper
1 pound asparagus spears, trimmed
1 recipe Olive Relish

1. Thaw fish, if frozen. Rinse fish; pat dry with paper towels. Cut fish in four serving-size pieces, if necessary. Preheat oven to 475°F. Lightly coat a 15×10×1-inch baking pan with some of the olive oil. In one side of pan arrange fillets, turning under any thin portions. Brush fish with 1 teaspoon of the remaining olive oil. Sprinkle fish with salt and pepper.

2. Bake for 5 minutes. Place asparagus in opposite side of pan; brush with remaining olive oil and sprinkle with salt and pepper. Bake for 7 to 10 minutes more or until

fish flakes easily when tested with a fork. Serve fish with asparagus and Olive Relish. **MAKES 4 SERVINGS**

Olive Relish: In a small bowl combine ¾ cup pimiento-stuffed green olives, coarsley chopped; ⅓ cup chopped onion; ¼ cup snipped fresh Italian (flat-leaf) parsley; 2 tablespoons capers, drained; 1 small jalapeño, seeded and chopped (see tip, page 63); and 1 tablespoon white wine vinegar. Season with black pepper.

Sicilian Tuna with Capers

PREP 10 minutes
MARINATE 15 minutes
BROIL 8 minutes

NUTRITION FACTS
PER SERVING

Calories 151
Fat 4 g
Cholesterol 51 mg
Sodium 271 mg
Carbohydrates 1 g
Fiber 0 g
Protein 27 g

4	4- to 5-ounce fresh or frozen skinless tuna steaks, 1 inch thick
2	tablespoons red wine vinegar
1	tablespoon snipped fresh dill or 1 teaspoon dried dill
2	teaspoons olive oil
¼	teaspoon salt
⅛	teaspoon cayenne pepper Nonstick cooking spray
½	cup chopped tomato (1 medium)
1	tablespoon capers, rinsed and drained
1	tablespoon chopped pitted ripe olives
1	clove garlic, minced

1. Thaw fish, if frozen. Rinse fish; pat dry with paper towels. Set aside.

2. For marinade, in a shallow dish combine vinegar, dill, olive oil, salt, and half the cayenne pepper. Add fish to marinade in dish, turning to coat fish. Cover and marinate in the refrigerator for 15 minutes.

3. Preheat broiler. Lightly coat the unheated rack of a broiler pan with cooking spray. In a small bowl combine tomato, drained capers, olives, garlic, and the remaining cayenne pepper.

4. Drain fish, reserving marinade. Place fish on prepared rack of broiler pan. Broil 4 inches from heat for 8 to 12 minutes or until fish flakes easily when tested with a fork, turning once and brushing with reserved marinade halfway through cooking. Serve fish topped with tomato and capers.

MAKES 4 SERVINGS

Chilly Bow Ties and Tuna

PREP 20 minutes
CHILL 4 to 24 hours

NUTRITION FACTS PER SERVING

Calories 254
Fat 3 g
Cholesterol 13 mg
Sodium 433 mg
Carbohydrates 43 g
Fiber 2 g
Protein 13 g

8   ounces dried farfalle pasta (bow ties)
⅓   cup light mayonnaise
⅓   cup bottled reduced-calorie Italian salad dressing
¼   cup thinly sliced green onions (2) (optional)
2   tablespoons orange juice
¼   teaspoon salt
¼   teaspoon black pepper
1   11-ounce can mandarin orange sections, drained
1   12-ounce can chunk white tuna (water pack), drained and broken in chunks
1   cup fresh pea pods, halved
    Milk (optional)

1. Cook pasta according to package directions; drain. Rinse with cold water; drain again.

2. Meanwhile, for dressing, in a large bowl combine mayonnaise, Italian dressing, green onions (if desired), orange juice, salt, and pepper.

3. Add cooked pasta to dressing in bowl. Toss well to coat. Gently stir in orange sections, tuna, and pea pods. Cover and refrigerate for 4 to 24 hours. Before serving, if necessary, stir in a little milk to moisten. **MAKES 6 SERVINGS**

Pasta with Tuna, Roasted Peppers, and Artichokes

START TO FINISH **20 minutes**

NUTRITION FACTS PER SERVING

Calories 415
Fat 10 g
Cholesterol 5 mg
Sodium 476 mg
Carbohydrates 61 g
Protein 19 g

1 pound dried tiny shell macaroni (conchigliette) or tiny bow ties (tripolini)
1 7-ounce jar roasted red sweet peppers, drained and cut in thin strips
1 6.5-ounce can chunk white tuna (water-pack), drained and broken in chunks
1 6-ounce jar marinated artichoke hearts, drained and halved
2 tablespoons olive oil
1 tablespoon capers, rinsed and drained
1 tablespoon snipped fresh parsley
2 teaspoons balsamic vinegar
1 clove garlic, minced
½ teaspoon salt
¼ teaspoon freshly ground black pepper

1. Cook pasta according to package directions. Drain. Return to pot. Cover and keep warm.

2. Meanwhile, in a large serving bowl combine roasted red peppers, tuna, artichoke hearts, olive oil, capers, parsley, balsamic vinegar, garlic, salt, and black pepper. Add the warm pasta; toss lightly to coat. Serve immediately.
MAKES 6 SERVINGS

Snapper Veracruz

START TO FINISH **30 minutes**

NUTRITION FACTS
PER SERVING

Calories 174
Fat 5 g
Cholesterol 42 mg
Sodium 260 mg
Carbohydrates 7 g
Fiber 6 g
Protein 24 g

1½ pounds fresh or frozen
   skinless red snapper or other
   fish fillets, ½ to ¾ inch thick
⅛ teaspoon salt
⅛ teaspoon black pepper
1   tablespoon vegetable oil
1   large onion, sliced and
   separated in rings
2   cloves garlic, minced
2   cups chopped tomatoes
   (2 large)
¼ cup sliced pimiento-stuffed
   green olives
¼ cup dry white wine
2   tablespoons capers, drained
1   to 2 fresh jalapeños or serrano
   chiles, seeded and chopped,
   or 1 to 2 canned jalapeños,
   rinsed, drained, seeded, and
   chopped (see tip, page 63)
½ teaspoon sugar
1   bay leaf

1. Thaw fish, if frozen. Rinse
fish; pat dry with paper towels.
Cut in six serving-size pieces, if
necessary. Sprinkle fish with salt
and black pepper.

2. For sauce, in a large skillet heat
oil over medium heat. Add onion
and garlic; cook until tender. Stir
in tomatoes, olives, wine, capers,
chiles, sugar, and bay leaf. Bring to
boiling. Add fish to skillet. Return
to boiling; reduce heat. Simmer,
covered, for 6 to 10 minutes or

until fish flakes easily when tested
with a fork. Using a slotted spatula,
carefully transfer fish from skillet
to a serving platter. Cover to keep
warm.

3. Bring sauce to boiling; cook for
5 to 6 minutes or until reduced to
about 2 cups, stirring occasionally.
Discard bay leaf. Spoon sauce over
fish. **MAKES 6 SERVINGS**

Tilapia with Grape Chutney

START TO FINISH 20 minutes

NUTRITION FACTS PER SERVING

Calories 305
Fat 9 g
Cholesterol 57 mg
Sodium 208 mg
Carbohydrates 37 g
Fiber 2 g
Protein 24 g

4   4-ounce fresh or frozen skinless tilapia or sole fillets
    Salt and black pepper
2   tablespoons vegetable oil
1   cup seedless green grapes, halved
½   cup tropical blend mixed dried fruit bits
⅓   cup sliced green onions
⅓   cup apricot spreadable fruit
    Hot cooked brown rice (optional)

1. Thaw fish if frozen. Rinse fish; pat dry with paper towels. Cut fish in four serving-size pieces, if necessary. Sprinkle fish with salt and pepper.

2. In a large skillet heat oil over medium-high heat. Cook fish in hot oil for 3 to 4 minutes or until fish flakes easily when tested with a fork, turning once. Transfer fish to a platter; cover to keep warm.

3. For grape chutney, add grapes, fruit bits, green onions, and spreadable fruit to skillet; cook and stir for 2 minutes. Season with additional salt and pepper. Spoon chutney over fish. If desired, serve with hot cooked rice.

MAKES 4 SERVINGS

Chicken with Grape Chutney: Prepare as above, except substitute 4 medium skinless, boneless chicken breast halves (about 1¼ pounds total) for the tilapia. Place each chicken breast half between two pieces of plastic wrap. Using the flat side of a meat mallet, lightly pound chicken to an even ¼ inch thickness. Remove and discard plastic wrap. Sprinkle with salt and pepper. Cook in hot oil over medium-high heat for 4 to 5 minutes or until no pink remains, turning once. Continue as directed in Step 3.

Tilapia with Ginger-Marinated Cucumbers

START TO FINISH **20 minutes**

NUTRITION FACTS PER SERVING

Calories 210
Fat 3 g
Cholesterol 59 mg
Sodium 388 mg
Carbohydrates 23 g
Fiber 0 g
Protein 26 g

4   4-ounce fresh or frozen skinless tilapia fillets, ½ to ¾ inch thick
½   cup cider vinegar
¼   cup packed brown sugar
2   teaspoons grated fresh ginger
½   teaspoon salt
3½ cups sliced cucumbers (2 medium)
2   tablespoons coarsely chopped fresh mint
1   6-ounce carton plain yogurt
1   teaspoon packed brown sugar
    Cracked black pepper
    Strips of lemon peel and lemon wedges (optional)

1. Thaw fish, if frozen. Rinse fish; pat dry with paper towels. Set aside. Preheat broiler. In a medium bowl stir together vinegar, the ¼ cup brown sugar, ginger, and salt until sugar is dissolved. Reserve ¼ cup of the vinegar mixture. Add cucumbers and 1 tablespoon of the mint to remaining vinegar mixture; toss to coat. Set aside.

2. Place fish on the greased unheated rack of a broiler pan. Brush the reserved ¼ cup vinegar mixture on the fish. Broil 4 inches from heat for 4 to 6 minutes or until fish flakes easily when tested with a fork.

3. Meanwhile, in another small bowl stir together yogurt, the remaining 1 tablespoon mint, and the 1 teaspoon brown sugar.

4. Using a slotted spoon, place cucumbers and fish on plates. Top fish with yogurt mixture. Sprinkle with cracked pepper and, if desired, lemon peel. If desired, serve with lemon wedges.

MAKES 4 SERVINGS

Cilantro-Lime Orange Roughy

PREP 10 minutes
BROIL 4 to 6 minutes per ½-inch thickness

NUTRITION FACTS PER SERVING

Calories 127
Fat 4 g
Cholesterol 36 mg
Sodium 259 mg
Carbohydrates 1 g
Fiber 0 g
Protein 21 g

1¼ pounds fresh or frozen skinless orange roughy, ocean perch, cod, or haddock fillets, ¾ to 1 inch thick
Salt and black pepper
Nonstick cooking spray
¼ cup snipped fresh cilantro
1 tablespoon butter, melted
1 teaspoon finely shredded lime peel
1 tablespoon lime juice

1. Thaw fish, if frozen. Preheat broiler. Rinse fish; pat dry with paper towels. Cut fish in four serving-size pieces, if necessary. Measure thickness of fish. Sprinkle fish with salt and pepper.

2. Lightly coat the unheated rack of a broiler pan with cooking spray. Place fish on broiler pan, tucking under any thin edges for uniform thickness.

3. Broil 4 inches from heat for 4 to 6 minutes per ½-inch thickness of fish or until fish flakes easily when tested with a fork, tuning once halfway through cooking if fish is 1 inch thick.

4. For sauce, in a small bowl stir together cilantro, melted butter, lime peel, and lime juice. Spoon sauce over fish. **MAKES 4 SERVINGS**

Wasabi-Glazed Whitefish with Vegetable Slaw

PREP 20 minutes
GRILL 6 minutes

NUTRITION FACTS PER SERVING

Calories 198
Fat 8 g
Cholesterol 62 mg
Sodium 539 mg
Carbohydrates 4 g
Fiber 1 g
Protein 24 g

4   4- to 5-ounce fresh or frozen skinless whitefish, cod, or flounder fillets, about ¾ inch thick
2   tablespoons soy sauce
¼   teaspoon wasabi powder or 1 tablespoon prepared horseradish
1   teaspoon toasted sesame oil
1⅓ cups coarsely shredded zucchini (1 medium)
1   cup sliced radishes
1   cup fresh snow pea pods, trimmed
3   tablespoons snipped fresh chives
3   tablespoons rice vinegar

1. Thaw fish, if frozen. Rinse fish; pat dry with paper towels. In a small bowl combine soy sauce, wasabi powder, and ½ teaspoon of the sesame oil. Brush both sides of fish with wasabi sauce.

2. For a charcoal grill, grill fish on the lightly greased rack of an uncovered grill directly over medium coals for 6 to 9 minutes or until fish flakes easily when tested with a fork, turning once halfway through grilling. (For a gas grill, preheat grill. Reduce heat to medium. Place fish on grill rack over heat. Cover and grill as above.)

3. Meanwhile, for vegetable slaw, in a medium bowl combine zucchini, radishes, pea pods, and 2 tablespoons of the chives. In a small bowl combine the remaining ½ teaspoon sesame oil and the vinegar. Drizzle over vegetable slaw; toss to combine.

4. To serve, sprinkle the remaining 1 tablespoon chives on fish. Serve fish with vegetable slaw.
MAKES 4 SERVINGS

Catfish with Succotash Salad

START TO FINISH **20 minutes**

NUTRITION FACTS PER SERVING

Calories 372
Fat 12 g
Cholesterol 53 mg
Sodium 509 mg
Carbohydrates 41 g
Fiber 5 g
Protein 24 g

4	4- to 6-ounce fresh or frozen catfish fillets, about ½ inch thick
2	cups frozen lima beans
	Olive oil
	Garlic salt
	Black pepper
1	cup purchased corn relish
1	cup fresh baby spinach

1. Thaw fish, if frozen. Rinse fish; pat dry with paper towels. Set aside. Cook lima beans according to package directions; drain in a colander. Rinse beans under cold water until cool; drain well.

2. Brush fish lightly with olive oil; sprinkle with garlic salt and pepper. Place fish in a well-greased grill basket. For a charcoal grill, place basket on the grill rack directly over medium coals. Grill for 6 to 9 minutes or until fish flakes easily when tested with a

fork, turning basket once halfway through grilling. (For a gas grill, preheat grill. Reduce heat to medium. Place basket on grill rack over heat. Cover and grill as above.)

3. Place fish on a serving platter. For succotash salad, in a large bowl toss together cooked lima beans, corn relish, and spinach. Serve salad with fish. **MAKES 4 SERVINGS**

Honey-Sauced Shrimp and Veggies

START TO FINISH **20 minutes**

NUTRITION FACTS PER SERVING

Calories 319
Fat 6 g
Cholesterol 172 mg
Sodium 361 mg
Carbohydrates 43 g
Fiber 5 g
Protein 26 g

1 pound fresh or frozen medium shrimp in shells
1 12-ounce package peeled fresh baby carrots
3 cups broccoli florets
1 tablespoon vegetable oil
1 cup cherry tomatoes
⅓ cup honey
2 tablespoons bottled chili garlic sauce
2 tablespoons orange juice

1. Thaw shrimp, if frozen. Peel and devein shrimp, removing tails. Rinse shrimp; pat dry with paper towels. Set aside.

2. In a large saucepan cook carrots, covered, in boiling lightly salted water for 5 minutes. Add broccoli; cook for 3 to 4 minutes more or just until vegetables are tender. Drain.

3. Meanwhile, in a large skillet heat oil over medium heat. Add shrimp and tomatoes to skillet. Cook and stir for 3 to 4 minutes or until shrimp are opaque. Transfer shrimp mixture to a serving platter; add cooked carrots and broccoli to platter. In the same skillet stir together honey, chili sauce, and orange juice; heat through. Spoon honey mixture over shrimp and vegetables.
MAKES 4 SERVINGS

Jerk-Spiced Shrimp with Wilted Spinach

START TO FINISH **25 minutes**

NUTRITION FACTS PER SERVING

Calories 159
Fat 8 g
Cholesterol 129 mg
Sodium 315 mg
Carbohydrates 2 g
Fiber 6 g
Protein 19 g

12 ounces fresh or frozen medium shrimp in shells
1½ teaspoons Jamaican jerk seasoning
2 tablespoons olive oil
3 cloves garlic, minced
8 cups torn fresh spinach

1. Thaw shrimp, if frozen. Peel and devein shrimp, removing tails. Rinse shrimp; pat dry with paper towels. In a small bowl toss together shrimp and jerk seasoning; set aside.

2. In a large skillet heat oil over medium-high heat. Add garlic; cook for 15 seconds. Add half the spinach. Cook and stir about 1 minute or just until spinach is wilted. Transfer to a serving platter. Cook and stir remaining spinach. Cover to keep warm.

3. Carefully add remaining oil to skillet. Add shrimp. Cook and stir for 2 to 3 minutes or until shrimp are opaque. Spoon shrimp over wilted spinach. **MAKES 4 SERVINGS**

Fettuccine with Peas and Shrimp

START TO FINISH **25 minutes**

NUTRITION FACTS PER SERVING

Calories 432
Fat 5 g
Cholesterol 172 mg
Sodium 340 mg
Carbohydrates 54 g
Fiber 2 g
Protein 34 g

8   ounces fresh or frozen medium shrimp in shells
4   ounces dried whole wheat or spinach fettuccine
1   teaspoon olive oil
2   cloves garlic, minced
½   cup dry white wine or reduced-sodium chicken broth
½   cup frozen peas, thawed
⅓   cup finely chopped plum tomato (1 medium)
½   teaspoon finely shredded lemon peel
¼   teaspoon ground nutmeg
⅛   teaspoon salt
1   teaspoon snipped fresh Italian (flat-leaf) parsley
    Whole grain baguette-style French bread, sliced (optional)

1. Thaw shrimp, if frozen. Peel and devein shrimp, leaving tails intact, if desired. Rinse shrimp; pat dry with paper towels; set aside. Cook pasta according to package directions. Drain. Return to pot. Cover to keep warm.

2. Meanwhile, in a medium skillet heat oil over medium heat. Add garlic. Cook and stir for 30 seconds. Add shrimp and wine to skillet. Cook and stir for 3 to 4 minutes or until shrimp are opaque. Stir in peas, tomato, lemon peel, nutmeg, and salt. Add warm pasta; toss lightly with shrimp. Heat through.

3. To serve, divide pasta and shrimp between two shallow bowls. Sprinkle with parsley. If desired, serve with bread.
MAKES 2 SERVINGS

Shrimp with Basil on Linguini

START TO FINISH **25 minutes**

NUTRITION FACTS
PER SERVING

Calories 332
Fat 9 g
Cholesterol 189 mg
Sodium 231 mg
Carbohydrates 33 g
Fiber 1 g
Protein 29 g

1½ pounds fresh or frozen
   medium shrimp in shell
6   ounces dried spinach linguini
   or regular fettucine
2   tablespoons butter
2   teaspoons snipped fresh basil
   or tarragon or 1 teaspoon
   dried basil or tarragon,
   crushed

1. Thaw shrimp, if frozen. Peel and devein shrimp, leaving tails intact. Cook pasta according to package directions. Drain. Return to pot. Cover to keep warm.

2. In a large skillet melt butter over medium-high heat. Add shrimp and basil. Cook, stirring frequently, for 2 to 3 minutes or until shrimp are opaque. Serve immediately over warm pasta.
MAKES 4 SERVINGS

Shrimp Tacos

START TO FINISH 35 minutes
OVEN 350°F

NUTRITION FACTS PER SERVING

Calories 274
Fat 7 g
Cholesterol 129 mg
Sodium 381 mg
Carbohydrates 33 g
Fiber 7 g
Protein 22 g

1   pound fresh or frozen medium shrimp in shells
8   6-inch corn tortillas
1½ cups chopped, seeded, peeled tomatoes (3 medium)
1   cup chopped, seeded cucumber (1 small)
⅓   cup thinly sliced green onions
¼   cup snipped fresh cilantro
3   tablespoons lime juice
¼   teaspoon salt
8   ounces fresh green beans, trimmed and halved crosswise
1   teaspoon Jamaican jerk seasoning
1   tablespoon olive oil

1. Thaw shrimp, if frozen. Peel and devein shrimp, removing tails. Rinse shrimp; pat dry with paper towels. Set aside.

2. Wrap tortillas in heavy foil. Heat in a 350°F oven for 10 minutes.*

3. Meanwhile, for salsa, in a medium bowl stir together tomatoes, cucumber, green onions, cilantro, lime juice, and salt; set aside.

4. In a medium bowl toss green beans with ½ teaspoon of the jerk seasoning. In another bowl toss shrimp with the remaining ½ teaspoon jerk seasoning. In a large skillet heat oil over medium-high heat. Add green beans; cook and stir for 3 minutes. Add shrimp; cook and stir for 2 to 3 minutes more or until shrimp are opaque.

5. To assemble tacos, fill each warm tortilla with about ⅓ cup of the shrimp mixture. Serve with salsa. MAKES 4 SERVINGS

*Tip: If you like, instead of warming the tortillas in the oven, heat them in the skillet. After removing the shrimp (cover to keep warm), heat tortillas, one at a time, over medium-high heat for 30 to 60 seconds or until lightly browned, turning once. Fill one tortilla as you heat the next.

Shrimply Divine Pasta

START TO FINISH **20 minutes**

NUTRITION FACTS
PER SERVING

Calories 333
Fat 7 g
Cholesterol 136 mg
Sodium 422 mg
Carbohydrates 39 g
Fiber 3 g
Protein 25 g

12 ounces fresh or frozen
    medium shrimp in shells
6   ounces dried rotini or other
    pasta
1   tablespoon olive oil
3   cloves garlic, minced
1   cup chicken broth
1   tablespoon cornstarch
1   teaspoon dried basil, crushed
1   teaspoon dried oregano,
    crushed
4   cups fresh baby spinach or
    torn spinach
    Finely shredded Parmesan
    cheese (optional)

1. Thaw shrimp, if frozen. Peel and devein shrimp, removing tails. Rinse shrimp; pat dry with paper towels. Set aside. Cook pasta according to package directions; drain. Return pasta to hot pan; cover to keep warm.

2. For sauce, in a large skillet heat olive oil over medium-high heat. Add garlic; cook for 15 seconds. Add shrimp; cook and stir for 2 to 3 minutes or until shrimp are opaque. Remove shrimp from skillet. Combine broth, cornstarch, basil, and oregano. Add to skillet. Cook and stir until thickened and bubbly. Add the spinach. Cook for 1 to 2 minutes or just until wilted. Return the shrimp to the skillet; stir to combine.

3. Toss shrimp and pasta together. If desired, sprinkle with Parmesan cheese. **MAKES 4 SERVINGS**

Shrimp and Watercress Salad

START TO FINISH 15 minutes

NUTRITION FACTS
PER SERVING

Calories 257
Fat 8 g
Cholesterol 227 mg
Sodium 360 mg
Carbohydrates 14 g
Fiber 2 g
Protein 33 g

1   pound asparagus spears, trimmed
4   cups watercress, tough stems removed
1   pound cooked peeled and deveined shrimp (tails on, if desired)
2   cups cherry tomatoes, halved
½   cup bottled light raspberry or berry vinaigrette salad dressing
    Cracked black pepper

1. In a large skillet cook asparagus, covered, in a small amount of boiling lightly salted water about 3 minutes or until crisp-tender; drain in a colander. Rinse asparagus under cold water until cool; drain well.

2. Divide asparagus among four plates; top with watercress, shrimp, and cherry tomatoes. Drizzle dressing evenly over salads. Sprinkle with cracked pepper. **MAKES 4 SERVINGS**

Scallops-Pecans Wilted Salad

START TO FINISH 20 minutes

NUTRITION FACTS PER SERVING

Calories 449
Fat 19 g
Cholesterol 56 mg
Sodium 1,153 mg
Carbohydrates 37 g
Fiber 2 g
Protein 33 g

1½ pounds fresh or frozen sea scallops*
½   cup pecan halves
    Salt and black pepper
2   tablespoons olive oil
1   tablespoon sesame seeds
6   cups baby arugula leaves
4   medium heads endive, leaves separated and sliced crosswise (3½ to 4 cups)
½   cup maple syrup
⅓   cup reduced-sodium soy sauce
¼   teaspoon cayenne pepper

1. Thaw scallops, if frozen. Rinse scallops; pat dry with paper towels. Halve any large scallops.

2. In a 12-inch skillet cook and stir pecans over medium-high heat for 3 to 4 minutes or until toasted. Transfer pecans to a medium bowl; set aside.

3. Sprinkle scallops with salt and black pepper. In the same skillet heat oil over medium-high heat. Add scallops; cook for 2 to 3 minutes or until scallops are opaque, turning once halfway through cooking. Transfer scallops to bowl with pecans; sprinkle with sesame seeds. Cover to keep warm.

4. In a large bowl toss together arugula and endive. For dressing, in a small saucepan combine maple syrup, soy sauce, and cayenne pepper. Bring to boiling; remove from heat. Toss greens with three-fourths of the warm dressing. Cover with plate for 30 to 60 seconds or until arugula begins to wilt. Drizzle the remaining dressing over scallop mixture; toss to coat. Divide greens among four plates; top with scallops.
MAKES 4 SERVINGS

*Tip: Bay scallops are the tiny scallops and sea scallops are the larger variety. For even cooking in this recipe, halve the scallops horizontally to about ½ inch thick.

CHAPTER 11

Meatless

Spinach and Cheese Roll-Ups

PREP 30 minutes
BAKE 25 minutes
OVEN 350°F

NUTRITION FACTS PER SERVING

Calories 231
Fat 3 g
Cholesterol 10 mg
Sodium 425 mg
Carbohydrates 39 g
Fiber 2 g
Protein 20 g

1 teaspoon olive oil
⅓ cup chopped onion (1 small)
1 clove garlic, minced
1 14.5-ounce can diced tomatoes, undrained
2 tablespoons tomato paste
3½ teaspoons snipped fresh basil or 1 teaspoon dried basil, crushed
¼ teaspoon sugar
Dash salt
Dash black pepper
8 dried lasagna noodles
¾ cup fat-free or reduced-fat ricotta cheese
½ cup shredded part-skim mozzarella cheese (2 ounces)
2 tablespoons finely shredded Parmesan cheese
1 10-ounce package frozen chopped spinach, thawed and well drained
1 egg white

1. Preheat over to 350°F. For sauce, in a medium saucepan heat olive oil over medium heat. Add onion and garlic; cook until onion is tender, stirring occasionally. Carefully stir in undrained tomatoes, the tomato paste, 1½ teaspoons of the fresh basil or ½ teaspoon dried basil, the sugar, salt, and pepper. Bring to boiling; reduce heat. Simmer, uncovered, about 5 minutes or until sauce is desired consistency, stirring occasionally.

2. Meanwhile, cook lasagna noodles according to package directions; drain. Rinse with cold water; drain again.

3. In a medium bowl stir together ricotta cheese, mozzarella cheese, Parmesan cheese, and the remaining 2 teaspoons fresh basil or ½ teaspoon dried basil. Add spinach and egg white; stir to combine.

4. To assemble, evenly spread about ¼ cup of the cheese mixture on each noodle. Roll up from one end. Place two rolls, seam sides down, into each of four individual casseroles. Top rolls evenly with sauce.

5. Bake, covered, about 25 minutes or until heated through.
MAKES 4 SERVINGS

Tortellini with Roasted Red Pepper Sauce

START TO FINISH **20 minutes**

NUTRITION FACTS PER SERVING

Calories 324
Fat 8 g
Cholesterol 55 mg
Sodium 633 mg
Carbohydrates 47 g
Fiber 2 g
Protein 16 g

2   9-ounce packages refrigerated meat- or cheese-filled tortellini or one 7- to 8-ounce package dried cheese-filled tortellini
2   12-ounce jars roasted red sweet peppers, drained
1   tablespoon olive oil
1   cup chopped onion (1 large)
4   cloves garlic, minced
2   tablespoons snipped fresh basil or 1 teaspoon dried basil, crushed
1   teaspoon sugar
½   teaspoon salt
¼   cup finely shredded Asiago cheese or Parmesan cheese (1 ounce)

1. Cook pasta according to package directions. Drain. Return to pot. Cover to keep warm.

2. Meanwhile, place sweet peppers in a food processor. Cover and process until almost smooth. Set aside.

3. For sauce, in a medium saucepan heat oil over medium heat. Add onion and garlic; cook until onion is tender. Add pureed peppers, basil, sugar, and salt. Cook and stir for 3 to 5 minutes or until heated through.

4. Pour sauce over warm pasta; gently toss to coat. Sprinkle with cheese. Serve immediately.
MAKES 6 SERVINGS

Ravioli with Spinach Pesto

START TO FINISH **20 minutes**

NUTRITION FACTS PER SERVING

Calories 218
Fat 6 g
Cholesterol 27 mg
Sodium 525 mg
Carbohydrates 31 g
Fiber 3 g
Protein 11 g

1 9-ounce package refrigerated four-cheese ravioli or tortellini
12 ounces baby pattypan squash, halved, or yellow summer squash, halved lengthwise and sliced ½ inch thick
3½ cups fresh baby spinach
½ cup torn fresh basil
¼ cup bottled Caesar Parmesan vinaigrette salad dressing
2 tablespoons water
    Shredded Parmesan cheese (optional)

1. Cook ravioli according to package directions, adding squash the last 2 minutes of cooking; drain.

2. Meanwhile, for pesto, in a blender combine spinach, basil, salad dressing, and the water. Cover and blend until smooth, stopping to scrape down blender as needed.

3. Toss ravioli and squash with pesto. Sprinkle with Parmesan cheese. **MAKES 4 SERVINGS**

Herbed Pasta Primavera

START TO FINISH **30 minutes**

NUTRITION FACTS PER SERVING

Calories 284
Fat 9 g
Cholesterol 0 mg
Sodium 375 mg
Carbohydrates 42 g
Fiber 7 g
Protein 12 g

1¾ cups dried multigrain or whole wheat penne pasta (8 ounces)
1 tablespoon olive oil
8 ounces packaged peeled baby carrots, halved lengthwise (1¾ cups)
8 ounces fresh green beans, trimmed and cut in 2-inch pieces (1½ cups)
½ cup sliced green onions (4) or ½ cup chopped onion (1 medium)
¾ cup chicken broth
2 cloves garlic, minced
1 medium zucchini and/or yellow summer squash, halved lengthwise and cut in ¼-inch slices (2 cups)
2 tablespoons snipped fresh basil or 1 teaspoon dried basil, crushed
¼ teaspoon salt
¼ cup sliced almonds, toasted (see tip, page 80)
   Grated or finely shredded Parmesan cheese (optional)
   Cracked black pepper

1. Cook pasta according to package directions. Drain. Return pasta to pot. Cover to keep warm.

2. Meanwhile, in a large skillet heat olive oil over medium heat. Add carrots; cook and stir for 5 minutes. Add green beans and green onions. Stir in broth and garlic; reduce heat. Simmer, uncovered, for 3 minutes, stirring occasionally. Stir in zucchini. Simmer, uncovered, for 4 to 5 minutes more or until vegetables are crisp-tender, stirring occasionally.

3. In a large serving bowl toss together warm pasta, vegetables, basil, and salt. Sprinkle with almonds, Parmesan cheese (if desired), and pepper. Serve immediately. **MAKES 4 SERVINGS**

Linguine with Zucchini Sauce

START TO FINISH **20 minutes**

NUTRITION FACTS PER SERVING

Calories 378
Fat 15 g
Cholesterol 28 mg
Sodium 593 mg
Carbohydrates 48 g
Fiber 4 g
Protein 16 g

1 pound dried linguine
2 tablespoons olive oil
3 cloves garlic, peeled and thinly sliced
2 pounds zucchini, coarsely shredded
½ teaspoon salt
⅛ teaspoon black pepper
1 cup shredded sharp cheddar cheese (4 ounces)
½ cup purchased Alfredo sauce
  Fresh basil leaves (optional)

1. Cook pasta according to package directions; drain. Return pasta to pan; cover to keep warm.

2. For zucchini sauce, in a large skillet heat olive oil over medium-high heat. Add garlic; cook and stir for 30 seconds. Increase heat to high. Stir in zucchini, salt, and pepper. Cook and stir about 3 minutes or until tender. Stir in cheese and Alfredo sauce; heat through.

3. Pour zucchini sauce over pasta in pan; toss to coat. If desired, garnish servings with fresh basil.
MAKES 6 SERVINGS

Weeknight Pasta Toss

START TO FINISH 25 minutes

NUTRITION FACTS PER SERVING

Calories 116
Fat 10 g
Cholesterol 3 mg
Sodium 102 mg
Carbohydrates 5 g
Fiber 2 g
Protein 3 g

8   ounces dried linguine, fettuccine, or malfalda pasta
3   cups fresh asparagus pieces, broccoli florets, or cauliflower florets
¼   cup olive oil
4   cloves garlic, minced
½   teaspoon crushed red pepper
¼   cup finely shredded Pecorino Romano or Parmesan cheese (1 ounce)
2   tablespoons snipped fresh Italian (flat-leaf) parsley
¼   teaspoon black pepper
Salt

1. Cook pasta according to package directions. Drain. Return to pot. Cover to keep warm.

2. Meanwhile, place a steamer basket in a saucepan. Add water to just below the bottom of the basket. Bring water to boiling. Add vegetables to the steamer basket. Cover and reduce heat. Steam until the vegetables are crisp-tender. For asparagus, allow 3 to 5 minutes; for broccoli or cauliflower, allow 8 to 10 minutes. Add steamed vegetables to warm pasta.

3. In a small saucepan heat olive oil over medium heat. Add garlic and crushed red pepper; cook for 30 seconds to 1 minute or until fragrant.

4. Add garlic mixture to warm pasta and vegetables; toss lightly. Add cheese, parsley, and black pepper; toss lightly to mix. Season with salt. Serve immediately.
MAKES 6 SERVINGS

Garden Pasta

START TO FINISH 25 minutes

NUTRITION FACTS PER SERVING

Calories 207
Fat 1 g
Cholesterol 1 mg
Sodium 460 mg
Carbohydrates 44 g
Fiber 5 g
Protein 11 g

8   ounces dried whole wheat linguine or whole grain spaghetti
1   medium zucchini, halved and sliced crosswise or 2 cups broccoli florets
1   15-ounce can cannellini beans (white kidney beans), rinsed and drained
1   14.5-ounce can diced tomatoes, undrained
2   tablespoons tomato paste
2   cloves garlic, minced
½   teaspoon kosher salt or ¼ teaspoon salt
¼   teaspoon black pepper
2   tablespoons snipped fresh Italian (flat-leaf) parsley
2   ounces Parmesan cheese, shaved

1. Cook pasta according to package directions, adding zucchini the last 2 minutes of cooking time. Drain. Return to pot. Cover to keep warm.

2. Meanwhile, for sauce, in a blender or food processor combine beans, undrained tomatoes, tomato paste, garlic, salt, and pepper. Cover and blend or process until smooth. Transfer sauce to a medium saucepan. Heat over medium-low heat about 5 minutes or until heated through. Stir in parsley.

3. Pour sauce over warm pasta; toss lightly to coat. Serve immediately with Parmesan cheese. **MAKES 6 SERVINGS**

Asian Noodle Slaw

START TO FINISH **25 minutes**

NUTRITION FACTS PER SERVING

Calories 285
Fat 7 g
Cholesterol 0 mg
Sodium 318 mg
Carbohydrates 45 g
Fiber 7 g
Protein 12 g

6   ounces dried multigrain spaghetti or soba (buckwheat) noodles
⅓   cup peanut sauce
⅓   cup carrot juice
1   tablespoon vegetable oil
1   tablespoon finely chopped fresh ginger
1   16-ounce package shredded broccoli (broccoli slaw mix)
¾   cup shredded carrot (1 large)

1. Cook pasta according to package directions; drain. Return pasta to pan. Using kitchen scissors, snip pasta in small pieces. Cover to keep warm. In a small bowl whisk together peanut sauce and carrot juice; set aside.

2. In a wok or large nonstick skillet heat oil over medium-high heat. Add ginger; cook and stir for 15 seconds. Add broccoli and carrot; cook and stir for 1 minute. Stir in peanut sauce mixture; cook and stir for 2 minutes more. Add pasta. Using tongs, toss to coat. Serve warm. **MAKES 4 SERVINGS**

Orzo Risotto with Roasted Vegetables

START TO FINISH 45 minutes
OVEN 425°F

NUTRITION FACTS
PER SERVING

Calories 385
Fat 9 g
Cholesterol 0 mg
Sodium 471 mg
Carbohydrates 64 g
Fiber 6 g
Protein 15 g

Nonstick cooking spray
½ of a 2-pound butternut squash, peeled, seeded, and cut in ¾- to 1-inch cubes
⅛ teaspoon black pepper
3 cups halved button or cremini mushrooms (8 ounces)
1 large onion, cut in thin wedges
1 tablespoon snipped fresh rosemary or oregano or 1 teaspoon dried rosemary or oregano, crushed
1 tablespoon olive oil
2 14.5-ounce cans reduced-sodium chicken or vegetable broth
8 ounces dried whole wheat orzo (1⅓ cups)
2 cloves garlic, minced
¼ cup chopped walnuts, toasted (see tip, page 80)
¼ cup crumbled feta cheese (optional)

1. Preheat oven to 425°F. Coat a 15×10×1-inch baking pan with cooking spray. Place squash pieces in pan. Sprinkle with pepper. Cover with foil; roast for 10 minutes. Uncover; add mushrooms, onion, rosemary, and oil; toss to coat. Roast, uncovered, for 15 to 20 minutes or until vegetables are tender and light brown, stirring once or twice.

2. Meanwhile, in a saucepan bring broth to boiling; reduce heat. Cover; keep broth simmering. Coat a large skillet with cooking spray. Cook orzo and garlic in hot skillet over medium heat for 2 to

3 minutes or until orzo is light brown, stirring frequently. Remove from heat.

3. Add ½ cup hot broth to orzo. Return to heat. Cook, stirring frequently, over medium heat until liquid is absorbed. Continue adding broth, ½ cup at a time, stirring frequently until liquid is absorbed before adding more. Cook and stir about 15 minutes or until orzo is tender and creamy.

4. Add roasted vegetables and the walnuts to orzo; stir gently to combine. Sprinkle servings with feta cheese. **MAKES 4 SERVINGS**

Vegetable Curry

START TO FINISH 20 minutes

NUTRITION FACTS PER SERVING

Calories 385
Fat 3 g
Cholesterol 0 mg
Sodium 939 mg
Carbohydrates 72 g
Fiber 9 g
Protein 14 g

1   16-ounce package frozen baby lima beans
½   cup water
1   15-ounce can tomato sauce with garlic and onion
1½ teaspoons curry powder
2   8.8-ounce pouches cooked Spanish-style rice
¼   cup sliced green onions (2) or snipped fresh cilantro
    Olive oil (optional)

1. In a medium saucepan combine beans and the water. Bring to boiling; reduce heat. Simmer, covered, for 5 minutes. Stir in tomato sauce and curry powder. Return to boiling; reduce heat. Simmer, covered, about 3 minutes or until beans are crisp-tender.

2. Meanwhile, heat rice according to package directions. Spoon rice on one side of four plates; spoon bean mixture alongside rice. Sprinkle with green onions. If desired, drizzle olive oil over all.
MAKES 4 SERVINGS

Vegetable Fried Rice

PREP 25 minutes
CHILL 1 hour

NUTRITION FACTS
PER SERVING

Calories 226
Fat 4 g
Cholesterol 0 mg
Sodium 538 mg
Carbohydrates 42 g
Fiber 2 g
Protein 6 g

2   cups water
1   cup uncooked long grain rice
1   tablespoon toasted sesame oil
4   cloves garlic, minced
    (2 teaspoons)
2   teaspoons grated fresh ginger
3   cups assorted cut-up fresh
    vegetables (such as sweet
    pepper strips, red onion,
    sliced fresh mushrooms, small
    broccoli florets, or matchstick
    carrots)
1½ cups coarsely chopped bok
    choy
¼   cup reduced-sodium soy sauce
¼   cup snipped fresh cilantro or
    thinly sliced green onions (2)

1. In a medium saucepan combine the water and rice. Bring to boiling. Simmer, covered, about 15 minutes or until water is absorbed and rice is tender. Transfer rice to a medium bowl. Cover and chill for at least 1 hour.

2. In a 12-inch nonstick skillet heat oil over medium heat. Add garlic and ginger. Cook and stir for 30 seconds. Add assorted vegetables and bok choy. Cook and stir for 3 to 4 minutes or until vegetables are crisp-tender.

3. Add chilled rice and soy sauce to vegetables. Cook and stir for 3 minutes more or until heated through. Sprinkle with cilantro. Serve immediately.
MAKES 4 SERVINGS

Zesty Vegetable Enchiladas

PREP 30 minutes
BAKE 15 minutes
OVEN 350°F

NUTRITION FACTS PER SERVING

Calories 450
Fat 15 g
Cholesterol 20 mg
Sodium 929 mg
Carbohydrates 57 g
Fiber 11 g
Protein 22 g

1⅓ cups water
½ cup dry brown lentils, rinsed and drained
   Nonstick cooking spray
8 8-inch flour tortillas
1 cup thinly sliced carrots (2 medium)
2 small zucchini or yellow summer squash, quartered lengthwise and sliced (2 cups)
1 teaspoon ground cumin
1 8-ounce can tomato sauce
1 cup shredded reduced-fat Monterey Jack cheese (4 ounces)
   Dash bottled hot pepper sauce (optional)
1 14.5-ounce can Mexican-style stewed tomatoes, undrained and cut up
   Fresh cilantro sprigs (optional)

1. In a medium saucepan combine the water and lentils. Bring to boiling; reduce heat. Simmer, covered, for 25 to 30 minutes or until lentils are tender; drain.

2. Preheat oven to 350°F. Coat a 2-quart rectangular baking dish with cooking spray; set aside. Stack tortillas and wrap tightly in foil. Heat about 10 minutes or until warm.

3. Lightly coat an unheated large skillet with cooking spray. Preheat over medium heat. Add carrots; cook and stir for 2 minutes. Add zucchini and cumin; cook and stir for 2 to 3 minutes or until

vegetables are crisp-tender. Remove from heat. Stir in drained lentils, the tomato sauce, ¾ cup of the cheese, and, if desired, hot pepper sauce.

4. Divide lentil mixture among warm tortillas; roll up tortillas. Arrange tortillas, seam sides down, in the prepared baking dish. Sprinkle with the remaining ¼ cup cheese. Spoon undrained tomatoes over tortillas.

5. Bake, uncovered, for 15 to 20 minutes or until heated through. If desired, garnish with cilantro. **MAKES 4 SERVINGS**

Meatless Tacos

START TO FINISH 30 minutes

NUTRITION FACTS PER TACO

Calories 148
Fat 7 g
Cholesterol 7 mg
Sodium 460 mg
Carbohydrates 16 g
Fiber 3 g
Protein 7 g

½ cup water
¼ cup dry brown lentils, rinsed and drained
¼ cup chopped onion
8 taco shells
1 8-ounce can tomato sauce
½ of a 1.125 or 1.25-ounce envelope (5 teaspoons) taco seasoning mix
8 ounces firm or extra-firm tub-style tofu (fresh bean curd), drained and finely chopped
1½ cups shredded lettuce
½ cup chopped tomato (1 medium)
½ cup shredded cheddar cheese (2 ounces)
½ cup salsa (optional)

1. In a medium saucepan combine the water, lentils, and onion. Bring to boiling; reduce heat. Simmer, covered, for 25 to 30 minutes or until lentils are tender and liquid is absorbed.

2. Meanwhile, heat taco shells according to package directions.

3. Stir tomato sauce and taco seasoning mix into lentils. Bring to boiling; reduce heat. Simmer, uncovered, for 5 minutes. Stir in tofu; heat through. Spoon tofu mixture into taco shells. Top with lettuce, tomato, and cheese. If desired, serve with salsa.
MAKES 8 TACOS

Bulgur Tacos: Prepare as directed, except increase the water to ¾ cup and substitute ¼ cup bulgur for lentils. Simmer water, bulgur, and onion, covered, for about 15 minutes or until bulgur is tender and liquid is absorbed.
NUTRITION FACTS PER TACO: *143 calories, 7 g fat, 7 mg cholesterol, 460 mg sodium, 16 g carbohydrates, 2 g fiber, 6 g protein.*

Vegetable Tacos: Prepare as above, except stir 1 cup frozen whole kernel corn and ¾ cup shredded carrot into the tomato sauce. Increase number of taco shells to 12.
NUTRITION FACTS PER TACO: *133 calories, 6 g fat, 5 mg cholesterol, 326 mg sodium, 17 g carbohydrates, 3 g fiber, 6 g protein.*

Bean Burgers

PREP 10 minutes
GRILL 10 minutes

NUTRITION FACTS PER BURGER

Calories 234
Fat 3 g
Cholesterol 36 mg
Sodium 994 mg
Carbohydrates 41 g
Fiber 5 g
Protein 10 g

2 15.5-ounce cans pinto beans, rinsed and drained
½ cup dry fine bread crumbs
½ cup bottled salsa
1 egg, lightly beaten
1 teaspoon chili powder
½ teaspoon ground cumin
½ cup coarsely crushed baked tortilla chips
   Nonstick cooking spray
3 pita bread rounds, halved
12 lettuce leaves
12 slices tomato
   Bottled salsa

1. Reserve 1 cup of the pinto beans. Place remaining beans in a food processor; process until smooth. (Or use a potato masher to mash beans in a large bowl.)

2. In large bowl combine the reserved 1 cup beans, the pureed beans, bread crumbs, the ½ cup salsa, egg, chili powder, and cumin. Stir in crushed chips; mix well. Form bean mixture in six patties. Coat both sides of each patty with cooking spray.

3. For a charcoal grill, grill burgers on the lightly greased rack of an uncovered grill directly over medium coals about 10 minutes or until an instant-read thermometer inserted in sides of burgers registers 160°F. (For a gas grill, preheat grill. Reduce heat to medium. Place burgers on grill rack over heat. Cover and grill as above.) Serve burgers in pita pockets with lettuce and tomato slices. Serve with additional salsa.
MAKES 6 BURGERS

Broiler directions: Place burgers on the unheated lightly greased rack of a broiler pan. Broil 4 to 5 inches from heat about 10 minutes or until an instant-read thermometer inserted into sides of burgers registers 160°F, turning once halfway through broiling.

Garden Veggie Burgers

PREP 10 minutes
GRILL 15 minutes

NUTRITION FACTS PER SERVING

Calories 350
Fat 14 g
Cholesterol 17 mg
Sodium 920 mg
Carbohydrates 37 g
Fiber 7 g
Protein 21 g

2	medium red onions
4	refrigerated or frozen meatless burger patties
¼	cup bottled vinaigrette salad dressing, at room temperature
1	tablespoon olive oil
4	cups fresh spinach
1	clove garlic, minced
½	cup crumbled feta cheese (2 ounces)
4	hamburger buns, split

1. For onion topping, cut onions in ½-inch slices. For a charcoal grill, grill onion slices on the rack of an uncovered grill directly over medium coals for 15 to 20 minutes or until tender, turning once halfway through grilling. Grill burger patties directly over the coals alongside the onions for 8 to 10 minutes or until heated through, turning once halfway through grilling. (For a gas grill, preheat grill. Reduce heat to medium. Place onion slices and burger patties on grill rack over heat. Cover and grill as above.) Brush grilled onions with the salad dressing.

2. Meanwhile, for spinach topping, in a large skillet heat oil over medium-high heat. Add spinach and garlic; cook and stir for 30 seconds or just until spinach is wilted. Remove skillet from heat. Stir in feta cheese.

3. To serve, place onion slices on buns. Top with burger patties, spinach mixture, and bun tops.
MAKES 4 SERVINGS

Veggie-Cheese Sandwiches

PREP 20 minutes
COOK 5 minutes

NUTRITION FACTS PER SANDWICH

Calories 194
Fat 7 g
Cholesterol 0 mg
Sodium 244 mg
Carbohydrates 22 g
Fiber 1 g
Protein 10 g

8	½-inch slices country French white bread
4	teaspoons olive oil
2	tablespoons honey mustard
4	ounces thinly sliced cheddar cheese
½	cup thinly sliced cucumber
½	cup fresh spinach
¼	cup thinly sliced red onion

1. Brush one side of each bread slice with oil; brush the other side with mustard. Top mustard sides of four bread slices with cheese, cucumber, spinach, and onion. Top with the remaining bread slices, mustard sides down.

2. Preheat indoor electric grill. Place sandwiches on grill. If using covered grill, close lid. Grill sandwiches until bread is golden. For covered grill, allow 3 to 5 minutes. For uncovered grill, allow 6 to 8 minutes, turning once halfway through grilling. Serve immediately. **MAKES 4 SANDWICHES**

Tomato-Parmesan Pizza

PREP 20 minutes
BAKE 20 minutes
OVEN 350°F/450°F

NUTRITION FACTS PER SERVING

Calories 367
Fat 11 g
Cholesterol 10 mg
Sodium 881 mg
Carbohydrates 54 g
Fiber 4 g
Protein 15 g

8   ¼-inch slices eggplant (5 to 6 ounces)
Olive oil nonstick cooking spray
¼   teaspoon herbes de Provence or dried Italian seasoning, crushed
⅛   teaspoon salt
Black pepper
1   13.8-ounce package refrigerated pizza dough
¼   cup purchased dried tomato pesto
2   medium plum tomatoes, thinly sliced
½   cup grated Parmesan cheese, shredded reduced-fat mozzarella cheese (2 ounces), and/or crumbled reduced-fat feta cheese (2 ounces)
2   tablespoons small fresh basil leaves or snipped fresh basil

1. Preheat oven to 350°F. Arrange eggplant slices on a large baking sheet; coat slices on both sides with cooking spray. Sprinkle with herbes de Provence, salt, and pepper. Bake for 10 to 12 minutes or just until eggplant is softened. Transfer pan to a wire rack.

2. Increase oven temperature to 450°F. Grease two extra-large baking sheets. Divide dough in half. On a lightly floured surface, roll each dough portion to a 13×5-inch rectangle. Transfer to prepared baking sheets.

3. Spread pesto on dough. Arrange eggplant slices and tomato slices on pesto, overlapping to fit. Sprinkle with cheese. Lightly coat with cooking spray.

4. Bake, one pizza at a time, about 10 minutes or until pizza crusts are golden brown. Just before serving, top with basil. **MAKES 4 SERVINGS**

CHAPTER 12

Sides

Garlic-Roasted Asparagus

PREP 15 minutes
ROAST 10 minutes
OVEN 450°F

NUTRITION FACTS PER SERVING

Calories 64
Fat 5 g
Cholesterol 0 mg
Sodium 99 mg
Carbohydrates 5 g
Fiber 2 g
Protein 3 g

1½ pounds fresh asparagus spears
2 to 3 cloves garlic, thinly sliced
2 to 3 tablespoons olive oil
¼ teaspoon salt
¼ teaspoon black pepper

1. Preheat oven to 450°F. Snap off and discard woody bases from asparagus. Place asparagus and garlic in a 15×10×1-inch baking pan. Drizzle with oil and sprinkle with salt and pepper. Toss to coat.

2. Roast for 10 to 15 minutes or until asparagus is crisp-tender, stirring once halfway through roasting. Serve immediately.
MAKES 6 SERVINGS

Green Beans with Lime

START TO FINISH 30 minutes

NUTRITION FACTS PER SERVING

Calories 66
Fat 4 g
Cholesterol 0 mg
Sodium 67 mg
Carbohydrates 9 g
Fiber 4 g
Protein 2 g

1 tablespoon vegetable oil or olive oil
1 pound fresh green beans, cut in 2-inch pieces (4 cups)
1 lime
  Salt

1. In a large skillet heat oil over medium heat. Add green beans; cook, uncovered, for 18 to 20 minutes or until crisp-tender and lightly browned, stirring occasionally.

2. Meanwhile, shred 1 teaspoon of peel from the lime. Cut lime in half.

3. Add lime peel to beans. Cook and stir for 1 minute more. Lightly season beans with salt. Squeeze juice from lime halves over beans. Serve immediately.
MAKES 4 SERVINGS

Garlic and Parsley Green Beans

PREP 25 minutes
COOK 10 minutes

NUTRITION FACTS PER SERVING

Calories 90
Fat 6 g
Cholesterol 15 mg
Sodium 80 mg
Carbohydrates 9 g
Fiber 4 g
Protein 2 g

1½ pounds green beans, trimmed
1   tablespoon salt
3   tablespoons unsalted butter
4   cloves garlic, minced
2   tablespoons snipped fresh parsley
    Salt and freshly ground black pepper
    Snipped fresh parsley (optional)

1. Fill a large pot with water and bring to boiling. Add green beans and the 1 tablespoon salt. Cook, uncovered, for 5 to 8 minutes or just until beans are tender and still vibrant green. Drain the beans then immediately submerge into a bowl of lightly salted ice water to cool quickly. Drain well.

2. In a large skillet melt butter over medium-high heat. Add the beans; cook and stir until heated through. Add the garlic and the 2 tablespoons parsley. Sprinkle with salt and pepper. Cook and stir for 1 minute more. If desired, sprinkle with additional parsley. Serve immediately.
MAKES 6 TO 8 SERVINGS

Make-Ahead Directions:
Prepare beans as directed through Step 1. Cover and refrigerate beans up to 1 day.

Wine-Poached Beets

PREP 25 minutes
COOK 45 minutes

NUTRITION FACTS PER SERVING

Calories 54
Fat 0 g
Cholesterol 0 mg
Sodium 119 mg
Carbohydrates 9 g
Fiber 2 g
Protein 1 g

¾ cup dry red wine, such as merlot or shiraz, or apple juice
½ cup water
1 tablespoon packed brown sugar
2½ pounds beets, peeled, and cut in bite-size pieces*
   Salt and black pepper
   Honey (optional)
1 tablespoon snipped fresh parsley
   Lemon wedges (optional)

1. In a large saucepan combine ½ cup of the wine, the water, and brown sugar. Bring to boiling, stirring to dissolve sugar. Add beets. Return to boiling; reduce heat. Simmer, covered, about 45 minutes or until beets are tender and can be pierced with a fork, stirring occasionally. Drain.

2. Transfer beets to a serving bowl. Season with salt and pepper. Drizzle remaining ¼ cup wine and, if desired, honey over beets. Sprinkle with parsley. If desired, serve with lemon wedges.
MAKES 8 TO 10 SERVINGS

*Tip: To avoid staining your hands, wear plastic gloves while peeling and cutting beets. Leave on 1 to 2 inches of tops during cooking or trim them just at the base of the tops.

Beet Greens with Walnuts and Blue Cheese

START TO FINISH **15 minutes**

NUTRITION FACTS
PER SERVING

Calories 55
Fat 5 g
Cholesterol 0 mg
Sodium 109 mg
Carbohydrates 3 g
Fiber 2 g
Protein 2 g

8   ounces fresh beet greens*
2   teaspoons vegetable oil
2   tablespoons chopped walnuts
1   tablespoon crumbled blue
    cheese
¼   teaspoon black pepper

1. Cut beet greens in 1-inch strips. In a large skillet heat oil over medium-high heat. Add walnuts; cook and stir for 2 minutes. Add beet greens. Cook and stir about 1 minute or just until wilted. Top with crumbled blue cheese and sprinkle with pepper.
MAKES 4 SERVINGS

*Tip: If desired, substitute fresh spinach or Swiss chard for the beet greens. Clean all greens well under cold running water to remove any dirt or sand. Drain well.

Caramelized Brussels Sprouts

PREP 25 minutes
COOK 21 minutes

NUTRITION FACTS PER SERVING

Calories 76
Fat 3 g
Cholesterol 8 mg
Sodium 155 mg
Carbohydrates 11 g
Fiber 2 g
Protein 2 g

10 cups small, firm fresh Brussels sprouts (about 2¾ pounds)
½ cup sugar
¼ cup butter
½ cup red wine vinegar
¾ cup water
¾ teaspoon salt

1. Prepare the Brussels sprouts by peeling off two or three of the dark outer leaves from each sprout; trim stem ends.

2. In a Dutch oven or very large skillet heat the sugar over medium-high heat until it begins to melt, shaking pan occasionally to heat sugar evenly. Once sugar starts to melt, reduce heat and cook until it begins to turn brown. Add butter; stir until melted. Add vinegar; cook and stir for 1 minute.

3. Carefully add the water and salt. Bring to boiling; add the Brussels sprouts. Return to boiling; reduce heat. Simmer, covered, for 6 minutes. Uncover and cook about 15 minutes more or until most of the liquid has been absorbed and the sprouts are coated with a golden glaze, gently stirring occasionally. **MAKES 16 SERVINGS**

Orange-Glazed Baby Carrots

START TO FINISH **15 minutes**

NUTRITION FACTS PER SERVING

Calories 77
Fat 3 g
Cholesterol 8 mg
Sodium 57 mg
Carbohydrates 13 g
Fiber 2 g
Protein 1 g

2   cups packaged peeled baby carrots
1   tablespoon butter
2   tablespoons orange marmalade
    Snipped fresh basil

1. In a medium-size covered saucepan cook carrots in a small amount of boiling, lightly salted water for 5 minutes; drain in a colander.

2. In the same saucepan melt butter over medium heat. Add carrots and orange marmalade. Cook and stir for 2 to 3 minutes or until carrots are tender and glazed. Sprinkle with snipped basil, if desired. **MAKES 4 SERVINGS**

Honey-Glazed Carrots

START TO FINISH **30 minutes**

NUTRITION FACTS PER SERVING

Calories 75
Fat 2 g
Cholesterol 5 mg
Sodium 180 mg
Carbohydrates 14 g
Fiber 3 g
Protein 1 g

6   cups water
3   pounds baby carrots with
     tops trimmed to 2 inches,
     peeled or scrubbed, or
     3 pounds packaged peeled
     baby carrots
2   tablespoons butter
3   to 4 tablespoons honey
1   teaspoon finely shredded
     lemon peel
½   teaspoon crushed red pepper
½   teaspoon salt
     Crushed red pepper
     (optional)

1. In a 12-inch skillet bring the water to boiling. Add carrots. Return to boiling; reduce heat. Simmer, covered, for 8 to 10 minutes or just until carrots are tender. Drain carrots. Pat dry with paper towels.

2. In the same skillet combine butter, honey, lemon peel, crushed red pepper, and salt. Stir constantly over medium heat until butter is melted and mixture bubbles. Carefully add carrots. Toss gently for 2 to 3 minutes or until carrots are well coated with glaze and heated through.

3. To serve, transfer carrots to shallow bowl or platter. Drizzle with any remaining glaze from pan. Sprinkle with additional crushed red pepper, if desired.
MAKES 12 SERVINGS

Make-Ahead Directions:
Prepare carrots as directed through Step 1. Cool cooked carrots, then cover and refrigerate up to one day. Bring to room temperature (takes about 1 hour) before glazing. Heat carrots in glaze for 4 to 5 minutes.

Roasted Vegetable Medley

PREP 15 minutes
ROAST 25 minutes
OVEN 425°F

NUTRITION FACTS PER SERVING

Calories 50
Fat 2 g
Cholesterol 0 mg
Sodium 150 mg
Carbohydrates 8 g
Fiber 2 g
Protein 1 g

3   medium red, yellow, and/or green sweet peppers, seeded and cut in ½-inch-wide strips
2   medium red onions, cut in 8 wedges
2   small yellow summer squash, cut in ½-inch slices
2   small zucchini, cut in ½-inch slices
4   cloves garlic, thinly sliced
2   tablespoons snipped fresh parsley
2   tablespoons balsamic vinegar
1   tablespoon olive oil
1   teaspoon dried oregano, crushed
½   teaspoon salt
¼   teaspoon black pepper

1. Preheat oven to 425°F. In a 13×9×2-inch baking pan combine sweet peppers, onions, yellow summer squash, zucchini, and garlic.

2. In a screw-top jar combine parsley, balsamic vinegar, olive oil, oregano, salt, and black pepper; cover and shake well. Pour over the vegetables; toss gently to coat.

3. Roast, uncovered, about 25 minutes or until vegetables are crisp-tender, stirring twice.
MAKES 8 SERVINGS

Grilled Potato Wedges

PREP 25 minutes
GRILL 8 minutes

NUTRITION FACTS
PER SERVING

Calories 145
Fat 4 g
Cholesterol 0 mg
Sodium 301 mg
Carbohydrates 26 g
Fiber 3 g
Protein 3 g

1⅓ pounds red-skinned potatoes
     and/or sweet potatoes
1   tablespoon olive oil
1   tablespoon water
4   cloves garlic, minced
1½ teaspoons paprika
½   teaspoon salt
¼   teaspoon black pepper

1. Cut potatoes lengthwise in quarters. In a large covered saucepan cook potatoes in enough lightly salted boiling water to cover about 10 minutes or just until tender; drain. Return potatoes to saucepan.

2. Meanwhile, in a small bowl combine oil, the water, garlic, paprika, salt, and pepper. Pour over potatoes; toss gently to coat. Place potatoes in a grill basket.

3. For a charcoal grill, grill potatoes in a basket on the rack of an uncovered grill directly over medium coals for 8 to 10 minutes or until edges start to brown, turning occasionally. (For a gas grill, preheat grill. Reduce heat to medium. Place potatoes in basket on grill rack over heat. Cover and grill as above.) **MAKES 4 SERVINGS**

Make-Ahead Directions: Cook potatoes as directed in Step 1. Drain; cover and refrigerate up to 24 hours. When ready to grill, toss potato wedges with oil mixture and grill for 12 to 15 minutes or until heated through and edges start to brown.

Brown-Sugar Sweet Potato Wedges

PREP 10 minutes
GRILL 15 minutes

NUTRITION FACTS PER SERVING

Calories 173
Fat 4 g
Cholesterol 4 mg
Sodium 159 mg
Carbohydrates 33 g
Fiber 4 g
Protein 2 g

6	small sweet potatoes (about 6 ounces each)
1	tablespoon butter
¼	cup chopped walnuts
⅓	cup packed light brown sugar
2	tablespoons cider vinegar
½	teaspoon salt
¼	teaspoon black pepper
¼	teaspoon ground allspice

1. Scrub sweet potatoes; pierce with a fork. Place potatoes on paper towels in a microwave oven. Microwave on high about 10 minutes or until partially cooked but still very firm, turning over halfway through cooking. Cool slightly. When sweet potatoes are cool enough to handle, cut potatoes lengthwise in quarters.

2. Meanwhile, in a small skillet melt butter over medium heat. Add walnuts, brown sugar, vinegar, salt, pepper, and allspice; cook and stir about 2 minutes or until the brown sugar is melted. Remove from heat. Brush cut sides of sweet potatoes with the brown sugar mixture, leaving the walnuts in the skillet.

3. For a charcoal grill, grill potatoes, cut sides down, on the rack of an uncovered grill directly over medium coals for 5 minutes.

Turn potatoes to second cut sides on the grill rack. Grill for 5 minutes more. Turn wedges skin sides down; brush cut sides with brown sugar mixture. Grill about 5 minutes more or until sweet potatoes are tender. (For a gas grill, preheat grill. Reduce heat to medium. Place potatoes on grill rack over heat as directed above. Cover and grill as above.)

4. Transfer sweet potatoes to a serving platter. Spoon remaining brown sugar mixture and walnuts over potatoes. **MAKES 8 SERVINGS**

Stovetop Method: Heat a stovetop grill pan over medium-high heat. Cook the sweet potato wedges in grill pan as directed above.

Roasted Apples

PREP 15 minutes
CHILL 24 hours
ROAST 30 minutes
OVEN 350°F

NUTRITION FACTS PER SERVING

Calories 100
Fat 3 g
Cholesterol 3 mg
Sodium 93 mg
Carbohydrates 16 g
Fiber 2 g
Protein 3 g

¾ cup plain lowfat yogurt*
   Nonstick cooking spray
1 teaspoon lemon juice
1 teaspoon honey
¼ teaspoon ground cinnamon
⅛ teaspoon kosher salt
2 medium Granny Smith apples,
   peeled, cored, and halved
2 tablespoons chopped toasted
   hazelnuts**
1 tablespoon snipped dried
   cherries

1. For yogurt cheese, line a sieve or small colander with three layers of 100%-cotton cheesecloth or a clean paper coffee filter. Suspend the lined sieve or colander over a bowl. (Or use a yogurt strainer.) Spoon yogurt into sieve or colander. Cover with plastic wrap. Refrigerate for at least 24 hours. Remove from refrigerator; discard liquid. Transfer yogurt cheese to a bowl; set aside.

2. Preheat oven to 350°F. Lightly coat a small baking sheet with cooking spray; set aside. In a small bowl combine lemon juice, honey, cinnamon, and kosher salt. Brush lemon juice mixture on apple halves. Place apple halves, cut sides down, on the prepared baking sheet.

3. Roast about 30 minutes or until apple halves are lightly browned and tender. Transfer apples to a cutting board. Thinly slice each apple half.

Divide slices among four plates, fanning slices. Serve with yogurt cheese; sprinkle with hazelnuts and dried cherries.
MAKES 4 SERVINGS

*Tip: Use a brand of yogurt that contains no gums, gelatin, or fillers. These ingredients may prevent the whey from separating from the curd to make yogurt cheese.

**Tip: To toast hazelnuts, preheat oven to 350°F. Place the nuts in a shallow baking pan. Bake about 10 minutes or until toasted. Place the warm nuts on a clean kitchen towel. Rub the nuts with the towel to remove the loose skins.

Peachy Baked Beans

PREP 20 minutes
STAND 1 hour
COOK 1 hour
BAKE 1 hour 15 minutes
OVEN 300°F

NUTRITION FACTS PER SERVING

Calories 229
Fat 2 g
Cholesterol 6 mg
Sodium 139 mg
Carbohydrates 43 g
Fiber 10 g
Protein 12 g

1   pound dry white beans, such as Great Northern, cannellini, or navy beans (about 2⅓ cups)
1   to 1½ pounds meaty smoked pork hocks
3   medium peaches, pitted and cut in wedges (about 3 cups)
1   cup chopped onion (1 large)
1   cup peach nectar or apple juice
¼   cup packed brown sugar
2   tablespoons snipped fresh sage or 2 teaspoons dried sage, crushed
½   teaspoon salt
½   teaspoon black pepper
1   or 2 medium peaches, pitted and sliced
    Fresh sage leaves (optional)

1. Rinse beans. In a large Dutch oven or pot combine beans and 8 cups water. Bring to boiling; reduce heat. Simmer for 2 minutes. Remove from heat. Cover and let stand for 1 hour. (Or place beans in water in Dutch oven. Cover and let soak in a cool place overnight.)

2. Drain and rinse beans. Return beans to Dutch oven. Add pork hocks. Stir in 8 cups fresh water. Bring to boiling; reduce heat. Simmer, covered, for 1 to 1½ hours or until beans are tender, stirring occasionally. Remove hocks; set aside. Drain beans. When cool enough to handle, cut meat off bones; coarsely chop meat.

3. Preheat oven to 300°F. In a 2½- to 3-quart casserole combine the beans, meat, the 3 cups peach wedges, and onion. Stir in peach nectar, brown sugar, snipped sage, salt, and pepper.

4. Bake, covered, for 1 hour. Uncover and bake 15 minutes more or until desired consistency, stirring occasionally. Before serving, top with the peach slices and, if desired, fresh sage leaves.
MAKES 10 TO 12 SERVINGS

Summer's Best BBQ Beans

PREP 15 minutes
COOK 25 minutes
STAND 15 minutes

NUTRITION FACTS
PER SERVING

Calories 140
Fat 0 g
Cholesterol 0 mg
Sodium 351 mg
Carbohydrates 32 g
Fiber 8 g
Protein 10 g

Nonstick cooking spray
1 medium onion, halved and thinly sliced
¾ cup chopped green or red sweet pepper (1 medium)
2 cups chopped tomatoes (2 large)
3 15- to 16-ounce cans light red kidney beans, rinsed and drained
1 8-ounce can tomato sauce
1 8-ounce can crushed pineapple, undrained
1 tablespoon Worcestershire sauce
1 tablespoon molasses
Italian (flat-leaf) parsley sprigs (optional)

1. Lightly coat a large saucepan or Dutch oven with cooking spray. Cook onion and sweet pepper in hot pan over medium heat for 5 to 10 minutes or until tender, stirring occasionally. Stir in tomatoes, beans, tomato sauce, undrained pineapple, Worcestershire sauce, and molasses. Bring to boiling; reduce heat. Simmer, covered, for 10 minutes. Uncover and simmer about 10 minutes more or until desired consistency.

2. Transfer beans to a serving bowl. Let stand for 5 to 10 minutes before serving. Sauce will thicken as it stands. If desired, garnish with parsley. **MAKES 10 SERVINGS**

Bulgur-Mushroom Pilaf

PREP 15 minutes
COOK 45 minutes
STAND 5 minutes

NUTRITION FACTS PER SERVING

Calories 197
Fat 7 g
Cholesterol 5 mg
Sodium 328 mg
Carbohydrates 29 g
Fiber 5 g
Protein 7 g

1   tablespoon olive oil
½   cup chopped onion (1 medium)
1   14.5-ounce can chicken broth
1   cup apple juice
½   cup uncooked wild rice, rinsed
2   cups quartered or sliced
     shiitake mushrooms,
     stemmed; cremini
     mushrooms; or button
     mushrooms
½   cup bulgur
¾   cup chopped red or green
     sweet pepper (1 medium)
½   cup snipped fresh Italian
     (flat-leaf) parsley
¼   cup chopped walnuts, toasted
     Freshly cracked black pepper
¼   cup crumbled feta cheese,
     crumbled (1 ounce)

1. In a large saucepan heat olive oil over medium heat. Add onion; cook about 5 minutes or until tender, stirring occasionally. Carefully add broth, apple juice, and wild rice. Bring to boiling; reduce heat. Simmer, covered, for 30 minutes.

2. Stir mushrooms and bulgur into rice mixture. Simmer, covered, for 10 to 15 minutes more or until rice and bulgur are tender and most of the liquid is absorbed. Stir in sweet pepper; remove from heat. Cover and let stand for 5 minutes. Stir in parsley and walnuts. Season with cracked black pepper. Sprinkle with feta cheese. **MAKES 6 SERVINGS**

Couscous with Seven Vegetables

PREP 30 minutes
COOK 15 minutes

NUTRITION FACTS PER SERVING

Calories 159
Fat 2 g
Cholesterol 0 mg
Sodium 134 mg
Carbohydrates 31 g
Fiber 3 g
Protein 5 g

1   tablespoon olive oil
1½ cups slivered yellow onions (2 medium)
2   cloves garlic, minced
1   cup sliced carrots (2 medium)
1   cup cubed, peeled sweet potato (1 small)
2   teaspoons ground turmeric
2   teaspoons ground cumin
½   teaspoon salt
¾   cup water
1   cup sliced yellow summer squash
1   cup sliced zucchini
1   cup chopped green sweet pepper (1 large)
1   cup chopped, seeded tomatoes (2 medium)
1   10-ounce package quick-cooking couscous
½   cup snipped fresh mint

1. In a large saucepan or 4-quart Dutch oven heat oil over medium heat. Add onions and garlic; cook until tender. Add carrots, sweet potato, turmeric, cumin, and salt. Add the water. Bring to boiling; reduce heat. Cook, covered, for 5 minutes, stirring occasionally. Add yellow summer squash, zucchini, and sweet pepper. Cover and cook 5 minutes or until vegetables are tender. Stir in chopped tomatoes.

2. Meanwhile, prepare couscous according to package directions. Transfer couscous to a very large bowl. Add vegetables; stir gently. Stir in mint. Serve immediately.
MAKES 10 SERVINGS

Parmesan-Cornmeal Pancakes

START TO FINISH 25 minutes

NUTRITION FACTS PER PANCAKE

Calories 92
Fat 3 g
Cholesterol 29 mg
Sodium 216 mg
Carbohydrates 12 g
Fiber 1 g
Protein 4 g

1   cup all-purpose flour
¾   cup yellow cornmeal
⅓   cup grated Parmesan cheese
1   tablespoon sugar (optional)
1   teaspoon baking soda
½   teaspoon salt
1¾ cups buttermilk or sour milk*
2   eggs, lightly beaten
⅓   cup finely chopped green
    onions
2   tablespoons vegetable oil

1. In a medium bowl stir together flour, cornmeal, cheese, sugar (if desired), baking soda, and salt. In another medium bowl combine buttermilk, eggs, green onions, and oil. Add buttermilk mixture all at once to flour mixture. Stir just until moistened (batter should be slightly lumpy).

2. For each pancake, pour about ¼ cup batter onto a hot, lightly greased griddle or heavy skillet, spreading batter if necessary. Cook over medium heat for 1 to 2 minutes on each side or until pancakes are golden brown, turning to second side when pancakes have bubbly surfaces and edges are slightly dry.

MAKES ABOUT 16 PANCAKES

*Tip: To make sour milk, place 2 tablespoons lemon juice or vinegar in a 2-cup glass measuring cup. Add enough milk to equal 1¾ cups total liquid. Let mixture stand for 5 minutes before using.

Spinach with Sweet Red Onion

START TO FINISH 25 minutes

NUTRITION FACTS PER SERVING

Calories 88
Fat 3 g
Cholesterol 7 mg
Sodium 153 mg
Carbohydrates 12 g
Fiber 3 g
Protein 1 g

2   tablespoons butter
2   large red onions, halved and sliced (3 cups)
1   cup red wine
¼   cup grenadine syrup or boysenberry syrup
2   tablespoons sugar
¼   teaspoon salt
2   5- to 6-ounce packages fresh baby spinach (16 cups)
    Salt and black pepper

1. In a large nonstick skillet melt butter over medium heat. Add onions; cook for 5 to 8 minutes or until tender, stirring occasionally. Add wine, syrup, sugar, and salt. Bring to boiling; reduce heat. Boil gently, uncovered, about 15 minutes or until the liquid is reduced and syrupy.

2. Meanwhile, place spinach in a very large serving bowl. Spoon the onions over spinach. Toss to combine. Season with salt and pepper. Serve immediately.
MAKES 10 SERVINGS

Chilled Asparagus Salad

PREP 15 minutes
CHILL 6 hours
COOK 3 minutes

NUTRITION FACTS PER SERVING

Calories 119
Fat 7 g
Cholesterol 7 mg
Sodium 181 mg
Carbohydrates 13 g
Fiber 2 g
Protein 3 g

½ cup light mayonnaise
½ teaspoon finely shredded orange peel
⅓ cup orange juice
¼ cup plain fat-free yogurt
⅛ teaspoon lemon-pepper seasoning
1 pound fresh asparagus spears
6 cups torn butterhead (Boston or bibb) lettuce
1 11-ounce can mandarin orange sections, drained
1 small red onion, cut in thin wedges

1. For dressing, in a small bowl combine mayonnaise, orange peel, orange juice, yogurt, and lemon-pepper seasoning. Cover and refrigerate up to 6 hours or until ready to serve.

2. Snap off and discard woody bases from asparagus. If desired, scrape off scales. In a large covered saucepan cook asparagus in a small amount of lightly salted boiling water for 3 to 5 minutes or until crisp-tender; drain. Immediately submerge cooked asparagus in a bowl of ice water to cool quickly. Drain again.

3. Divide lettuce among six salad plates. Arrange asparagus, drained mandarin orange sections, and onion wedges on top of lettuce. Drizzle with dressing.
MAKES 6 SERVINGS

Asian Broccoli Slaw

PREP 10 minutes
CHILL 2 hours or overnight

NUTRITION FACTS PER SERVING

Calories 117
Fat 9 g
Cholesterol 0 mg
Sodium 332 mg
Carbohydrates 9 g
Fiber 3 g
Protein 2 g

2   12-ounce packages shredded broccoli (broccoli slaw mix)
1   cup shredded carrots (2 medium)
⅔   cup sliced green onions (6)
1   8-ounce can sliced water chestnuts, drained
6   tablespoons salad oil
6   tablespoons rice wine vinegar
5   tablespoons reduced-sodium soy sauce
4   teaspoons toasted sesame oil
1   tablespoon sugar
2   teaspoons grated fresh ginger
½   teaspoon salt

1. In large bowl stir together shredded broccoli, carrots, green onions, and water chestnuts.

2. For dressing, in a medium bowl whisk together oil, rice vinegar, soy sauce, sesame oil, sugar, ginger, and salt. Pour dressing over slaw; toss to coat. Cover and chill for 2 hours or overnight.
MAKES 12 SERVINGS

Two-Toned Coleslaw

PREP 20 minutes
CHILL 2 to 48 hours

NUTRITION FACTS PER SERVING

Calories 78
Fat 5 g
Cholesterol 5 mg
Sodium 195 mg
Carbohydrates 10 g
Fiber 2 g
Protein 1 g

⅔ cup light mayonnaise
3 tablespoons cider vinegar
1 tablespoon snipped fresh dill or 1 teaspoon dried dill
½ teaspoon salt
½ teaspoon coarsely ground black pepper
7 cups shredded green cabbage (1 medium)
3 medium apples, cored and thinly sliced
1 cup chopped sweet onion (1 large)
   Fresh dill sprigs (optional)

1. For dressing, in a very large bowl stir together the mayonnaise, vinegar, dill, salt, and pepper.

2. Add cabbage, apples, and onion to dressing in bowl; toss to coat. Cover and refrigerate for 2 to 48 hours. If desired, garnish with fresh dill sprigs. **MAKES 12 SERVINGS**

Vegetable Potato Salad with Dill

PREP 45 minutes
CHILL 2 to 24 hours

NUTRITION FACTS PER SERVING

Calories 117
Fat 3 g
Cholesterol 4 mg
Sodium 84 mg
Carbohydrates 20 g
Fiber 3 g
Protein 4 g

1½ pounds tiny new potatoes, quartered (about 18)
1 pound fresh asparagus spears or fresh green beans, cut in 1-inch pieces (2⅔ cups)
2 medium carrots, cut in thin matchstick-size strips (1 cup)
⅓ cup light mayonnaise
⅓ cup plain lowfat yogurt
¼ cup thinly sliced green onions (2)
2 tablespoons white wine vinegar
1 tablespoon snipped fresh dill or 1 teaspoon dried dill
¼ teaspoon coarsely ground black pepper
Fresh dill sprigs (optional)

1. Bring 1 cup water and ¼ teaspoon salt to boiling in a large saucepan. Add potatoes and cook, covered, for 8 minutes. Add asparagus and carrots; cover and cook for 4 to 6 minutes more or just until potatoes are tender and asparagus and carrots are crisp-tender. Drain well. Arrange vegetables in a shallow serving bowl. Cover and refrigerate for 2 to 24 hours.

2. For dressing, in a medium bowl stir together mayonnaise, yogurt, green onions, vinegar, the 1 tablespoon fresh dill or 1 teaspoon dried dill, and the pepper. Cover and refrigerate up to 24 hours. Just before serving, spoon dressing over vegetables. If desired, garnish with fresh dill sprigs. **MAKES 8 SERVINGS**

Berry-Best Salad

START TO FINISH **15 minutes**

NUTRITION FACTS PER SERVING

Calories 86
Fat 4 g
Cholesterol 0 mg
Sodium 208 mg
Carbohydrates 13 g
Fiber 3 g
Protein 1 g

¼ cup orange juice
1 tablespoon salad oil
2 teaspoons honey mustard or Dijon mustard
1 teaspoon sugar
¼ teaspoon salt
4 cups torn lettuce
1½ cups fresh blueberries, raspberries, and/or quartered strawberries
2 tablespoons bite-size cheese crackers or 1 tablespoon sunflower kernels

1. For dressing, in a screw-top jar combine orange juice, oil, mustard, sugar, and salt. Cover and shake well. Place lettuce in a medium bowl. Drizzle with dressing; toss gently to coat.

2. Divide lettuce among four salad plates. Top with berries and sprinkle with crackers.
MAKES 4 SERVINGS

Summer Strawberry Salad

CHILL 1 hour
START TO FINISH 20 minutes

NUTRITION FACTS
PER SERVING

Calories 111
Fat 4 g
Cholesterol 0 mg
Sodium 35 mg
Carbohydrates 20 g
Fiber 4 g
Protein 2 g

6 cups chopped romaine lettuce
(½ of a large head)
3 cups sliced fresh strawberries
2 cups cubed fresh pineapple
(½ of a small)
¾ cup sliced banana (1 medium)
¼ cup water
¼ cup canned unsweetened
cream of coconut
2 tablespoons lemon juice
1 tablespoon yellow mustard
½ teaspoon ground ginger
¼ cup sliced almonds, toasted
(see tip, page 80) (optional)

1. In a very large bowl toss together romaine, strawberries, pineapple, and banana. If desired, cover and refrigerate up to 1 hour.

2. For dressing, in a small bowl whisk together the water, the cream of coconut, lemon juice, mustard, and ginger.

3. To serve, pour dressing over greens; toss to coat. If desired, sprinkle with almonds.
MAKES 6 TO 8 SERVINGS

Apple-Rice Salad

PREP 20 minutes
COOK 40 minutes
CHILL 2 hours

NUTRITION FACTS PER SERVING

Calories 191
Fat 6 g
Cholesterol 0 mg
Sodium 143 mg
Carbohydrates 32 g
Fiber 4 g
Protein 4 g

1¾ cups water
⅓ cup uncooked brown rice
⅓ cup uncooked wild rice, rinsed and drained
2 cups chopped apples (3 medium)
1 cup thinly sliced celery (2 stalks)
¼ cup sunflower kernels
¼ cup dried currants or dried cranberries
1 recipe Orange-Balsamic Vinaigrette
Lettuce leaves (optional)

1. In a medium saucepan combine the water, brown rice, and wild rice. Bring to boiling; reduce heat. Simmer, covered, for 40 to 45 minutes or until rice is tender. Drain off any liquid. Transfer to a large bowl; cover and refrigerate for at least 2 hours.

2. Stir apples, celery, sunflower kernels, and currants into cooked rice. Drizzle with Orange-Balsamic Vinaigrette; toss gently to coat. If desired, serve on lettuce-lined salad plates. **MAKES 6 SERVINGS**

Orange-Balsamic Vinaigrette:
In a screw-top jar combine 2 tablespoons balsamic vinegar; 1 tablespoon olive oil; 2 teaspoons honey; 2 teaspoons brown mustard or Dijon mustard; 2 teaspoons finely shredded orange peel; 1 clove garlic, minced; and ¼ teaspoon salt. Cover and shake well.

CHAPTER 13

Appetizers, Beverages & Snacks

Sweet-and-Sour Turkey Meatballs

PREP 50 minutes
BAKE 15 minutes
OVEN 400°F

NUTRITION FACTS PER 3 MEATBALLS

Calories 82
Fat 5 g
Cholesterol 39 mg
Sodium 152 mg
Carbohydrates 2 g
Fiber 0 g
Protein 8 g

Nonstick cooking spray
1   egg, lightly beaten
8   slices bacon, crisp-cooked and finely crumbled (about ½ cup)
½   cup fine dry bread crumbs
½   cup snipped fresh basil
¼   cup plain yogurt or sour cream
½   teaspoon black pepper
¼   teaspoon salt
2   pounds uncooked ground turkey
1   recipe Sweet-and-Sour Sauce

1. Preheat oven to 400°F. Line two 15×10×1-inch baking pans with foil. Lightly coat foil with cooking spray; set aside.

2. In a large bowl stir together egg, bacon, bread crumbs, basil, yogurt, pepper, and salt. Add ground turkey; mix well. Shape mixture into 75 one-inch meatballs (about 1 tablespoon each). Place on prepared pans.

3. Bake on separate oven racks for 15 to 20 minutes or until done (165°F).*

4. Meanwhile, prepare Sweet-and-Sour Sauce. Transfer meatballs to saucepan with Sweet-and-Sour Sauce. Stir gently to coat.
MAKES 25 SERVINGS

Sweet-and-Sour Sauce: In a large saucepan combine one 10-ounce bottle sweet-and-sour sauce; ⅓ cup mango nectar; 1 teaspoon chili powder; 1 large clove garlic, minced; ½ teaspoon finely shredded lime peel; and ¼ teaspoon salt. Heat through over medium-low heat, stirring occasionally.

*Tip: The internal color of a meatball is not a reliable doneness indicator. A turkey or chicken meatball cooked to 165°F is safe, regardless of color. To measure doneness, insert an instant-read thermometer into a few of the meatballs.

Pizza Meatballs

PREP 25 minutes
BAKE 20 minutes
OVEN 350°F

NUTRITION FACTS PER 2 MEATBALLS

Calories 122
Fat 4 g
Cholesterol 29 mg
Sodium 225 mg
Carbohydrates 8 g
Fiber 1 g
Protein 12 g

Nonstick cooking spray
1 cup fresh cremini or button mushrooms, finely chopped
½ cup finely chopped green sweet pepper (1 small)
½ cup finely chopped onion (1 medium)
2 cloves garlic, minced
¾ cup soft whole wheat bread crumbs (about 1 slice)
1 egg white, lightly beaten
1½ teaspoons dried Italian seasoning, crushed
⅛ teaspoon black pepper
8 ounces uncooked bulk turkey sausage
8 ounces uncooked ground turkey breast
1 cup shredded reduced-fat Italian blend cheeses (4 ounces)
1½ cups purchased low-sodium pasta sauce

1. Preheat oven to 350°F. Coat a large nonstick skillet with cooking spray; heat skillet over medium heat. Add mushrooms, green pepper, and onion. Cook for 5 to 8 minutes or until vegetables are tender, stirring frequently. Stir in garlic; set aside.

2. In a large bowl combine bread crumbs, egg white, Italian seasoning, and black pepper. Stir in mushroom mixture. Add turkey sausage, turkey breast, and cheese. Mix well.

3. Line a 15×10×1-inch baking pan with foil. Spray foil with cooking spray; set aside. Using wet hands, shape meat mixture into twenty-four 1½-inch diameter meatballs. Place meatballs in prepared pan. Bake about 20 minutes or until done (165°F).*

4. Meanwhile, in a small saucepan heat pasta sauce over medium heat, stirring occasionally. Serve with meatballs. MAKES 12 SERVINGS

*Tip: The internal color of a meatball is not a reliable doneness indicator. A turkey or chicken meatball cooked to 165°F is safe, regardless of color. To measure doneness, insert an instant-read thermometer into a few of the meatballs.

Shrimp-Avocado Nachos

PREP 20 minutes
CHILL 10 minutes to 1 hour

NUTRITION FACTS
PER SERVING

Calories 140
Fat 8 g
Cholesterol 43 mg
Sodium 134 mg
Carbohydrates 11 g
Fiber 4 g
Protein 7 g

16 fresh or frozen peeled cooked medium shrimp
1   medium avocado, halved, seeded, peeled, and chopped
1   small plum tomato, seeded and chopped
2   tablespoons bottled green salsa or salsa
1½ teaspoons snipped fresh oregano
1   clove garlic, minced
16 baked tortilla chips

1. Thaw shrimp, if frozen. Rinse shrimp; pat dry with paper towels. In a medium bowl combine shrimp, avocado, tomato, salsa, oregano, and garlic. Cover and refrigerate for 10 minutes to 1 hour.

2. Arrange chips on a serving platter. Spoon 1 shrimp and some salsa on each chip. Serve immediately. **MAKES 4 SERVINGS**

Shrimp Pinwheels

PREP 30 minutes
CHILL up to 4 hours

NUTRITION FACTS PER SERVING

Calories 82
Fat 4 g
Cholesterol 19 mg
Sodium 137 mg
Carbohydrates 8 g
Fiber 1 g
Protein 4 g

1 avocado, halved, seeded, and peeled
½ of a 8-ounce package cream cheese, softened
¼ cup ketchup
1 tablespoon prepared horseradish
1 teaspoon finely shredded lemon peel
2 tablespoons lemon juice
½ teaspoon chili powder
6 9- to 10-inch tomato, spinach, and/or plain flour tortillas
3 cups shredded spinach leaves
⅔ cup smoked almonds, chopped
10 ounces cooked peeled and deveined shrimp, chopped

1. In a medium bowl mash avocado with potato masher or fork. Add cream cheese; stir until smooth. Stir in ketchup, horseradish, lemon peel, lemon juice, and chili powder.

2. For each pinwheel, spread ¼ cup avocado mixture on a tortilla to within 1 inch of edges. Top with a layer of spinach. Sprinkle with a scant 2 tablespoons almonds and about ¼ cup shrimp. Roll up tightly.

3. Place rolled tortillas on a tray or platter. Cover and refrigerate up to 4 hours. To serve, cut each rolled tortilla in 1-inch slices, trimming ends. If necessary, secure with party picks. Arrange pinwheels on a serving platter.

MAKES ABOUT 36 PINWHEELS

Shrimp Crostini

START TO FINISH 20 minutes

NUTRITION FACTS PER CROSTINI

Calories 52
Fat 2 g
Cholesterol 28 mg
Sodium 112 mg
Carbohydrates 4 g
Fiber 0 g
Protein 4 g

16 large fresh or frozen peeled
    and deveined cooked shrimp
    (about 8 ounces total)
⅓ cup shredded fresh basil
1 tablespoon olive oil
2 teaspoons white wine vinegar
¼ teaspoon salt
¼ teaspoon black pepper
16 ¼-inch slices baguette-style
    French bread
2 large cloves garlic, halved
4 teaspoons olive oil

1. Thaw shrimp, if frozen. Rinse shrimp; pat dry with paper towels. Preheat broiler. In a medium bowl combine shrimp, basil, the 1 tablespoon oil, vinegar, salt, and pepper; set aside.

2. Arrange bread slices on baking sheet. Broil 3 to 4 inches from heat about 2 minutes or until lightly toasted, turning once halfway through broiling. Rub one side of toast with cut sides of garlic cloves; brush with the 4 teaspoons oil. Arrange toast, brushed sides up, on serving platter.

3. Using a slotted spoon, spoon a shrimp onto each toast. Serve immediately. **MAKES 16 CROSTINI**

Tomato, Basil, and Mozzarella Crostini

START TO FINISH **20 minutes**
OVEN **425°F**

NUTRITION FACTS
PER CROSTINI

Calories 95
Fat 5 g
Cholesterol 6 mg
Sodium 169 mg
Carbohydrates 9 g
Fiber 1 g
Protein 3 g

1   8-ounce loaf baguette-style
    French bread, cut in ½-inch
    slices
2   to 3 tablespoons olive oil
⅛   teaspoon black pepper
4   ounces fresh mozzarella
    cheese, thinly sliced
12 red or yellow cherry
    tomatoes, halved
12 yellow or red pear-shape
    tomatoes, halved
1   tablespoon snipped or
    shredded fresh basil
2   tablespoons olive oil
¼   teaspoon salt

1. Preheat oven to 425°F. For
crostini, lightly brush both sides of
bread with the 2 to 3 tablespoons
olive oil; sprinkle with pepper.
Place on a large baking sheet.
Toast for 5 to 7 minutes or until
crisp and light brown, turning
once halfway through toasting.

2. Top crostini with mozzarella
cheese, tomatoes, and basil.
Drizzle with the 2 tablespoons
olive oil; sprinkle with salt.
MAKES 16 CROSTINI

Herbed Feta Cheese Spread

START TO FINISH 10 minutes

NUTRITION FACTS
PER SERVING

Calories 119
Fat 8 g
Cholesterol 18 mg
Sodium 245 mg
Carbohydrates 8 g
Fiber 0 g
Protein 3 g

1   8-ounce package reduced-fat
    cream cheese (Neufchâtel)
1   4-ounce package crumbled
    feta cheese with garlic and
    herb
1   tablespoon milk
    Several dashes black pepper
    Pita chips, sweet pepper
    wedges, other vegetable
    dippers, or crackers

1. In a small mixing bowl stir
together cream cheese, feta cheese,
milk, and black pepper. Beat with
an electric mixer on medium until
mixture is well combined and of
spreading consistency. Serve with
pepper wedges, vegetable dippers,
or crackers.
MAKES 15 TO 20 SERVINGS

Arugula-Cannellini Bean Dip

START TO FINISH **10 minutes**

NUTRITION FACTS
PER 2-TABLESPOONS DIP

Calories 64
Fat 5 g
Cholesterol 0 mg
Sodium 154 mg
Carbohydrates 6 g
Fiber 2 g
Protein 2 g

3   cups lightly packed arugula leaves
¼   cup olive oil
2   tablespoons lemon juice
2   cloves garlic, halved
½   teaspoon salt
1   15-ounce can cannellini beans (white kidney beans), rinsed and drained
½   cup chopped seeded tomato (1 medium)
    Assorted crackers, toasted baguette slices, or cut-up vegetables

1. In a food processor or blender combine arugula, olive oil, lemon juice, garlic, and salt. Cover and process or blend until nearly smooth. Add beans. Cover and process or blend just until coarsely chopped and mixture is combined (mixture should be slightly chunky).

2. Transfer bean mixture to a serving bowl. Gently stir in tomato. Serve immediately or cover and refrigerate up to 24 hours. Serve with crackers, baguette slices, or vegetables.
MAKES 1½ CUPS (ABOUT 12 TWO-TABLESPOON SERVINGS)

Avocado-Feta Cheese Salsa

PREP 20 minutes
CHILL 2 to 6 hours

NUTRITION FACTS PER ¼-CUP SALSA

Calories 63
Fat 5 g
Cholesterol 8 mg
Sodium 106 mg
Carbohydrates 3 g
Fiber 1 g
Protein 2 g

⅔ cup chopped plum tomatoes (2 medium)
1 avocado, halved, seeded, peeled, and chopped
¼ cup finely chopped red onion
1 tablespoon snipped fresh parsley
1 tablespoon snipped fresh oregano
1 tablespoon olive oil
1 tablespoon red or white wine vinegar
1 clove garlic, minced
4 ounces feta cheese, coarsely crumbled
  Pita chips or tortilla chips

1. In a medium bowl combine tomatoes, avocado, red onion, parsley, oregano, olive oil, vinegar, and garlic. Stir gently to mix. Gently stir in feta cheese. Cover and chill for 2 to 6 hours. Serve with pita chips or tortilla chips.
MAKES 3 CUPS (SIX ¼-CUP SERVINGS)

Basil Guacamole

START TO FINISH **25 minutes**

NUTRITION FACTS PER 2-TABLESPOONS DIP

Calories 40
Fat 4 g
Cholesterol 0 mg
Sodium 40 mg
Carbohydrates 2 g
Fiber 1 g
Protein 1 g

2 ripe, medium avocados, halved, seeded, and peeled
¾ cup snipped fresh basil
½ cup chopped seeded tomato
2 tablespoons chopped green onion (1)
1 tablespoon lime juice
¼ to ½ teaspoon salt
¼ teaspoon crushed red pepper or few drops bottled hot pepper sauce
   Tortilla chips

1. In a large mortar mash avocados with a pestle. (Or in a medium bowl mash avocados with a fork.) Stir in basil, tomato, green onion, lime juice, salt, and crushed red pepper. Serve immediately with tortilla chips. **MAKES 2 CUPS (ABOUT 16 TWO-TABLESPOON SERVINGS)**

Creamy Dill Dip

PREP 10 minutes
CHILL 1 hour

NUTRITION FACTS
PER 2-TABLESPOONS DIP

Calories 100
Fat 8 g
Cholesterol 28 mg
Sodium 204 mg
Carbohydrates 2 g
Fiber 0 g
Protein 4 g

1 8-ounce package reduced-fat cream cheese (Neufchâtel), softened
1 8-ounce carton light sour cream
2 tablespoons finely chopped green onion (1)
2 to 3 tablespoons snipped fresh dill or 2 to 3 teaspoons dried dill
½ teaspoon seasoned salt or salt
   Milk (optional)
   Fresh dill sprig (optional)
   Assorted spring vegetable dippers (such as baby carrots, radishes, pea pods, blanched asparagus spears, and/or jicama strips)

1. In a medium mixing bowl beat cream cheese, sour cream, green onion, the snipped dill, and salt with an electric mixer on low until fluffy. Cover and refrigerate at least 1 hour.

2. If dip is too thick after chilling, stir in 1 to 2 tablespoons milk until dipping consistency. If desired, garnish with a dill sprig. Serve with vegetable dippers.
MAKES 2¼ CUPS (ABOUT 10 TWO-TABLESPOON SERVINGS)

Make-Ahead Directions:
Prepare dip as directed in Step 1. Cover and refrigerate up to 24 hours. Cut up vegetable dippers and place in resealable plastic bags; refrigerate up to 24 hours.

Summer Fruits with Ricotta Dip

START TO FINISH 15 minutes

NUTRITION FACTS PER SERVING

Calories 94
Fat 4 g
Cholesterol 14 mg
Sodium 72 mg
Carbohydrates 12 g
Fiber 1 g
Protein 3 g

½ cup lowfat ricotta cheese
4 ounces cream cheese, softened
3 tablespoons orange juice
2 tablespoons powdered sugar
1 6-ounce container vanilla lowfat yogurt
6 cups assorted fresh fruit (such as sliced plums, cubed cantaloupe, cubed honeydew melon, pitted dark sweet cherries, and/or sliced strawberries)

1. For dip, in a food processor or blender combine ricotta cheese, cream cheese, orange juice, and powdered sugar. Cover and process or blend until smooth.

2. In a medium bowl stir together cheese mixture and yogurt. Serve immediately or cover and refrigerate up to 24 hours. Serve with fruit. **MAKES 12 SERVINGS**

Wasabi Party Mix

PREP 15 minutes

NUTRITION FACTS PER ¼-CUP SERVING

Calories 99
Fat 6 g
Cholesterol 0 mg
Sodium 134 mg
Carbohydrates 9 g
Fiber 1 g
Protein 3 g

5 cups wasabi-flavor dehydrated peas*
4 cups bite-size toasted rice cracker mix
4 cups sesame sticks
4 cups honey-roasted peanuts
2 cups shredded coconut

1. In a very large bowl stir together all ingredients. Store in an airtight container at room temperature up to 2 weeks or in the freezer up to 4 months. **MAKES 80 SERVINGS**

*Tip: To make wasabi-flavor peas, place 5 cups of dried peas in a large bowl. Lightly coat peas with nonstick cooking spray. Sprinkle with 2 to 3 teaspoons wasabi powder; toss to coat.

Savory Bites

PREP 10 minutes
BAKE 15 minutes
OVEN 300°F

NUTRITION FACTS
PER SERVING

Calories 70
Fat 2 g
Cholesterol 0 mg
Sodium 109 mg
Carbohydrates 12 g
Fiber 1 g
Protein 2 g

1   5¼-ounce package plain melba
    toast rounds (3 cups)
4   teaspoons olive oil
2   teaspoons white wine
    Worcestershire sauce
2   teaspoons water
½   teaspoon dried basil, crushed
¼   teaspoon garlic powder
    Dash cayenne pepper

1. Preheat oven to 300°F. Place toast rounds in a medium bowl; set aside. In a small bowl stir together olive oil, white wine Worcestershire sauce, the water, basil, garlic powder, and cayenne pepper. Drizzle oil mixture over toast rounds, tossing to coat. Spread toast rounds in an even layer in a shallow baking pan.

2. Bake for 15 minutes. Cool in pan on a wire rack. Store in an airtight container at room temperature up to 1 week.
MAKES 10 SERVINGS

Easy Olive Focaccia

PREP 20 minutes
BAKE 20 minutes
COOL 10 minutes
OVEN 375°F

NUTRITION FACTS PER SERVING

Calories 73
Fat 2 g
Cholesterol 8 mg
Sodium 166 mg
Carbohydrates 11 g
Fiber 0 g
Protein 2 g

1 16-ounce package hot roll mix
3 tablespoons olive oil
2 cloves garlic, minced
1 tablespoon snipped fresh rosemary
½ to 1 teaspoon kosher salt
¼ teaspoon black pepper
½ cup crumbled blue cheese (2 ounces)
½ cup chopped pitted ripe olives

1. Lightly grease a 15×10×1-inch baking pan; set aside.

2. Prepare hot roll mix according to package directions, except substitute 2 tablespoons of the olive oil for the butter or margarine called for on the package. Knead dough and allow to rest as directed.

3. Preheat oven to 375°F. On a lightly floured surface, roll dough in a 15×10-inch rectangle. Carefully transfer dough to prepared baking pan. Use your fingers to push dough into corners and sides of pan. Using your fingertips, randomly press indentations into dough.

4. In a small bowl stir together the remaining 1 tablespoon olive oil and the garlic; brush on dough. In another small bowl stir together the rosemary, salt, and pepper; sprinkle on dough. Sprinkle dough with blue cheese and olives; gently press cheese and olives into the dough.

5. Bake about 20 minutes or until golden. Cool in pan on a wire rack for 10 minutes. Using a wide spatula, lift focaccia from baking pan; place on a wire rack and cool completely. Serve within 2 hours.
MAKES 32 SERVINGS

Make-Ahead Directions: Place cooled focaccia in an airtight container or freezer bag; seal. Freeze up to 3 months. To reheat, wrap loosely in foil. Heat in a 350°F oven for 20 to 25 minutes or until warmed through.

Spicy Cheddar Twists

PREP **45 minutes**
BAKE **10 minutes**
OVEN **425°F**

NUTRITION FACTS PER 5-INCH TWIST

Calories 51
Fat 4 g
Cholesterol 3 mg
Sodium 53 mg
Carbohydrates 3 g
Fiber 0 g
Protein 1 g

1   teaspoon paprika
½   teaspoon garlic powder
½   teaspoon onion powder
½   teaspoon ground ginger
½   teaspoon ground cardamom
      (optional)
⅛   to ¼ teaspoon cayenne pepper
1   egg white
1   tablespoon water
1   17.3-ounce package (2 sheets)
      frozen puff pastry, thawed
1½ cups shredded smoked or
      regular cheddar cheese
      (6 ounces)

1. Preheat oven to 425°F. In a small bowl stir together paprika, garlic powder, onion powder, ginger, cardamom (if using), and cayenne pepper; set aside. In a small bowl gently beat egg white with the water; set aside. Lightly grease baking sheets; set aside.

2. On a lightly floured surface, unfold pastry sheets. Brush each sheet with some of the egg white mixture; sprinkle each with ¼ cup of the shredded cheese. Fold sheets in half. Using a rolling pin, roll each folded sheet in a 12×8-inch rectangle.

3. Brush tops with more of the egg white mixture; sprinkle each with ½ cup of the remaining cheese. Sprinkle evenly with spice mixture. Fold in half; roll each sheet in a 14×5-inch rectangle, pressing edges together to seal.

4. Cut each rectangle crosswise in ½-inch-wide strips (or cut lengthwise for long twists). Twist ends of each strip in opposite directions several times. Place twists on prepared baking sheets, pressing ends of strips onto the baking sheet. Lightly brush twists with remaining egg white mixture.

5. Bake for 10 to 12 minutes or until brown. Serve warm or cooled to room temperature.*
MAKES 56 (5-INCH) OR 20 (14-INCH) TWISTS

*__Tip:__ You can make these twists an hour or two ahead. To reheat, place twists in a single layer on a baking sheet. Reheat in a 350°F oven about 5 minutes.

Coconut Lemonade

PREP **10 minutes**
CHILL **4 to 24 hours**

NUTRITION FACTS PER SERVING

Calories 150
Fat 0 g
Cholesterol 0 mg
Sodium 7 mg
Carbohydrates 39 g
Fiber 2 g
Protein 1 g

3   cups water
⅔   cup lemon juice
½   cup sugar
2   tablespoons coconut beverage
     flavoring syrup (such as
     Monin or Torani) or cream
     of coconut
½   cup frozen unsweetened
     blueberries
½   cup frozen red raspberries
1   small fresh carambola (star
     fruit), thinly sliced crosswise
     Ice cubes (optional)

1. In a large bowl combine the water, lemon juice, sugar, and coconut syrup. Stir until sugar is well dissolved. Cover and refrigerate for 4 to 24 hours.

2. To serve, transfer lemonade to a serving bowl or pitcher. Add blueberries, raspberries, and carambola. If desired, serve over ice cubes. **MAKES 4 SERVINGS**

Cranberry Apple Crush

START TO FINISH 15 minutes

NUTRITION FACTS PER SERVING

Calories 182
Fat 0 g
Cholesterol 0 mg
Sodium 28 mg
Carbohydrates 46 g
Fiber 0 g
Protein 0 g

5   cups apple cider or apple juice
5   cups cranberry juice
1½ cups guava juice or mango
    nectar
¼   cup lime juice
1   teaspoon ground ginger
½   teaspoon ground cinnamon
½   teaspoon ground allspice
    Honey (optional)
    Lime slices (optional)

1. In a 4-quart Dutch oven combine apple cider, cranberry juice, guava juice, lime juice, ginger, cinnamon, and allspice. Bring to boiling; reduce heat. Simmer, uncovered, for 5 minutes, stirring occasionally. If desired, sweeten to taste with honey.

2. To serve, pour into mugs. If desired, garnish with lime slices.
MAKES 8 TO 10 SERVINGS

Apricot Slush

PREP 15 minutes
STAND 30 minutes
FREEZE 24 hours

NUTRITION FACTS PER SERVING

Calories 115
Fat 0 g
Cholesterol 0 mg
Sodium 9 mg
Carbohydrates 29 g
Fiber 1 g
Protein 1 g

1   46-ounce bottle apricot nectar
3   cups pineapple juice
1   12-ounce can frozen orange juice concentrate, thawed
⅓   cup frozen lemonade concentrate, thawed
1   2-liter bottle ginger ale, chilled
    Apricot slices (optional)

1. In a 3-quart plastic freezer container combine apricot nectar, pineapple juice, orange juice concentrate, and lemonade concentrate. Seal and freeze at least 24 hours or up to 1 week.

2. To serve, let frozen mixture stand at room temperature for 30 minutes. Scrape into a slush. For each serving, fill a glass two-thirds with slush. Carefully add ginger ale, stirring gently to mix. If desired, garnish with an apricot slice. **MAKES ABOUT 24 SERVINGS**

Pomegranate Fizzes

PREP 15 minutes
CHILL 8 to 24 hours

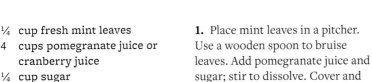

NUTRITION FACTS PER SERVING

Calories 49
Fat 0 g
Cholesterol 0 mg
Sodium 15 mg
Carbohydrates 12 g
Fiber 0 g
Protein 1 g

¼ cup fresh mint leaves
4 cups pomegranate juice or cranberry juice
¼ cup sugar
Ice
1 2-liter bottle diet lemon-lime carbonated beverage or three 750-milliliter bottles champagne, chilled
Mint leaves
Pomegranate seeds (arils)

1. Place mint leaves in a pitcher. Use a wooden spoon to bruise leaves. Add pomegranate juice and sugar; stir to dissolve. Cover and chill for 8 to 24 hours.

2. Use a slotted spoon to remove mint leaves; discard.* For each serving, fill a glass with ice. Pour ¼ cup of the juice over ice. Top with about ½ cup carbonated beverage. Garnish with mint leaves and pomegranate seeds.

MAKES 16 SERVINGS

*Tip: After the mint has been removed, the syrup may be stored in the refrigerator up to 48 hours.

Spiced Fruit Tea

PREP 15 minutes
CHILL 4 hours to 3 days
FREEZE 4 hours

NUTRITION FACTS PER SERVING

Calories 157
Fat 0 g
Cholesterol 0 mg
Sodium 9 mg
Carbohydrates 39 g
Fiber 0 g
Protein 1 g

5   cups boiling water
5   bags orange-flavor spiced
    herb tea
⅓   cup sugar
¼   teaspoon ground cinnamon
1   46-ounce can unsweetened
    pineapple juice
2   cups cranberry juice
⅓   cup lime juice
    Kumquat slices (optional)
    Orange slices, mint sprigs,
    lime slices, and/or fresh
    pineapple chunks (optional)

1. Pour the boiling water into a very large bowl. Add the tea bags. Let steep for 5 minutes. Remove and discard tea bags. Stir in sugar and cinnamon until sugar is dissolved. Stir in pineapple juice, cranberry juice, and lime juice. Remove 3 cups of the juice. Cover and refrigerate the remaining juice at least 4 hours or up to 3 days.

2. Pour the 3 cups of juice into two clean ice cube trays, adding kumquat slices, if desired. Cover and freeze until firm.

3. To serve, divide prepared ice cubes among glasses. Add chilled juice. If desired, garnish with fruit and/or mint.
MAKES 8 TO 10 SERVINGS

Chocolate Heart-Shape Cakes

PREP 35 minutes
BAKE 30 minutes
COOL 1 hour
OVEN 350°F

NUTRITION FACTS
PER SERVING

Calories 202
Fat 7 g
Cholesterol 0 mg
Sodium 41 mg
Carbohydrates 35 g
Fiber 2 g
Protein 8 g

¾   cup granulated sugar
½   cup water
4   ounces bittersweet chocolate,
     chopped
2   tablespoons refrigerated or
     frozen egg product, thawed,
     or 2 egg yolks, lightly beaten
1   teaspoon vanilla
⅓   cup all-purpose flour
¼   cup unsweetened cocoa
     powder
¼   cup ground flax seeds
¼   teaspoon baking powder
5   egg whites
¼   cup apricot spreadable fruit
2   tablespoons sliced almonds,
     toasted (see tip, page 80) and
     coarsely chopped
     Powdered sugar (optional)
     Fresh raspberries (optional)
     Fresh mint leaves (optional)
     Slivered almonds (optional)

1. Preheat oven to 350°F. Grease and lightly flour a 9×9×2-inch baking pan; set aside. In a medium saucepan stir together granulated sugar and the water. Cook and stir over medium heat until sugar is dissolved and mixture nearly boils. Remove from heat. Stir in chocolate until melted. Place egg product in a large bowl. Gradually stir in chocolate mixture and vanilla (mixture may appear slightly grainy). Set aside.

2. In a small bowl stir together flour, cocoa powder, flax seeds, and baking powder. Stir flour mixture into chocolate until smooth. In a medium mixing bowl beat egg whites with mixer on medium to high until stiff peaks form (tips stand straight). Gradually stir a small amount of the beaten egg whites into chocolate to lighten. Fold in the remaining beaten egg whites. Pour batter into the prepared pan, spreading evenly.

3. Bake about 30 minutes or until a toothpick inserted near center comes out clean. Cool in pan on a wire rack for 10 minutes. Remove cake from pan; cool completely on rack.

4. Transfer cake to a cutting board. Using a 3¼-inch heart-shape cookie cutter, cut six individual cakes. For filling, in a small bowl combine spreadable fruit and almonds. Spread filling on three of the cakes; top with the remaining three cakes. If desired, sprinkle with powdered sugar and garnish with raspberries, mint, and almonds. To serve, cut each cake in half. **MAKES 6 SERVINGS**

Tip: If desired, prepare and cut individual cakes as directed except do not fill and stack cakes. Serve single-layer cakes with toppings, filling, spread, and garnishes.

Citrus Angel Cake

PREP 50 minutes
BAKE 40 minutes
COOL 2 hours
OVEN 350°F

NUTRITION FACTS PER SERVING

Calories 152
Fat 0 g
Cholesterol 0 mg
Sodium 51 mg
Carbohydrates 34 g
Fiber 0 g
Protein 4 g

1½ cups egg whites (10 to 12 large)
1½ cups powdered sugar
1 cup cake flour or all-purpose flour
1 teaspoon cream of tartar
3 tablespoons frozen juice concentrate (limeade, lemonade, or orange juice), thawed
¾ cup granulated sugar

1. Allow egg whites to stand at room temperature for 30 minutes. Meanwhile, remove top oven rack; preheat oven to 350°F. Sift powdered sugar and flour together three times; set aside.

2. In an extra-large mixing bowl combine egg whites and cream of tartar. Beat with mixer on medium until soft peaks form (tips curl). Add juice concentrate. Gradually add granulated sugar, about 2 tablespoons at a time, beating on high until stiff peaks form (tips stand straight).

3. Sift about one-fourth of the flour mixture over beaten egg whites; fold in gently. Repeat, folding in the remaining flour mixture by fourths.

4. Pour batter into an ungreased 10-inch tube pan. Gently cut through batter with a narrow metal spatula to remove any large air pockets. Bake on the lowest oven rack for 40 to 45 minutes or until top springs back when lightly touched. Immediately invert cake; cool completely in the inverted pan.*

5. Loosen side and center of cake from pan; remove cake. Using a serrated knife, cut into wedges.
MAKES 12 SERVINGS

*Tip: If the cake has risen higher than the pan, invert it over a jar or bottle to prevent the top of the cake from touching the countertop.

Date-Ginger Cake

PREP 25 minutes
BAKE 30 minutes
OVEN 350°F

NUTRITION FACTS PER SERVING

Calories 247
Fat 6 g
Cholesterol 1 mg
Sodium 85 mg
Carbohydrates 46 g
Fiber 2 g
Protein 4 g

1   cup all-purpose flour
1   teaspoon baking powder
¼   teaspoon baking soda
½   cup sugar
¼   cup vegetable oil
1   teaspoon grated fresh ginger
    or ½ teaspoon ground ginger
½   cup orange or lemon low-fat
    yogurt
¼   cup refrigerated or frozen egg
    product, thawed, or 1 egg,
    lightly beaten
2   tablespoons fat-free milk
¾   cup pitted whole dates,
    snipped
2   tablespoons all-purpose flour
1   recipe Orange Sauce

1. Preheat oven to 350°F. Grease and lightly flour an 8×8×2-inch baking pan; set aside. In a small bowl stir together the 1 cup flour, baking powder, and baking soda; set aside.

2. In a medium bowl combine sugar, oil, and ginger. Stir in yogurt, egg product, and milk. Add flour mixture to yogurt mixture, stirring just until combined.

3. In a small bowl combine dates and the 2 tablespoons flour; toss gently to coat. Fold into batter. Pour batter into the prepared pan, spreading evenly.

4. Bake for 30 to 35 minutes or until a toothpick inserted in center comes out clean. Serve warm with Orange Sauce. **MAKES 9 SERVINGS**

Orange Sauce: In a small saucepan combine ¼ cup sugar, 2 teaspoons cornstarch, 1 teaspoon grated fresh ginger or ½ teaspoon ground ginger, and ¼ teaspoon finely shredded orange peel. Stir in ¾ cup orange juice. Cook and stir over medium heat until thickened and bubbly. Cook and stir for 2 minutes more. Serve warm.

Chocolate-Cream Cheese Cupcakes

PREP 30 minutes
BAKE 25 minutes
COOL 1 hour
OVEN 350°F

NUTRITION FACTS PER CUPCAKE

Calories 166
Fat 5 g
Cholesterol 1 mg
Sodium 62 mg
Carbohydrates 27 g
Fiber 0 g
Protein 3 g

½ of an 8-ounce package fat-free cream cheese, softened
⅓ cup sugar
¼ cup fresh or frozen egg product, thawed, or 1 egg, lightly beaten
⅓ cup miniature semisweet chocolate pieces
1½ cups all-purpose flour
1 cup sugar
¼ cup unsweetened cocoa powder
1 teaspoon baking powder
¼ teaspoon baking soda
⅛ teaspoon salt
1 cup water
⅓ cup vegetable oil
1 tablespoon vinegar
1 teaspoon vanilla
½ cup plain low-fat granola

1. Preheat oven to 350°F. Line eighteen 2½-inch muffin cups with paper bake cups; set aside.

2. In a small mixing bowl beat cream cheese with a mixer on medium until smooth. Add the ⅓ cup sugar and the egg product; beat until combined. Stir in chocolate pieces; set aside.

3. In a large bowl stir together flour, the 1 cup sugar, the cocoa powder, baking powder, baking soda, and salt. Add the water, oil, vinegar, and vanilla. Beat on medium for 2 minutes, scraping bowl occasionally. Spoon batter into the prepared muffin cups, filling each about half full. Spoon about 1 tablespoon of the cream cheese mixture into each cup. Sprinkle with granola.

4. Bake for 25 to 30 minutes or until tops spring back when lightly touched. Cool in muffin cups on wire racks for 10 minutes. Remove from muffin cups; cool completely on racks. **MAKES 18 CUPCAKES**

Double Pumpkin Bars

PREP **15 minutes**
BAKE **20 minutes**
COOL **1 hour**
OVEN **350°F**

Nonstick cooking spray
1   cup rolled oats
½   cup whole wheat pastry flour
    or white whole wheat flour
½   teaspoon baking soda
½   teaspoon ground cinnamon
½   teaspoon ground allspice
¼   teaspoon salt
1   egg, lightly beaten
½   cup canned pumpkin
¼   cup sugar
¼   cup canola oil
1   teaspoon vanilla
½   cup chopped pitted whole
    dates
¼   cup pumpkin seeds (pepitas)
    or chopped walnuts

1. Preheat oven to 350°F. Lightly coat an 8×8×2-inch baking pan with cooking spray; set aside.

2. In a medium bowl stir together oats, flour, baking soda, cinnamon, allspice, and salt. In a small bowl combine egg, pumpkin, sugar, oil, and vanilla. Stir pumpkin mixture into flour mixture until combined. Stir in dates and pumpkin seeds. Spread batter evenly in the prepared pan.

3. Bake about 20 minutes or until top is firm and a toothpick inserted near center comes out clean. Cool in pan on a wire rack. Cut four squares, then cut diagonally for eight triangles. **MAKES 8 BARS**

To Store: Place bars in a single layer in an airtight container; cover. Store in the refrigerator up to 1 week.

Oaty Doodle Hearts

PREP 30 minutes
BAKE 8 minutes per batch
OVEN 400°F

NUTRITION FACTS
PER COOKIE

Calories 82
Fat 4 g
Cholesterol 11 mg
Sodium 45 mg
Carbohydrates 11 g
Fiber 1 g
Protein 1 g

2   cups rolled oats
1½ cups all-purpose flour
½   cup whole wheat flour
4   teaspoons ground cinnamon
1   teaspoon baking soda
½   teaspoon cream of tartar
¼   teaspoon salt
½   cup butter, softened
½   cup butter-flavor shortening
1½ cups sugar
2   eggs
1   teaspoon vanilla
⅓   cup sugar

1. Preheat oven to 400°F. Line cookie sheets with parchment paper or foil; set aside. In a food processor process oats until finely ground. In a medium bowl stir together ground oats, all-purpose flour, whole wheat flour, cinnamon, baking soda, cream of tartar, and salt; set aside.

2. In a large mixing bowl beat butter and shortening with mixer on medium to high for 30 seconds. Add the 1½ cups sugar and beat until combined, scraping bowl. Beat in eggs and vanilla until combined. Beat in as much of the flour mixture as you can with the mixer. Stir in any remaining flour mixture.

3. Using a heaping teaspoon for each, shape dough into balls. Roll balls in the ⅓ cup sugar. Place 2 inches apart on the prepared cookie sheets. Flatten balls to a little less than ½ inch thick. Use your fingers to shape into hearts.

4. Bake for 8 to 10 minutes or until set and lightly browned. Cool on cookie sheets for 1 minute. Transfer to wire racks to cool.
MAKES ABOUT 60 COOKIES

To Store: Place cookies in layers separated by waxed paper in an airtight container; cover. Store at room temperature up to 3 days or freeze up to 3 months.

Fruit and Chip Cookies

PREP 25 minutes
BAKE 10 minutes per batch
OVEN 350°F

NUTRITION FACTS PER COOKIE

Calories 109
Fat 5 g
Cholesterol 15 mg
Sodium 54 mg
Fiber 1 g
Protein 2 g

1   cup butter, softened
¾   cup packed brown sugar
½   cup granulated sugar
1   teaspoon baking soda
2   eggs
1   teaspoon vanilla
2   cups all-purpose flour
2   cups granola cereal
1   6-ounce package mixed dried fruit bits (1½ cups)
1   cup white baking pieces

1. Preheat oven to 350°F. In a large mixing bowl beat butter with a mixer on medium for 30 seconds. Add brown sugar, granulated sugar, and baking soda; beat until combined. Beat in eggs and vanilla until combined. Beat in as much of the flour as you can with the mixer. Stir in any remaining flour and the granola with a wooden spoon. Stir in dried fruit bits and baking pieces.

2. Drop dough by rounded teaspoons 2 inches apart onto an ungreased cookie sheet. Flatten slightly.

3. Bake about 10 minutes or until edges are golden. Cool on cookie sheet for 1 minute. Transfer to wire racks and cool completely.
MAKES ABOUT 60 COOKIES

To Store: Place cookies in layers separated by waxed paper in an airtight container; cover. Store at room temperature up to 3 days or freeze up to 3 months.

Malted Milk Ball Cookies

PREP **35 minutes**
BAKE **8 minutes per batch**
OVEN **375°F**

**NUTRITION FACTS
PER COOKIE**

Calories 122
Fat 5 g
Cholesterol 17 mg
Sodium 100 mg
Carbohydrates 19 g
Fiber 1 g
Protein 1 g

¾   cup butter, softened
1¼ cups packed brown sugar
1   cup granulated sugar
1½ teaspoons baking soda
½   teaspoon salt
3   eggs
¼   cup vegetable oil
1½ teaspoons vanilla
3½ cups all-purpose flour
1½ cups whole bran cereal
3   cups malted milk balls,
      crushed (12 ounces)

1. Preheat oven to 375°F. In a large mixing bowl beat butter with a mixer on medium to high for 30 seconds. Add brown sugar, granulated sugar, baking soda, and salt. Beat until well combined, scraping bowl occasionally. Beat in eggs, oil, and vanilla. Beat in as much of the flour as you can with the mixer. Stir in any remaining flour and the cereal. If desired, reserve ½ cup crushed malted milk balls to sprinkle on top. Stir remaining malted milk balls into dough.

2. Shape dough in 1½-inch balls. Place balls 2 inches apart on an ungreased cookie sheet.

3. Bake for 8 to 10 minutes or until golden. Place cookie sheet on a wire rack. If desired, immediately sprinkle tops of warm cookies with reserved crushed malted milk balls. Cool on cookie sheet for 2 minutes. Transfer to a wire rack and cool completely.
MAKES ABOUT 60 COOKIES

To Store: Place cookies in layers separated by waxed paper in an airtight container; cover. Store at room temperature up to 3 days or freeze up to 3 months.

Snickerdoodles

PREP 25 minutes
CHILL 1 hour
BAKE 10 minutes per batch
OVEN 375°F

NUTRITION FACTS PER COOKIE

Calories 69
Fat 3 g
Cholesterol 13 mg
Sodium 38 mg
Carbohydrates 10 g
Fiber 0 g
Protein 1 g

½   cup butter, softened
1   cup sugar
¼   teaspoon baking soda
¼   teaspoon cream of tartar
1   egg
½   teaspoon vanilla
1½ cups all-purpose flour
2   tablespoons sugar
1   teaspoon ground cinnamon

1. In a medium mixing bowl beat butter with a mixer on medium to high for 30 seconds. Add the 1 cup sugar, baking soda, and cream of tartar. Beat until combined, scraping bowl occasionally. Beat in egg and vanilla until combined. Beat in as much of the flour as you can with the mixer. Using a wooden spoon, stir in any remaining flour. Cover and chill about 1 hour or until dough is easy to handle.

2. Preheat oven to 375°F. In a small bowl combine the 2 tablespoons sugar and the cinnamon. Shape dough in 1-inch balls. Roll balls in sugar mixture to coat. Place 2 inches apart on an ungreased cookie sheet.

3. Bake for 10 to 11 minutes or until edges are golden. Transfer to a wire rack and cool completely.
MAKES ABOUT 36 COOKIES

To Store: Place cookies in layers separated by waxed paper in an airtight container; cover. Store at room temperature up to 3 days or freeze up to 3 months.

Ginger Squares

PREP 25 minutes
FREEZE 30 minutes
BAKE 8 minutes per batch
OVEN 375°F

NUTRITION FACTS
PER COOKIE

Calories 44
Fat 1 g
Cholesterol 8 mg
Sodium 37 mg
Carbohydrates 7 g
Fiber 0 g
Protein 1 g

⅓ cup molasses
⅓ cup butter
2 cups all-purpose flour
⅓ cup packed brown sugar
1½ teaspoons ground ginger
½ teaspoon baking soda
½ teaspoon ground cinnamon
¼ teaspoon salt
¼ teaspoon black pepper
   (optional)
⅛ teaspoon ground cloves
1 egg, lightly beaten
   Powdered sugar (optional)

1. In a small saucepan combine molasses and butter. Cook and stir over low heat until butter is melted. Pour molasses mixture into a large bowl; cool to room temperature. In a medium bowl stir together flour, brown sugar, ginger, baking soda, cinnamon, salt, pepper (if desired), and cloves. Set aside. Stir egg into cooled molasses mixture. Stir in flour mixture until combined.

2. Divide dough in half; shape in two 5½×1½-inch square logs. Wrap in plastic wrap or waxed paper. Freeze about 30 minutes or until dough is firm enough to slice.

3. Preheat oven to 375°F. Cut logs in ⅛-inch slices (reshaping logs as necessary). Place slices 1 inch apart on an ungreased cookie sheet. Prick each slice several times with a fork.

4. Bake for 8 to 10 minutes or until edges are firm and light brown. Transfer to a wire rack and cool completely. Sprinkle cooled cookies with powdered sugar.
MAKES ABOUT 4 DOZEN COOKIES

To Store: Place cookies in layers separated by waxed paper in an airtight container; cover. Store at room temperature up to 3 days or freeze up to 3 months.

Peanut Butter Macaroons

PREP 20 minutes
BAKE 10 minutes per batch
STAND 15 minutes
OVEN 300°F

NUTRITION FACTS PER MACAROON

Calories 57
Fat 3 g
Cholesterol 0 mg
Sodium 50 mg
Carbohydrates 7 g
Fiber 0 g
Protein 2 g

2   egg whites
⅛   teaspoon cream of tartar
      Dash salt
½   cup sugar
½   cup creamy peanut butter
2   cups chocolate-flavor crisp
      rice cereal
⅓   cup chopped honey-roasted
      peanuts
      Melted chocolate (optional)

1. Preheat oven to 300°F. Lightly grease two cookie sheets or line with parchment paper; set aside.

2. In a medium mixing bowl beat egg whites, cream of tartar, and salt with a mixer on high until soft peaks form (tips curl). Gradually add sugar, 1 tablespoon at a time, beating until stiff peaks form (tips stand straight). Gently fold in peanut butter. Fold in cereal. Drop dough by rounded teaspoons 2 inches apart onto prepared cookie sheets. Sprinkle with chopped peanuts.

3. Bake for 10 minutes. Turn off oven and let cookies stand in oven with door closed for 15 minutes. Transfer to a wire rack and cool completely. Drizzle with melted chocolate, if desired.
MAKES ABOUT 30 MACAROONS

To Store: Place cookies in layers separated by waxed paper in an airtight container; cover. Store at room temperature up to 3 days or freeze up to 3 months.

Choco-Berry Thumbprints

PREP 30 minutes
BAKE 10 minutes
COOL 1 hour
OVEN 350°F

NUTRITION FACTS PER TASSIE

Calories 122
Fat 6 g
Cholesterol 15 mg
Sodium 57 mg
Carbohydrates 18 g
Fiber 1 g
Protein 1 g

Nonstick cooking spray
1⅔ cups all-purpose flour
⅓ cup unsweetened cocoa powder
¼ teaspoon baking powder
¼ teaspoon baking soda
¼ teaspoon salt
1 cup bittersweet chocolate pieces
½ of a 14-ounce can (⅔ cup) sweetened condensed milk
½ cup coconut, toasted*
½ cup seedless red raspberry jam
½ cup butter, softened
¾ cup granulated sugar
1 egg
1½ teaspoons vanilla
Whole fresh raspberries
Powdered sugar (optional)

1. Preheat oven to 350°F. Lightly coat thirty-six 1¾-inch muffin cups with cooking spray; set aside. In a medium bowl stir together flour, cocoa powder, baking powder, baking soda, and salt; set aside.

2. For filling, in a medium saucepan combine chocolate and sweetened condensed milk. Cook and stir over low heat just until chocolate is melted. Remove from heat. Stir in coconut and jam. Cover and set aside.

3. In a large mixing bowl beat butter with a mixer on medium to high for 30 seconds. Add granulated sugar. Beat until combined, scraping bowl occasionally. Beat in egg and vanilla until combined. Add flour mixture; beat on low just until combined.

4. Divide dough into 36 pieces; shape in balls. Press evenly into the bottoms and up the sides of the prepared muffin cups. Divide filling among cups.

5. Bake for 10 to 12 minutes or until pastry is golden and set. Cool in muffin cups on wire racks for 15 minutes. Carefully remove tassies from muffin cups; cool completely on racks. Top with rasberries and, if desired, sprinkle with powdered sugar.
MAKES 36 TASSIES

***Tip:** To toast coconut, spread it in a shallow baking pan. Bake at 350°F about 5 minutes or until lightly toasted, shaking the pan occasionally and watching closely to avoid burning.

To Store: Place tassies in layers separated by waxed paper in an airtight container; cover. Store at room temperature up to 3 days or in the refrigerator up to 1 week.

Pudding Tartlets

START TO FINISH **15 minutes**

NUTRITION FACTS
PER TARTLET

Calories 54
Fat 2 g
Cholesterol 3 mg
Sodium 47 mg
Carbohydrates 8 g
Fiber 0 g
Protein 1 g

2   individual oblong creme-filled
    sponge cakes, or fifteen ½-inch
    cubes frozen pound cake,
    thawed
1   2.1-ounce package baked
    miniature phyllo dough shells
    (15 shells)
½   cup any-flavor pudding
    Whipped cream or frozen
    whipped dessert topping,
    thawed
    Unsweetened cocoa powder

1. Slice sponge cakes in half
lengthwise then crosswise into
about 1-inch pieces. Place one
cake piece in each phyllo cup (may
have a piece or two left over).
Spoon pudding on cake. Cover and
refrigerate for 5 minutes. Before
serving, top with whipped cream
and sprinkle with cocoa powder.
MAKES 15 TARTLETS

Cranberry Tart

PREP 35 minutes
BAKE 25 minutes
COOL 1 hour
CHILL 2 to 4 hours
OVEN 350°F

NUTRITION FACTS PER SERVING

Calories 192
Fat 7 g
Cholesterol 40 mg
Sodium 142 mg
Carbohydrates 18 g
Fiber 1 g
Protein 4 g

1   cup fresh cranberries
¼   cup sugar
1   tablespoon orange juice
1   8-ounce package cream cheese, softened
⅓   cup sugar
1   egg
1   egg white
1   teaspoon vanilla
    Butter-flavor nonstick cooking spray
6   sheets frozen phyllo dough (14×9-inch rectangles), thawed
1   ounce white baking chocolate with cocoa butter, melted (optional)

1. Preheat oven to 350°F. For filling in a small saucepan combine cranberries, the ¼ cup sugar, and the orange juice. Cook over medium heat about 6 minutes, until cranberries pop and sauce is slightly thickened, stirring frequently. Set aside.

2. In a medium mixing bowl combine cream cheese, the ⅓ cup sugar, the egg, egg white, and vanilla. Beat with a mixer on medium until smooth, scraping bowl occasionally. Set aside.

3. Coat a 9-inch tart pan or pie plate with cooking spray. Place one sheet of phyllo dough on a clean work surface. (As you work, cover the remaining phyllo dough with plastic wrap to prevent it from drying out.) Lightly coat the phyllo sheet with cooking spray. Fold in half crosswise to a 9×7-inch rectangle. Press gently into the prepared tart pan, allowing excess phyllo to extend over side of pan. Lightly coat with cooking spray. Coat and fold another phyllo sheet; place on first sheet, rotating slightly to stagger corners. Lightly coat with cooking spray. Repeat with remaining phyllo sheets. Bake for 5 minutes.

4. Spoon cream cheese mixture into phyllo crust, spreading evenly. Spoon cranberry sauce over cream cheese mixture. Using a knife, marble filling slightly.

5. Bake for 20 to 25 minutes or until phyllo crust is light brown and filling is set. Cool on a wire rack for 1 hour. Cover and refrigerate for 2 to 4 hours before serving. If desired, drizzle edge of phyllo crust with melted white chocolate. **MAKES 10 SERVINGS**

Easy Apple Dumplings

PREP 15 minutes
BAKE 25 minutes
OVEN 375°F

NUTRITION FACTS PER DUMPLING

Calories 201
Fat 9 g
Cholesterol 8 mg
Sodium 245 mg
Carbohydrates 28 g
Fiber 1 g
Protein 2 g

½ cup apple juice
⅓ cup packed brown sugar
2 tablespoons butter
2 tablespoons granulated sugar
1 teaspoon ground cinnamon
1 large cooking apple, peeled (if desired), cored, and cut in 8 wedges
1 8-ounce package (8) refrigerated crescent rolls
1 teaspoon coarse or granulated sugar
   Vanilla or cinnamon ice cream (optional)

1. Preheat oven to 375°F. Lightly grease a 2-quart square baking dish; set aside. In a small saucepan combine apple juice, brown sugar, and butter. Cook over medium-low heat until butter is melted, stirring to dissolve brown sugar. Set aside.

2. In a medium bowl stir together the 2 tablespoons granulated sugar and cinnamon. Add apple; toss gently to coat.

3. Unroll dough and separate at perforations. Place a coated apple wedge along the wide edge of each dough piece. Roll up dough around apple wedge. Arrange in the prepared baking dish. Drizzle apple juice evenly over dumplings. Sprinkle dumplings with coarse sugar.

4. Bake for 25 to 30 minutes or until pastry is golden and apple is tender. Serve warm. If desired, serve with ice cream.
MAKES 8 DUMPLINGS

Apples and Peanut Butter Crisp

PREP 20 minutes
BAKE 30 minutes
OVEN 375°F

NUTRITION FACTS
PER SERVING

Calories 174
Fat 6 g
Cholesterol 0 mg
Sodium 51 mg
Carbohydrates 28 g
Fiber 4 g
Protein 4 g

6   cups thinly sliced peeled (if desired) red and/or green cooking apples (6 medium)
2   tablespoons all-purpose flour
1   tablespoon brown sugar
⅔   cup quick-cooking rolled oats
2   tablespoons all-purpose flour
2   tablespoons packed brown sugar
¼   cup peanut butter
2   tablespoons chopped peanuts

1. Preheat oven to 375°F. Place apple slices in a 2-quart square baking dish; set aside. In a small bowl stir together the 2 tablespoons flour and the 1 tablespoon brown sugar. Sprinkle flour mixture on apple slices; toss to coat. Cover dish with foil.

2. Bake, covered, for 15 minutes. Meanwhile, for topping in a medium bowl stir together oats, 2 tablespoons flour, and the 2 tablespoons brown sugar. Using a fork, stir in peanut butter until mixture resembles coarse crumbs. Stir in peanuts.

3. Uncover apples; sprinkle with topping. Bake, uncovered, for 15 to 20 minutes or until apple is tender and topping is golden. Serve warm.
MAKES 8 SERVINGS

Chocolate-Filled Lemon Meringues

PREP 50 minutes
BAKE 25 minutes
STAND 1 hour
OVEN 300°F

NUTRITION FACTS PER SERVING

Calories 181
Fat 7 g
Cholesterol 18 mg
Sodium 29 mg
Carbohydrates 29 g
Fiber 2 g
Protein 5 g

2   egg whites
⅔   cup sugar
1   teaspoon finely shredded lemon peel
¼   teaspoon cream of tartar
4   teaspoons sugar
1   tablespoon unsweetened cocoa powder
⅓   cup mascarpone cheese or reduced-fat cream cheese (Neufchâtel) (about 3 ounces), softened
½   teaspoon vanilla
2   to 3 tablespoons fat-free milk
1   cup fresh raspberries and/or blueberries
    Finely shredded lemon peel and/or unsweetened cocoa powder (optional)

1. Allow egg whites to stand at room temperature for 30 minutes. Meanwhile, preheat oven to 300°F. Line a large baking sheet with parchment paper or foil. Draw twelve 2-inch circles 3 inches apart on the paper or foil; set aside.

2. For meringue, in a small bowl stir together the ⅔ cup sugar and the 1 teaspoon lemon peel; set aside. In a large mixing bowl combine egg whites and cream of tartar. Beat with a mixer on medium until soft peaks form (tips curl). Add sugar mixture, 1 tablespoon at a time, beating on high until stiff peaks form (tips stand straight). Spread meringue on circles on paper, building up sides to form shells.

3. Bake for 25 minutes. Turn off oven; let meringues dry in oven with door closed for 1 hour. Lift meringues off paper. Transfer to a wire rack; cool.

4. For filling, in a small bowl stir together the 4 teaspoons sugar and cocoa powder. In another small bowl combine mascarpone cheese and vanilla. Stir in cocoa mixture and enough of the milk to reach spreading consistency.

5. Spread filling in meringue shells. Top with berries. If desired, garnish with additional lemon peel and/or cocoa powder.
MAKES 6 SERVINGS

Make-Ahead Directions:
Prepare as directed through Step 3. Transfer meringues to an airtight container; cover. Store at room temperature up to 1 week. To serve, prepare filling and serve as directed.

Dream Cream Puffs

PREP 25 minutes
BAKE 30 minutes
COOL 1 hour 10 minutes
OVEN 400°F

NUTRITION FACTS PER SERVING

Calories 112
Fat 4 g
Cholesterol 62 mg
Sodium 231 mg
Carbohydrates 13 g
Fiber 0 g
Protein 5 g

Nonstick cooking spray
½ cup water
2 tablespoons butter
½ cup all-purpose flour
2 eggs
1 4-serving-size package sugar-free fat-free chocolate instant pudding and pie filling mix
2 cups fat-free milk
⅛ teaspoon peppermint extract
Powdered sugar or unsweetened cocoa powder (optional)

1. Preheat oven to 400°F. Lightly coat a baking sheet with cooking spray; set aside.

2. For puff shells, in a small saucepan combine the water and butter. Bring to boiling. Add flour all at once, stirring vigorously. Cook and stir until mixture forms a ball. Remove from heat. Cool for 10 minutes. Add eggs, one at a time, beating well with a wooden spoon after each addition. Drop dough in 8 mounds, 3 inches apart, onto the prepared baking sheet.

3. Bake about 30 minutes or until golden and firm. Transfer to a wire rack; cool.

4. Meanwhile, for filling, prepare pudding mix according to package directions using the fat-free milk. Stir in peppermint extract. Cover surface with plastic wrap and refrigerate until ready to serve.

5. To serve, cut tops from cream puffs; remove soft dough from insides. Spoon about ¼ cup of the filling into each cream puff. Replace tops. If desired, sprinkle lightly with powdered sugar.
MAKES 8 SERVINGS

Mocha Cream Puffs: Prepare as directed, except omit peppermint extract. Add 2 teaspoons instant espresso coffee powder or instant coffee crystals with the milk when preparing the pudding.

Meyer Lemon Sorbet

PREP 10 minutes
FREEZE According to
manufacturer's directions
+ 4 hours
CHILL Overnight
STAND 5 minutes

NUTRITION FACTS PER SERVING

Calories 118
Fat 0 g
Cholesterol 0 mg
Sodium 1 mg
Carbohydrates 31 g
Fiber 0 g
Protein 0 g

1½ cups sugar
1½ cups water
1 tablespoon finely shredded
   Meyer lemon peel or lemon
   peel
1 cup Meyer lemon juice or
   lemon juice
   Finely shredded Meyer lemon
   peel or lemon peel (optional)

1. For syrup, in a small saucepan bring the sugar and the water to boiling, stirring to dissolve sugar. Cover and refrigerate overnight or place saucepan in a bowl of ice water and stir until sugar syrup is completely chilled.

2. Stir the 1 tablespoon lemon peel and lemon juice into syrup. Pour lemon mixture into a 1-quart ice cream freezer.* Freeze according to the manufacturer's directions.

3. Transfer sorbet to an airtight container; ripen in the freezer for 4 hours. Before serving, let sorbet stand at room temperature for 5 minutes. If desired, garnish servings with additional lemon peel. **MAKES 10 SERVINGS**

*Tip: If you don't have an ice cream freezer, pour the sorbet into a 2-quart square baking dish. Cover; freeze for 5 to 6 hours or until almost firm. Break frozen sorbet into chunks. Transfer to a chilled mixing bowl. Beat with a mixer on medium until fluffy but not melted. Return to baking dish. Cover and freeze at least 1 hour.

Banana Crunch Pops

PREP 15 minutes
FREEZE 2 hours
STAND 10 minutes

NUTRITION FACTS PER SERVING

Calories 104
Fat 1 g
Cholesterol 1 mg
Sodium 37 mg
Carbohydrates 23 g
Fiber 2 g
Protein 3 g

1	6-ounce carton fat-free yogurt (any flavor)
¼	teaspoon ground cinnamon
1	cup granola with dried fruit
2	medium bananas
4	crafts sticks

1. Line a baking sheet with waxed paper; set aside. Place yogurt in a small shallow dish; stir in cinnamon. Place granola in another small shallow dish.

2. Cut bananas in half crosswise. Insert a wooden crafts stick into one end of each banana half. Roll banana in yogurt mixture, completely covering each. Roll in granola to coat. Place on the prepared baking sheet.

3. Freeze about 2 hours or until firm. Let stand at room temperature for 10 to 15 minutes before serving. **MAKES 4 SERVINGS**

Make-Ahead Directions:
Prepare as directed. Place each frozen banana crunch pop in a small resealable freezer bag; seal bag. Freeze up to 1 week.

Frozen Chocolate-Banana Bites

PREP 15 minutes
FREEZE 1 to 2 hours

NUTRITION FACTS PER SERVING

Calories 109
Fat 4 g
Cholesterol 1 mg
Sodium 1 mg
Carbohydrates 20 g
Fiber 2 g
Protein 1 g

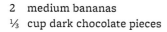

2 medium bananas
⅓ cup dark chocolate pieces

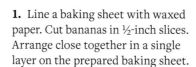

1. Line a baking sheet with waxed paper. Cut bananas in ½-inch slices. Arrange close together in a single layer on the prepared baking sheet.

2. In a small saucepan melt and stir chocolate over low heat. Cool slightly. Drizzle melted chocolate over banana slices. Cover and freeze for 1 to 2 hours or until firm.
MAKES 4 SERVINGS

Make-Ahead Directions:
Prepare as directed. Divide frozen banana among four small freezer containers or resealable freezer bags; cover containers or seal bags. Freeze up to 3 days.

Fruit Kabobs with Creamy Dipping Sauce

START TO FINISH 15 minutes

NUTRITION FACTS PER SERVING

Calories 142
Fat 3 g
Cholesterol 11 mg
Sodium 51 mg
Carbohydrates 27 g
Fiber 2 g
Protein 3 g

2   fresh kiwifruit, peeled and quartered
8   fresh pineapple chunks
8   fresh strawberries
16 large fresh blueberries
1   6-ounce carton strawberry or blueberry lowfat yogurt
½ cup light sour cream
2   tablespoons strawberry or blueberry spreadable fruit

1. Alternately thread fruit on eight 6-inch skewers; set aside.

2. For creamy dipping sauce, in a small bowl stir together yogurt, sour cream, and spreadable fruit. Serve kabobs with dipping sauce.
MAKES 4 SERVINGS

Caramelized Apple Tostadas

PREP 35 minutes
BAKE 10 minutes
OVEN 400°F

NUTRITION FACTS PER SERVING

Calories 199
Fat 2 g
Cholesterol 0 mg
Sodium 72 mg
Carbohydrates 29 g
Fiber 5 g
Protein 2 g

4 6- to 7-inch flour tortillas
   Butter-flavor nonstick cooking spray or nonstick cooking spray
2 teaspoons granulated sugar
¼ teaspoon pumpkin pie spice
4 cups peeled and sliced apples or pears (4 medium)
2 tablespoons packed brown sugar
1 teaspoon pumpkin pie spice
1 5.5-ounce can apple juice
2 tablespoons dried currants
   Powdered sugar (optional)

1. Preheat oven to 400°F. Place tortillas on a baking sheet. Lightly coat with cooking spray. In a small bowl stir together granulated sugar and the ¼ teaspoon pumpkin pie spice; sprinkle on tortillas. Bake about 10 minutes or until crisp. Cool on a wire rack.

2. Meanwhile, lightly coat a large nonstick skillet with cooking spray; heat skillet over medium heat. Add apples, brown sugar, and the 1 teaspoon pumpkin pie spice. Cook and stir about 10 minutes or until golden. Add apple juice and currants. Cook about 20 minutes or until liquid is nearly evaporated, stirring occasionally.

3. To serve, spoon apples on tortillas. If desired, sprinkle with powdered sugar. **MAKES 4 SERVINGS**

Sweet Basil Peaches

START TO FINISH 22 minutes

NUTRITION FACTS PER SERVING

Calories 73
Fat 0 g
Cholesterol 0 mg
Sodium 0 mg
Carbohydrates 13 g
Fiber 2 g
Protein 1 g

5   medium peaches or nectarines
½   cup sweet white wine (such as
    Gewürztraminer or Riesling)
    or apple juice
⅓   cup fresh basil leaves
1   to 2 tablespoons sugar
    (optional)
    Snipped and/or whole fresh
    basil leaves

1. Remove pits from two unpeeled peaches; chop. Set aside remaining whole peaches.

2. For sauce, in a medium saucepan combine chopped peaches, wine, the ⅓ cup basil, and the sugar, if necessary, to sweeten. Bring to boiling; reduce heat. Simmer, uncovered, for 12 to 15 minutes or until sauce is slightly thickened.

3. Remove and discard basil. Pour peaches into a food processor or blender; cover and process or blend until smooth.

4. Remove pits from remaining peaches; cut in wedges. Serve with peach sauce and additional basil. **MAKES 4 SERVINGS**

Dark Chocolate Dipped Apples

PREP 30 minutes
STAND 30 minutes

NUTRITION FACTS PER APPLE

Calories 239
Fat 11 g
Cholesterol 0 mg
Sodium 3 mg
Carbohydrates 40 g
Fiber 6 g
Protein 3 g

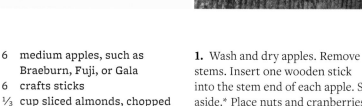

6   medium apples, such as Braeburn, Fuji, or Gala
6   crafts sticks
⅓   cup sliced almonds, chopped pistachios, and/or chopped walnuts, toasted
⅓   cup snipped dried cranberries
4   ounces bittersweet or dark chocolate, chopped
4   ounces semisweet chocolate, chopped, or 1 cup semisweet chocolate chips
½   teaspoon ground cinnamon
¼   teaspoon ground anise seeds (optional)
2   ounces white chocolate, chopped (optional)

1. Wash and dry apples. Remove stems. Insert one wooden stick into the stem end of each apple. Set aside.* Place nuts and cranberries in a deep bowl; set aside.

2. In a small heavy saucepan melt bittersweet chocolate, semisweet chocolate, cinnamon, and, if desired, anise seeds over low heat until chocolate is melted, stirring constantly. Remove from heat.

3. Dip the bottom half of each apple into the chocolate, using a spoon to spread chocolate evenly. Allow excess chocolate to drip off. Immediately dip apples into almonds and dried cranberries. Place apples, nut sides down, on waxed paper for 30 minutes or until set. Discard any remaining chocolate.

4. If desired, in a small heavy saucepan melt white chocolate over low heat, stirring constantly. Transfer melted chocolate to a small plastic bag. Snip a small hole in one corner of the bag. Hold apples by sticks and drizzle white chocolate over the coated portion of apples. Return apples to waxed paper and let stand at room temperature for 30 minutes or in the refrigerator for 15 minutes, until white chocolate is set.
MAKES 6 SERVINGS

Tip* If desired, refrigerate apples. Chocolate clings better to cold apples.

Strawberry Cream Pie

PREP 30 minutes
CHILL 4 hours

NUTRITION FACTS
PER SERVING

Calories 130
Fat 3 g
Cholesterol 39 mg
Sodium 48 mg
Carbohydrates 22 g
Fiber 1 g
Protein 4 g

2½ cups strawberries
¼ cup sugar
1 envelope unflavored gelatin
2 tablespoons frozen limeade concentrate or frozen lemonade concentrate, thawed
3 egg whites, slightly beaten
1 tablespoon tequila or orange juice
1 3-ounce package ladyfingers, split
2 tablespoons orange juice
½ of an 8-ounce container frozen light whipped dessert topping, thawed
  Sliced strawberries (optional)
  Fresh mint leaves (optional)

1. Place the 2½ cups strawberries in a blender or food processor. Cover and blend or process until nearly smooth. Measure blended strawberries (you should have about 1½ cups.)

2. For filling, in a medium saucepan stir together sugar and gelatin. Stir in blended strawberries and limeade concentrate. Cook and stir over medium heat until mixture bubbles and gelatin is dissolved. Gradually stir about half the gelatin mixture into the egg whites. Return mixture to the saucepan. Cook over low heat about 3 minutes or until slightly thickened, stirring constantly. (Do not boil.) Pour into a medium bowl; stir in tequila. Refigerate until filling mounds when spooned, stirring occasionally (about 2 hours).

3. Meanwhile, cut half the split ladyfingers in half crosswise; stand on end around the edge of a 9-inch tart pan with a removable bottom or a 9-inch springform pan. Arrange remaining split ladyfingers in the bottom of the pan. Drizzle the 2 tablespoons orange juice over the ladyfingers.

4. Fold whipped topping into chilled strawberry filling. Spoon into prepared pan. Cover and refigerate about 2 hours or until set. If desired, garnish with sliced strawberries and mint leaves.
MAKES 8 SERVINGS

Double-Melon Bowls

PREP **25 minutes**
STAND **20 minutes**
FREEZE **Overnight**

NUTRITION FACTS PER SERVING

Calories 188
Fat 4 g
Cholesterol 13 mg
Sodium 59 mg
Carbohydrates 36 g
Fiber 1 g
Protein 4 g

2   cups cubed seeded watermelon
1   medium cantaloupe (about 3 pounds), halved and seeded
1   quart vanilla frozen yogurt or vanilla ice cream, softened*
    Sea salt (optional)

1. Place watermelon cubes in a single layer on a tray or in a shallow baking pan; freeze for 2 to 3 hours or until firm. Transfer to a freezer bag or container and freeze until ready to use.

2. With a large spoon scoop out flesh from cantaloupe, leaving a ¼-inch shell; set fruit aside. Cut a thin slice from the bottom of each shell, to stand flat. Place shells, upside down, on a paper towel-lined tray; set aside.

3. Place cantaloupe flesh in a food processor or blender; cover and process or blend until smooth. Place pureed cantaloupe in a fine-mesh sieve set over a bowl. Let stand for 5 minutes to drain excess liquid; discard liquid. You should have about 1 cup pulp.

4. In a large bowl gently fold the cantaloupe pulp into the softened yogurt just until combined. Spoon the yogurt mixture into the cantaloupe shells. Place shells on a baking sheet or tray. Cover and freeze overnight or until very firm.

5. Before serving, let melon bowls stand at room temperature for 20 to 30 minutes to soften slightly. Top with frozen watermelon cubes. If desired, lightly sprinkle watermelon with sea salt. Scoop from melon bowls into serving bowls. **MAKES 6 TO 8 SERVINGS**

*Tip: To soften frozen yogurt or ice cream, place frozen yogurt in a large chilled bowl. Stir with a wooden spoon until soft, pressing yogurt against side of bowl.

Index & Metric

How Recipes Are Analyzed

The Better Homes and Gardens® Test Kitchen uses nutrition-analysis software to determine the nutritional value of a single serving of a recipe. Here are some factors to keep in mind regarding each analysis:

- Analyses do not include optional ingredients.
- The first serving size listed is analyzed when a range is given. For example, if a recipe makes 4 to 6 servings, the Nutrition Facts are based on 4 servings.
- When ingredient choices (such as butter or margarine) appear in a recipe, the first one mentioned is used for analysis.
- When milk is a recipe ingredient, the analysis has been calculated using fat-free (skim) milk unless otherwise noted.

Metric Information

The charts on this page provide a guide for converting measurements from the U.S. customary system, which is used throughout this book, to the metric system.

Product Differences

Most of the ingredients called for in the recipes in this book are available in most countries. However, some are known by different names. Here are some common American ingredients and their possible counterparts:

- Sugar (white) is granulated, fine granulated, or castor sugar.
- Powdered sugar is icing sugar.
- All-purpose flour is enriched, bleached, or unbleached white household flour. When self-rising flour is used in place of all-purpose flour in a recipe that calls for leavening, omit the leavening agent (baking soda or baking powder) and salt.
- Light-color corn syrup is golden syrup.
- Cornstarch is cornflour.
- Baking soda is bicarbonate of soda.
- Vanilla or vanilla extract is vanilla essence.
- Green, red, or yellow sweet peppers are capsicums or bell peppers.
- Golden raisins are sultanas.

Volume and Weight

The United States traditionally uses cup measures for liquid and solid ingredients. The chart below shows the approximate imperial and metric equivalents. If you are accustomed to weighing solid ingredients, the following approximate equivalents will be helpful.

- 1 cup butter, castor sugar, or rice = 8 ounces = ½ pound = 250 grams
- 1 cup flour = 4 ounces = ¼ pound = 125 grams
- 1 cup icing sugar = 5 ounces = 150 grams

Canadian and U.S. volume for a cup measure is 8 fluid ounces (237 ml), but the standard metric equivalent is 250 ml.

1 British imperial cup is 10 fluid ounces.

In Australia, 1 tablespoon equals 20 ml, and there are 4 teaspoons in the Australian tablespoon.

Spoon measures are used for smaller amounts of ingredients. Although the size of the tablespoon varies slightly in different countries, for practical purposes and for recipes in this book, a straight substitution is all that's necessary. Measurements made using cups or spoons always should be level unless stated otherwise.

Common Weight Range Replacements

IMPERIAL / U.S.	METRIC
½ ounce	15 g
1 ounce	25 g or 30 g
4 ounces (¼ pound)	115 g or 125 g
8 ounces (½ pound)	225 g or 250 g
16 ounces (1 pound)	450 g or 500 g
1¼ pounds	625 g
1½ pounds	750 g
2 pounds or 2¼ pounds	1,000 g or 1 Kg

Oven Temperature Equivalents

FAHRENHEIT SETTING	CELSIUS SETTING*	GAS SETTING
300°F	150°C	Gas Mark 2 (very low)
325°F	160°C	Gas Mark 3 (low)
350°F	180°C	Gas Mark 4 (moderate)
375°F	190°C	Gas Mark 5 (moderate)
400°F	200°C	Gas Mark 6 (hot)
425°F	220°C	Gas Mark 7 (hot)
450°F	230°C	Gas Mark 8 (very hot)
475°F	240°C	Gas Mark 9 (very hot)
500°F	260°C	Gas Mark 10 (extremely hot)
Broil	Broil	Grill

*Electric and gas ovens may be calibrated using celsius. However, for an electric oven, increase celsius setting 10 to 20 degrees when cooking above 160°C. For convection or forced air ovens (gas or electric), lower the temperature setting 25°F/10°C when cooking at all heat levels.

Baking Pan Sizes

IMPERIAL / U.S.	METRIC
9×1½-inch round cake pan	22- or 23×4-cm (1.5 L)
9×1½-inch pie plate	22- or 23×4-cm (1 L)
8×8×2-inch square cake pan	20×5-cm (2 L)
9×9×2-inch square cake pan	22- or 23×4.5-cm (2.5 L)
11×7×1½-inch baking pan	28×17×4-cm (2 L)
2-quart rectangular baking pan	30×19×4.5-cm (3 L)
13×9×2-inch baking pan	34×22×4.5-cm (3.5 L)
15×10×1-inch jelly roll pan	40×25×2-cm
9×5×3-inch loaf pan	23×13×8-cm (2 L)
2-quart casserole	2 L

U.S. / Standard Metric Equivalents

⅛ teaspoon = 0.5 ml	
¼ teaspoon = 1 ml	
½ teaspoon = 2 ml	
1 teaspoon = 5 ml	
1 tablespoon = 15 ml	
2 tablespoons = 25 ml	
¼ cup = 2 fluid ounces = 50 ml	
⅓ cup = 3 fluid ounces = 75 ml	
½ cup = 4 fluid ounces = 125 ml	
⅔ cup = 5 fluid ounces = 150 ml	
¾ cup = 6 fluid ounces = 175 ml	
1 cup = 8 fluid ounces = 250 ml	
2 cups = 1 pint = 500 ml	
1 quart = 1 litre